Proficiency Testbuilder 2

Mark Harrison

MACMILLAN
HEINEMANN
English Language Teaching

Macmillan Heinemann English Language Teaching
Between Towns Road, Oxford OX4 3PP, UK
A division of Macmillan Publishers Limited
Companies and representatives throughout the world

ISBN 0 435 24067 6 (with key)
0 435 24066 8 (without key)

First published 1998

The author and publishers would like to thank the following for permission to reproduce their material:
Sophie Campbell for extract from 'Is my bottom sticking out?' in The Sunday Telegraph Review, 5 May 1996 (p25); Faber and Faber Limited, extract from 'Dead Lagoon' by Michael Dibdin (p72); Graham Ison for extract from 'The way it was' in The Daily Telegraph, 21 May 1996 (p110); Ewan MacNaughton Associates, extracts from 'Chapter or curse - the ghost's story' by Elizabeth Grice in The Daily Telegraph, 8 December 1995 (p76) and 'And money came tumbling down' by Steve Jackson in The Daily Telegraph, 13 April 1996 (p20); Rick Maybury for extract from 'The future that never was' in the Daily Telegraph, 23 July 1996 (p53); News International Syndication, extract from 'They need a good talking to' by A.A.Gill in The Sunday Times, 20 October 1996 (p16), and extract from Matthew Parris' column in The Times, 9 October 1995 (p44); Newspaper Publishing Plc., extracts from 'How to stop the traffic' by Simon Evans in The Independent, 28 September 1995 (p81), 'The human face of genius' by James Gleick in The Independent, 4 April 1993 (p86), 'Time to take the bull by the horns' by Richard D North in The Independent, 18 July 1995 (p115) and '100 years of solitude' by David Thomson, in The Independent on Sunday, 13 August 1995 (p104); The Orion Publishing Group Ltd., extract from 'Judicial Whispers' by Caro Fraser (p10); Penguin Books Canada Ltd., extract from 'Talk, Talk, Talk' by Jay Ingram (p106); The Peters Fraser and Dunlop Group Ltd. and Victor Gollancz Limited, extract from 'Fever Pitch' by Nick Hornby (1992) (p12); Random House UK Limited, extracts from 'The Railway Man' by Eric Lomax for Jonathon Cape 1995 (p102), 'Crying With Laughter' by Bob Monkhouse for Arrow Books 1994 (p42), 'Orwell: The Authorised Biography' by Michael Sheldon for William Heinemann 1991 (p77) and 'The Lost Continent' by Bill Bryson for Martin Secker and Warburg 1989 (p46). Rogers, Coleridge and White on behalf of Nicholson Baker, his article 'Reading Aloud' from 'The Size of Thoughts', (p58).
Sample summaries:
Camila F Amaraj, 1st UK group (p30); Elena, 2nd IH group (p91); Lefrothea Papazafeiriou, Daniildou School (p120)

Recording acknowledgements:
Extracts from radio programmes are reproduced by kind permission of the BBC.

Susie Maguire, Guy Masterson, Stu Who, Clare Coulter, 'The Afternoon Shift', (BBC Radio 4, 20 November 1996), (p64); André Previn, 'The Music Machine', (BBC Radio 3, 9 December 1996), (p121); Hunter Davies, 'Ruscoe on Five', interview, (BBC Radio 5, 23 October 1996), (p31); Karen Moore, June Heffernon, 'The New Recruit', (BBC Radio 4, 7 November 1996), (p92); 'Ad Lib', (BBC Radio 4, 28 December 1996), (p32); Candis Magazine, article, 'The Private World of Mrs. Beeton', April 1996, (p92); Halifax Building Society Magazine, article, 'House of Lores', Spring 1995 (p32).

Whilst every effort has been made to trace the owners of copyright material in this book, there have been some cases when the publishers have been unable to contact the owners. We would be grateful to hear from anyone who recognizes their copyright material and who is unacknowledged. We shall be pleased to make the necessary ammendments in future editions of the book.

Cassettes produced by James Richardson at Studio AVP

Photograph acknowledgements:
Getty Images, p35(t,b), 66(t), 95(all), 126(all), Image Bank, p35(c), 66(c), Pictor International, p66(b)

Printed in China

2004 2003 2002 2001
12 11 10 9 8 7 6 5 4

CONTENTS

THE PROFICIENCY TESTBUILDER

The Proficiency Testbuilder is more than a book of Practice Tests. It is designed not only to enable students to practise doing tests of exactly the kind they will encounter in the exam itself, but also to provide them with valuable further practice, guidance and explanation.This will enable them to prepare thoroughly for the exam and increase their ability to perform well in it.

The Proficiency Testbuilder contains:

Four complete Practice Tests for the Cambridge Certificate of Proficiency in English

These tests reflect the level and types of question to be found in the real exam.

Further Practice and Guidance pages

These are included for each paper or section of paper of each test.

For Reading Comprehension, Use of English and Listening Comprehension, they contain exercises, questions and tips directly related to each paper or section. These encourage students to draw their own conclusions as to what the answers in the test should be.Their step-by-step approach enables students to develop and apply the right processes when answering questions in the exam.

For Composition and for Use of English Section B they contain suggestions and assessments of authentic sample compositions and summaries.

For Interview, there is practice in talking about pictures and passages, exercises for vocabulary development and suggestions for useful language.

Key and Explanation

This contains full explanations of every answer in the Tests and Further Practice and Guidance pages, together with a great deal of further information relevant to them. For questions where candidates must choose from a number of options, there are highly detailed explanations not only of the correct choice but also of why the other choices are incorrect.There is also a guide to examiner's assessment criteria for papers 2 and 5 on page 188.

How to use the Proficiency Testbuilder

Teachers and students who have the edition with key can use the book in these ways:

- simply follow the instructions

Clear directions are given as to the order in which to do things, enabling you to work through the book page by page. If you do this, you:

1. complete the whole of or a section of each Paper, perhaps under exam conditions;
2. complete the Further Practice and Guidance page or pages which follow this;
3. return to the relevant part of the test and check, and possibly change, the answers given, as a result of what has been learned from doing the Further Practice.

- Vary the order

You may wish to do some of the Further Practice and Guidance pages before answering the questions to which they apply or immediately after them, rather than completing the whole paper or section first. In addition, teachers may wish to do the Further Practice and Guidance pages as discussion or pairwork, or ask students to prepare them before class.

The Certificate of Proficiency

PAPER 1: Reading Comprehension (1 hour)

SECTION A: 25 multiple-choice questions in which candidates must choose which one of four words or phrases correctly completes a gap in a sentence.

SECTION B: 3 passages on which a total of 15 multiple-choice questions are asked. Candidates write their answers on a separate answer sheet.

PAPER 2: Composition (2 hours)

Two compositions to be written from a choice of topics. Each of the choices is for a composition of up to 350 words in length, except for one, which is 250-300 words long. Candidates write their compositions on paper provided.

Note: In this book, four choices are given. In the exam, there is a fifth choice relating to the three books which candidates have the option of reading. These books are specified in the examination regulations each year and candidates may write about one of them. As the books set change from year to year, this option is omitted in this book.

PAPER 3: Use of English (2 hours)

SECTION A:
1 A short passage with 20 gaps, each of which must be filled with one word.
2 A number of sentences that must be completed so that they mean the same as those printed above each one.
3 A number of sentences with gaps that must be filled with a phrase.
4 A number of sentences which must be rewritten using a word printed below each one.

SECTION B: A passage followed by:
1 up to 15 questions that must be answered with a phrase or sentence, with no choices given;
2 a question requiring a summary of the whole passage or part of it, 70-90 words in length. Candidates write their answers on the question paper.

PAPER 4: Listening Comprehension (about 30 minutes)

A cassette recording of (usually) three pieces, each of which is heard **twice.** A variety of accents are heard and speech is close to or at the speed of native speakers. Pieces include broadcasts, interviews, conversations, announcements, talks, etc.

Question types include filling in information, completing sentences, answering multiple-choice questions, matching, etc. Candidates are tested on their understanding of facts and information and the attitudes and opinions of speakers.

Note: In the exam there is a 45 second pause (60 seconds for multiple-choice questions) between the instructions and listening texts for candidates to read the questions. In these practice tests pauses and repeats have not been included. Candidates are given 5 minutes at the end to transfer their answers onto a separate answer sheet, (see p187).

PAPER 5: Interview (15-20 minutes)

There are usually three parts, all of which relate to a common topic.
1 Candidates are shown and asked questions about one or more photographs. This may lead to discussion of the topic.
2 Candidates are shown and asked questions about one or more short passages.
3 Candidates are shown further material as the basis for a discussion of the topic.

The interview may be done individually, in pairs or in groups of three. When done individually, the candidate speaks only to the examiner; when done in pairs or groups of three candidates speak both to each other and to the examiner and a second examiner may be there to assess the interview.

In addition, candidates may choose to talk about one of the set books.

TEST ONE

PAPER 1 READING COMPREHENSION 1 hour

SECTION A

In this section you must choose the word or phrase which best completes each sentence. On your answer sheet indicate the letter **A***,* **B***,* **C** *or* **D** *against the number of each item* **1** *to* **25** *for the word or phrase you choose. Give one answer only to each question.*

1 The problem .... because neither side was prepared to compromise.

A amassed **B** escalated **C** proliferated **D** enhanced

2 She relies .... on her parents for financial support.

A profusely **B** amply **C** heavily **D** severely

3 Emma found it impossible to .... her anger and started shouting.

A restrict **B** inhibit **C** reserve **D** contain

4 A meeting was held so that staff could .... their views freely.

A divulge **B** vent **C** utter **D** air

5 I was at .... to make it clear that I wasn't blaming either of them.

A efforts **B** trouble **C** pains **D** endeavours

6 After years of making unsuccessful films, she is hoping that this one will .... her career.

A revive **B** renew **C** refresh **D** reinstate

7 It's difficult to keep .... with all the recent changes in the law.

A pace **B** track **C** progress **D** step

8 Not even losing all the time could .... his enthusiasm for tennis.

A recede **B** dampen **C** erode **D** belittle

9 If I were you, I wouldn't .... any importance to such a trivial incident.

A put **B** attach **C** lay **D** pay

10 It was a .... lie and nobody at all believed it.

A blatant **B** salient **C** conspicuous **D** pronounced

11 I wouldn't .... too much into her comments, I'm sure they were meant as a joke.

A draw **B** see **C** take **D** read

12 You'll just have to .... yourself to the fact that you can't always have what you want.

A acknowledge **B** reconcile **C** concede **D** allow

13 The interests of her family .... all other considerations for her.

A outweigh **B** monopolize **C** overrun **D** surpass

14 Anne is rather childish and tends to .... if she can't have what she wants.

A ponder **B** sulk **C** hush **D** muse

15 I didn't want to make a decision ...., so I said I'd like to think about it.

A in one go **B** there and then **C** at a stroke **D** on and off

16 I don't like him and he doesn't like me, so the feeling is entirely ....

A respective **B** mutual **C** joint **D** collective

17 Once I had .... myself that they could be trusted, I signed the contract.

A assured **B** confirmed **C** ascertained **D** guaranteed

18 How did you come .... that wonderful painting over there?

A about **B** in for **C** by **D** out with

19 Tom's normally very efficient but he's been making a lot of mistakes ....

A of late **B** for now **C** in a while **D** shortly

20 Clare is completely .... to other people's opinions of her.

A casual **B** disinterested **C** detached **D** indifferent

21 We were under no .... about how difficult it would be to achieve our aims.

A fantasies **B** daydreams **C** illusions **D** deceptions

22 Suddenly I slipped and ended up .... on the floor.

A slouching **B** lounging **C** sprawling **D** drooping

23 I'm afraid that the facts don't .... your theory.

A pull off **B** check out **C** show off **D** bear out

24 I wouldn't like to .... a guess as to how much this might cost.

A speculate **B** hazard **C** advance **D** envisage

25 In .... with your request, I am happy to enclose our brochure.

A assent **B** obedience **C** accordance **D** concession

Before you check your answers to this section of the test, go on to pages 8 and 9.

COLLOCATION

Some of the questions in this part of the test require you to decide which of the four options can be used together with other words before or after the gap to form phrases.
The numbers of the exercises below refer to questions 1–10 of the test on page 6, which are questions of this type.

In each of the exercises, choose which of the four options given in the test fits each gap. This may help you to eliminate some of the incorrect options in the questions they refer to and to check or learn collocations involving the options.

1 | *amassed* | *escalated* | *proliferated* | *enhanced* |

A As tourism grew, new hotels .... along the coast.

B As the cost of living ...., more and more people struggled to survive.

C He .... an enormous personal fortune from clever business dealings.

D This building greatly .... his reputation as an architect.

2 | *amply* | *heavily* | *severely* | *profusely* |

A The injury has .... damaged his chances of playing in the next match.

B People in that profession are .... rewarded for their services.

C When I pointed out her mistake, she was .... apologetic.

D This area has always been .... dependent on agriculture for its survival.

3 | *contain* | *restrict* | *inhibit* | *reserve* |

A I couldn't .... my feelings any longer, I had to say what I thought.

B As the meeting is nearly over, could you .... yourself to a brief comment?

C Her shyness tends to .... her, which is why she seldom gives opinions.

D I shall .... judgement until I have heard all the facts.

4 | *divulge* | *air* | *vent* | *utter* |

A I intend to .... my grievances in a letter of complaint to the manager.

B She didn't .... a word the whole evening; she just sat in silence.

C He was not willing to .... the contents of the secret document.

D I knew it was unfair to him, but I had to .... my anger somehow.

5 | *pains* | *trouble* | *effort* | *endeavours* |

A The .... I made to improve the situation only made it worse.

B I was at .... to point out that I wasn't criticizing him personally.

C My best .... weren't enough to get the job.

D I took a lot of .... to make sure that the party went well.

6 | *revive* | *refresh* | *renew* | *reinstate* |

A Do you remember what we said last week or should I .... your memory?

B It was nice to .... my acquaintance with them after such a long time.

C He was dropped from the team but later the selectors decided to .... him.

D Unemployment is high and steps will have to be taken to .... the economy.

7 | *track* | *step* | *progress* | *pace* |

A I followed the .... of the court case in the newspaper.

B We must keep in .... with modern developments in our industry.

C He spoke so quickly that I couldn't keep .... with him.

D Linda travels so much that it's hard to keep .... of her whereabouts.

8 | *dampened* | *receded* | *eroded* | *belittled* |

A I was looking forward to the holiday, but the awful journey .... my spirits.

B Persistent criticism of his work .... his confidence.

C Fears of an outbreak of violence have .... today.

D People at work .... the contribution she made, so she left.

9 | *put* | *attach* | *lay* | *pay* |

A They'll probably .... the blame on me, although it's not my fault.

B I suggest that you .... heed to the advice that you've been given.

C Don't .... too much emphasis on the negative aspects of life.

D You always .... too much importance to trivial problems.

10 | *blatant* | *conspicuous* | *pronounced* | *salient* |

A In his strange hat, he was a .... figure wherever he went.

B It was a .... foul but the referee didn't blow his whistle.

C She walks with a .... limp, which is the result of a car accident.

D I put all the .... points in my report and left out the minor details.

Now check your answers to these exercises. When you have done so, decide whether you wish to change any of your answers to questions 1–10 in the test. Then check your answers to the test.

SECTION B

*In this section you will find after each of the passages a number of questions or unfinished statements about the passage, each with four suggested answers or ways of finishing. You must choose the one which you think fits best. On your answer sheet, indicate the letter **A**, **B**, **C** or **D** against the number of each item **26** to **40** for the answer you choose. Give **one answer only** to each question.*

FIRST PASSAGE

'Miss Dean and I have been waiting for you, Felicity,' said Mr Lamb in cold and meaningful tones, 'for ten minutes'.

'Oh, have you, Mr Lamb?' replied Felicity. 'Ever so sorry.' She held out her hand in greeting to her new boss. 'Hello, I'm Felicity.'

Rachel Dean looked at Felicity as she shook her hand, and saw a pretty, untidy-looking creature with garish clothes. She smiled warmly at Felicity because one couldn't help smiling at her, but her first impression was that this scatty-looking creature did not give the appearance of being a model of efficiency. Rachel had had secretaries in the past; some had been a positive asset, some a liability. Felicity, she suspected, fell into the latter category.

Felicity, looking at Rachel, marvelled at what she saw. I wish I was that slim, she thought, and had cheekbones like that and smooth black hair all swept back. Dead sophisticated. I want to be like that. I want to wear a suit like that and have a knockout smile. Some hope, she thought. She smiled bravely at Rachel and watched her walk round behind her desk, wondering how much her shoes had cost.

' I'll take you round in a bit, if you like, introduce you to the chaps, show you where everything is,' said Felicity brightly.

'Miss Dean has met most of her colleagues already, Felicity,' said Mr Lamb, 'and I think you've wasted enough time this morning chatting your way round the building'. He turned to Rachel and gave her his best smile. 'I'll leave you to get on, Miss Dean.' And he strutted out.

'They're not all like him,' said Felicity. 'He's a prize one, he is, Miss Dean.'

'Please call me Rachel.'

'It wouldn't go down too well with Mr Lamb if he heard me calling you Rachel,' said Felicity. 'He's a real one for form. He'll never call you anything but Miss Dean.'

'I hope not,' said Rachel. 'Still, office managers are a breed apart, aren't they?'

'I don't like to think about them much,' said Felicity with a giggle, and Rachel laughed, too.

'So,' said Felicity, 'what d'you want me to do then?'

'Well, I don't exactly know. With luck I should get some files from my old firm later. They'll need to be photocopied and the originals sent back. I have some letters to get out – do you want me to dictate a few to give you something to be getting on with?'

'If you like,' said Felicity. 'I don't really mind.'

'Well, I have to send out a standard letter to a list of different people, telling them where I am and so on. Not very exciting, but I suppose you like to keep busy, don't you?'

Felicity's eyes widened. 'Well – yes, generally,' she murmured. God, this one seemed a bit keen. Working for Mr O'Connell had been a doddle but Miss Dean seemed quite a different proposition. Oh, well, she'd just have to stick to her resolution. She would become amazingly efficient. 'Anyway,' she added, thinking of what Rachel had said, 'why can't you just ring your old firm up and tell them to get your stuff round here?'

'Well, there's a certain protocol about these things – I mean, a way of doing it,' .....she added, seeing Felicity's blank expression. 'I'm effectively leaving one firm and taking quite a bit of business with me. Not that there are any hard feelings about it, but they're not likely to fall over themselves to pass things on.'

'Right,' murmured Felicity. And the phone rang.

'Speak of the devil,' said Rachel, and picked it up. Felicity trotted out, deciding to pop down to accounts and have a little natter with Moira. Mr Lamb could hardly have a go at her for not getting on with things when there was nothing to be got on with.

26 What was Rachel's initial impression of Felicity?

A that she was unlikely to get on well with her personally
B that she looked like other secretaries she had worked with
C that she took no interest in her own appearance
D that she was unlikely to be a valuable assistant to her

27 What did Felicity think when she first saw Rachel?

A that she was a somewhat frightening person
B that she could never be like her
C that she was different from what she had expected
D that she would be very efficient

28 During their conversation after Mr Lamb left,

A Felicity realized that Rachel was impressed by Mr Lamb.
B Felicity realized that Rachel expected her to work hard.
C Rachel decided to change the atmosphere in the office.
D Rachel started to have doubts about accepting the job.

29 What happened when Rachel mentioned 'protocol'?

A She realized that the word wasn't in Felicity's vocabulary.
B Felicity began to suspect that she was dishonest.
C She realized that she hadn't acted very diplomatically.
D Felicity showed that she thought it was an important issue.

30 What do we learn about Felicity and Mr Lamb in the passage?

A Felicity thought Mr Lamb had too much power in the office.
B Mr Lamb was more unpleasant to Felicity than anyone else.
C Felicity wasn't sure how she could impress Mr Lamb.
D Mr Lamb thought Felicity was always avoiding work.

Now check your answers to these questions.

SECOND PASSAGE

I don't recall much about the football that first afternoon. One of those tricks of memory enables me to see the only goal clearly: the referee awards a penalty (he runs into the area, points a dramatic finger, there's a roar); a hush as Terry Neill takes it and scores. But I'm sure this picture has been built up from what I have long known about similar incidents, and actually I was aware of none of this. All I really saw on the day was a bewildering chain of incomprehensible incidents, at the end of which everyone around me stood and shouted. If I did the same it must have been an embarrassing ten seconds after the rest of the crowd.

But I do have other, more reliable, and probably more meaningful memories. I remember the overwhelming *maleness* of it all – cigar and pipe smoke, foul language (words I had heard before, but not from adults, not at that volume), and I remember looking at the crowd more than at the players. From where I was sitting I could probably have counted twenty thousand heads; only the sports fan (or a rock star or politician) can do that. My father told me that there were nearly as many people in the stadium as lived in my town, and I was suitably awed.

It wasn't the size of the crowd that impressed me most, however, or the way that adults were allowed to shout abuse at the players as loudly as they wanted without attracting any attention. What impressed me most was just how much most of the men around me *hated*, really *hated*, being there. As far as I could tell, nobody seemed to enjoy, in the way that I understood the word, anything that happened during the entire afternoon. Within minutes of the kick-off there was real anger (You're a DISGRACE, Holt He's a DISGRACE' 'A hundred quid a week? A HUNDRED QUID A WEEK They should give that to me for watching you.'); as the game went on, the anger turned into outrage, and then seemed to curdle into sullen, silent discontent. When I went to other grounds I saw the same thing: that the natural state of the football fan is bitter disappointment, no matter what the score.

I'd been to public entertainments before, of course; I'd been to the cinema and the pantomime and to see my mother sing in the chorus of the *White Horse Inn* at the Town Hall. But that was different. The audiences I had hitherto been a part of had paid to have a good time and, though occasionally one might spot a fidgety child or a yawning adult, I hadn't ever noticed faces contorted by rage or despair or frustration. Entertainment as pain was an idea entirely new to me, and it seemed to be something I'd been waiting for.

It might not be too fanciful to suggest that it was an idea which shaped my life. I have always been accused of taking the things I love – football, of course, but also books and records – much too seriously, and I do feel a kind of anger when I hear a bad record, or when someone is lukewarm about a book that means a lot to me. Perhaps it was these bitter men in the West Stand at Arsenal who taught me how to get angry in this way; and perhaps it is why I earn some of my living as a critic – maybe it's those voices I can hear when I write. 'You're NO GOOD, X.' 'A LITERARY PRIZE? A LITERARY PRIZE? They should give one to me for having to read you.'

31 The writer thinks he doesn't remember much about the game because
A only one goal was scored.
B it was a new experience for him.
C he was too nervous in the crowd to watch what happened.
D he wanted to follow what the others in the crowd did.

32 The writer recalls more clearly that when he went to the game,
A he got embarrassed about coming from a small town.
B he became more confident about using bad language.
C he wished he could be like the men in the crowd.
D he was staggered at the number of people in the crowd.

33 What struck the writer about the attitude of the crowd?
A their envy of the players' earnings
B their constant changes of mood
C their unhappiness regardless of events
D their unfairness towards the players

34 The writer says that at other entertainments he had attended,
A the audience had had different expectations.
B the audience had behaved in a way he found more acceptable.
C he had not wanted to admit that he was bored.
D he had paid less attention to the reactions of the audience.

35 What does the writer say about himself in the last paragraph?
A He is not very good as a critic.
B His opinions on certain things might be considered too strong.
C Certain accusations against him are unfair.
D He has been influenced too much by his experiences of football crowds.

Before you check your answers to these questions, go on to pages 14 and 15.

A DETAILED STUDY

The questions on these pages will help you to make sure that you have chosen the correct options for the questions on the second text, on pages 12–13.

Question 31 *Look at the first paragraph of the text and answer these questions.*

1 Is the writer sure that only one goal was scored in the whole game?

....

2 Does the writer refer to being scared in the crowd? If so, where?

....

3 Is the writer sure that he copied the behaviour of the crowd?

....

4 What do the adjectives 'bewildering' and 'incomprehensible' suggest?
a the writer's sense of danger at the football match
b the writer's desire to understand the conventions of football matches
c the writer's unfamiliarity with what happened at football matches
d the writer's disinterest in what was going on around him

....

Question 32 *Look at the second paragraph of the text and answer these questions.*

1 Does the writer refer to using bad language himself? If so, where?

....

2 Which of the following is closest in meaning to 'awed'?
a pleased
b disturbed
c amazed
d educated

....

3 Does the writer mention a feeling about his town? If so, where?

....

4 What does the writer mean by 'the overwhelming maleness of it all'?

....

Question 33 *Look at the third paragraph of the text and answer these questions.*

1 Does the writer say that a crowd's mood changes if their team is winning? If so, where?

....

2 Does the writer refer to feeling sympathy with the players? If so, where?

....

3 Does the man who shouts at Holt compare his earnings with those of Holt? If so, how?

....

4 Find as many words as you can in the paragraph which are closely connected in meaning with feeling angry.

....

Question 34 *Look at the fourth paragraph of the text and answer these questions.*

1 What does the writer mean by the phrase 'Entertainment as pain'?

....

2 What did audiences at other entertainments expect when they went to them?

....

3 Does the writer suggest that he looked at the audience at other entertainments? If so, where?

....

4 Does the writer say that he fidgeted or yawned at other entertainments? If so, where?

....

5 Does the writer suggest a preference concerning the crowds at football matches and the audience at other entertainments? If so, which did he prefer?

....

Question 35 *Look at the last paragraph of the text and answer these questions.*

1 What does the writer say about his attitude as a critic?

....

2 What has he been accused of?

....

3 How does he react to bad records and other people's opinions of books he likes?

....

4 Does he suggest that he thinks going to football matches as a boy had a bad effect on him? If so, where?

....

Now check your answers to the questions on these pages. Then decide whether you wish to change any of the answers that you gave to the questions on the second passage, on pages 12–13.

Then check your answers to the questions in the test on the second passage.

THIRD PASSAGE

Most journalists hate conducting one-to- one interviews. I hate them. I'm not very good at them. People never know how to edit their own lives. They don't understand what it is about them that makes a good story; they have no comprehension that five minutes' talk comes out at a thousand words. They'll go on for two hours and expect to see every sentence in print, verbatim. And they're obsessed with minutiae.

Journalists who do relish writing interviews are rare. And the good ones are worth their weight in sales figures. One of them told me that the trick is to keep as much of your personality out of the talk as possible. An interview isn't a dinner-party conversation. The most common failure for journalists is that they want their subjects to like them, and it is this that's at the heart of the dreadful fiasco that has become the TV chat show. Now, before you skip down the page to find something you haven't heard a million times before, this is not another slap in the face of the genre: this is more in the nature of constructive criticism.

There is in television a big divide between political current affairs interviews and social celebrity ones. It's a self-imposed and artificial division. On the whole, news-driven interviewers are pretty good. They consider themselves journalists and behave and ask questions like journalists. On the other hand, chat-show hosts want to see themselves as celebrities who are allowing the public to eavesdrop on mutual celebrity inanity and warmth. The questions are supposed to be as interesting as the answers. It's the fame of familiarity. And it's dull beyond screaming. The editorial supposition is that the viewers will be eternally enthralled by the electric propinquity of fame, and will just stare like children watching pandas at the zoo.

This might have been true once. But it is equally true that there never was a golden age of chat. The present hosts are just as ingratiating as they ever were. But the audience isn't. You and I have changed, grown up, grown sophisticated and blasé, and the nature of celebrities has changed. In the 1960s and 1970s, celebrity came with its own cachet. But not any more. The population explosion in fame and notoriety has devalued the currency. Chat shows have invented so much celebrity, made it so ubiquitous, that simply coming on and saying 'Hi, let me giggle for a couple of minutes', isn't enough.

Surely there must come a time when celebrities with new films, books, records will stop doing these shows, simply because the audience will actively hate them for it, for wasting their time. No professional entertainer would dare offer the disengaged, low-calibre performance of these shows if their name were above the heading and the public had to buy tickets.

36 According to the writer, one-to-one interviews are difficult because
- **A** interviewees don't realize what journalists need.
- **B** interviewees avoid talking about what journalists want to talk about.
- **C** journalists rapidly get bored when listening to most interviewees.
- **D** what interviewees say sometimes doesn't make sense.

37 The writer implies that readers might 'skip down the page' because
- **A** his comparison between journalism and chat shows will be complicated.
- **B** they think he is going to repeat a familiar point of view.
- **C** he has already written many articles about chat shows.
- **D** they are not interested in either journalism or chat shows.

38 According to the writer, what is assumed by programme makers about chat shows?
- **A** that viewers like to feel they are entering the world of the famous
- **B** that political interviewers do not make good chat-show hosts
- **C** that their hosts will enable celebrities to seem more interesting than they are
- **D** that viewers prefer them to political current affairs programmes

39 What is different from the 1960s and 1970s, according to the writer?
- **A** The kind of people hosting chat shows has changed.
- **B** The guests on chat shows are no longer as famous as guests used to be.
- **C** There are a great many more famous people than there used to be.
- **D** The same guests keep appearing on chat shows.

40 What is the writer's conclusion about chat shows?
- **A** They will be forced to improve in quality.
- **B** Famous people will refuse to appear on them.
- **C** Viewers have formed a low opinion of them.
- **D** They are the worst form of entertainment.

Now check your answers to these questions.

PAPER 2 COMPOSITION 2 hours

*Write **two only** of the composition exercises. Your answers must follow exactly the instructions given. Write in pen, not pencil. You are allowed to make alterations, but make sure your work is clear and easy to read.*

1 Describe someone who you believe to be one of the most significant figures of the 20th century. Why is/was this person so significant in their field? (About 350 words)

2 'The thing that annoys me most is ......' Write a composition that begins with these words. (About 350 words)

3 Write a story entitled 'The happiest day of my life.' You may describe a real day or an imaginary one. (About 350 words)

4 You are organizing a special event at your school, college or place of work. Write a notice giving details of what the event will involve. (About 300 words)

Before you write your compositions, go on to pages 18 and 19.

PLANNING A COMPOSITION

One of the questions in Paper 2 requires you to **describe** something or someone.

Look at question 1 on page 17 and then answer the following. This will enable you to get some ideas and make some notes that will form the plan for your composition for that question. It is advisable to practise each of the types of composition.

1 Decide which of the following the person is/was involved in.

- ☐ the Arts
- ☐ politics
- ☐ sport
- ☐ medicine
- ☐ the military
- ☐ science/technology
- ☐ religion
- ☐ other (specify below)

....

2 Name the person you have chosen.

....

3 Note the person's main achievement(s) briefly.

....

....

....

....

....

....

....

4 Note brief reasons why this or these are or were so significant.

....

....

....

5 Note briefly what this person's motives are/were.

....

....

....

6 What are/were some of the person's main qualities?

- ☐ patience
- ☐ originality
- ☐ forward thinking
- ☐ determination
- ☐ eccentricity
- ☐ modesty
- ☐ confidence
- ☐ other (specify below)

....

....

....

Now use these notes to write your composition. You may, of course, wish to include other points or not include some of the points noted here.

Then write one or more of the other compositions.

Now read through the following sample composition for question 1. When you have done so, answer the questions that follow it.

When at the age of fifteen Albert Einstein found pedagogic methods useless and irritating nobody suspected that he would be one of the most characteristic figures in the field of science and mathematics and virtually the founder of the theory of the Universe.

At the age of nine he stuttered and his family saw no future in him. At the age of fifteen he was compelled by his teachers to leave school, so he started engaging himself in mathematics and geometry. At 1900 he graduated from Zurich's Polytechnic School, without any distinction. He got a poorly paid job, but with a lot of leisure time to work on his own projects and personal worries.

At the age of twenty-six he published three theses, about photoelectric phenomenon, Brown activity and the theory of relativity, and he received two Nobel prizes. The theory of relativity is one of the most significant achievements of humanity. Einstein once said about his theory: 'There is no number of experiments that can prove I'm right, but one single experiment can prove I'm wrong'.

Einstein also helped in the construction of the atomic bomb, urged by the need to oppose to Nazi's menace. But he was a great pacifist and he believed in the peaceful and beneficial use of atomic energy. He was engaged in all the great and thorny problems of our century, such as global peace and the opposition to energy to every form of violence, justice, reciprocal respect between people and with all the social and political problems.

Therefore and because of his jewish origin he was persecuted all his life by the Nazi. He fought for the protection and freedom of the Jews and the retrieval of their country. He protested against Nazi's violence and he made every possible effort to provide help and shelter to the victims of Nazi's brutality.

But his dilemma was tragic: he either would continue to deny his support to the fight against the Nazi or he would abandon the beliefs that all his life he had supported. He chose the second and helped humanity exterminate its worst enemy.

1 Does the composition actually answer the question set or does it contain irrelevant parts, 'waffle' – writing that is simply intended to fill the space but does not really say anything – or 'padding' – writing that is repetitious in order to reach the required number of words?

2 Is the composition well-organized? Is it divided into paragraphs appropriately? Explain what each paragraph contains.

3 Are appropriate linking words and phrases used for connecting sentences and paragraphs? Give examples of some that are; if some are not, correct them.

4 Does it have a good range of appropriate vocabulary or is the vocabulary used mostly too simple? Give examples and correct any inappropriate or incorrect vocabulary.

5 Is there a good range of accurate structures forming sentences that are not just simple or are the structures used mostly too basic? Give examples and correct any incorrect structures or other mistakes.

6 Is the style appropriate for this type of composition?

Now check your assessment of and corrections to this sample composition.

PAPER 3 USE OF ENGLISH 2 hours

SECTION A

1 *Fill each of the numbered blanks in the passage with* **one** *suitable word.*

JENGA

A delivery man who called (1) .... the interview for this article spotted the wooden blocks on the table. 'Hey, I know (2) .... game,' he exclaimed. And so he was (3) .... to Leslie Scott, inventor of *Jenga*. 'Great game,' he said. 'But let's (4) .... it, it's money for nothing.'

His quip (5) .... to its simplicity. Wooden bricks are arranged in a tower (6) .... each player must find a loose brick, push it out and replace it (7) .... top. The (8) .... this goes on, the more unstable the tower becomes, until eventually the (9) .... lot comes crashing down.

Leslie first played the game as a child, (10) .... living in Ghana. The pieces had been bought (11) .... building blocks for a younger brother. They used them to play a game called *Takoradi Bricks*, (12) .... after a nearby port. When Leslie returned to England, her friends loved the game and, (13) .... up a promising career as a marketing manager, she went (14) .... business producing it. Its name was (15) .... to *Jenga*, a Swahili word (16) .... 'to build'.

A sympathetic bank manager (17) .... to a loan to finance the venture. She exhibited *Jenga* at a toy fair but didn't sell a (18) .... copy. Her lucky break came when a Canadian businessman played the game, liked it and (19) .... it on. It has sold in millions, but (20) .... Leslie has made a fortune from *Jenga*, she still invents games.

Before you check your answers to this part of the test, go on to page 21.

FILL IN THE MISSING WORD

Look again at Part 1 of this test on page 20.

– First of all, decide **what kind of word** must fill the gap (a verb? a preposition? etc.) Then decide which of the choices given below could fill each gap.

– You may need to **change the form** of the words given below in order to fill the gap. Some of the choices below do not fill any of the gaps. None of the choices fills more than one gap.

You may wish to change some of the answers you gave in the test after you have done this. However, if an answer that you gave in the test is not among the choices here, this does not necessarily mean that it is wrong.

VERBS	CONJUNCTIONS	ADJECTIVES	DETERMINERS	PREPOSITIONS
agree	whereas	full	that	as
show	although	single	the	on
mean	so	long	one	for
refer	while	complete		at
name	and	high		up
take	despite	whole		into
face	though	total		for
allow		tall		during
regard		great		
give				
stand				
introduce				
change				
call				

Now check your answers to these questions and to Part 1 of the test. Then go on to Part 2 of the test on page 22.

2 *Finish each of the following sentences in such a way that it is as similar as possible in meaning to the sentence printed before it.*

Example: She said that he was a brilliant musician.
Answer: She described *him as a brilliant musician.*

a Arguing with her won't get you anywhere.

It won't do ....

b I have only had to have this car repaired once.

On only ....

c All the other guests were embarrassed when he told a disgusting joke.

To ....

d I hope it's not inconvenient for me to phone you so late.

I hope I'm not putting..

e Fortunately, I found another job shortly afterwards.

I had..

f We only came to this restaurant because you insisted that we did so.

It was at ....

g She was definitely displeased when I told her.

She was anything ....

h His description of the incident was completely different from what really happened.

His description of the incident bore ....

Before you check your answers to this part, go on to page 23.

COMPLETE THE SENTENCES

Look again at Part 2 of this test on page 22, and then decide which of the following choices for each question could be the next word in each sentence. Sometimes only one of the choices could come next and sometimes more than one of them could come next. You may wish to change some of the answers you gave in the test when you have made your choice or choices. However, if the first word of the answer that you gave there is not included among the choices here, your answer is not necessarily incorrect.

a **1** you
2 good
3 no
4 any
5 some

b **1** an
2 one
3 but
4 a
5 the

c **1** the
2 make
3 a
4 all
5 tell

d **1** for
2 you
3 it
4 on
5 to

e **1** a
2 rather
3 an
4 the
5 so

f **1** your
2 only
3 this
4 the
5 our

g **1** else
2 but
3 than
4 instead
5 not

h **1** an
2 difference
3 no
4 any
5 complete

Now check your answers to these questions and to Part 2 of the test.

Then go on to Part 3 of the test on page 24.

3 *Fill each of the blanks with a suitable word or phrase.*

Example: She had difficulty making up her mind which one to buy.

a For ...., Andrew is annoyed with me, but I don't know what it is.

b Short .... in my resignation and walking out, there was nothing I could do.

c There's nothing out .... about this sort of thing, it happens all the time.

d They were talking so loud that I .... overhearing what they said.

e To .... worse, it started to rain as soon as the car broke down.

f Let's reach an agreement .... all, so that we don't have to discuss this ever again.

Now check your answers to this part of the test.

---

4 *For each of the sentences below, write a new sentence as similar as possible in meaning to the original sentence, but using the word given. This word* ***must not be altered*** *in any way.*

Example: She paid no attention to his warning.
notice
Answer: *She took no notice of his warning.*

a I'll have to find out about the background to the problem before I can comment.
acquaint

....

b Tom remained in a deep sleep throughout the thunderstorm.
sound

....

c I tried as hard as I could to make their stay here enjoyable.
utmost

....

d If I were you, I wouldn't spend more than you can afford too often.
habit

....

e The whole enterprise was very dangerous.
fraught

....

f I admire Julie totally.
nothing

....

g It's clear to everyone that he's excellent at his job.
denying

....

h I told the manager very clearly that I would not tolerate such appalling service.
uncertain

....

Now check your answers to this part of the test.

SECTION B

Read the following passage, then answer the questions which follow it.

Travel writer-turned-TV presenter

The scene is a canal in Venice. A barge nudges the pavement; an artichoke salesman deftly trims his wares. Houses and tourists shimmer upside-down in the water. Or they would if I was being a travel writer. As a travel presenter, all I can see is the muzzle of a camera, the crate of tomatoes where I am shortly to start my first piece to camera, and the plastic bottle marking where I must stop. And about 50 grinning schoolchildren who have paused to watch the fun.

'In your own time,' calls John, the director, and for a second I think about legging it out of shot and down the nearest alley. Instead, I head for the tomatoes and start to speak. I fluff my lines immediately and walk back to the beginning. 'Replay,' says a teenager slyly, leaning against the wall. I start again. This time some of the elderly shoppers turn to stare; I am wearing a radio mike, and if you are short-sighted enough not to spot the camera it looks as though I am talking to myself.

The assistant producer dives into a bar and I assume that he is phoning Manchester ('She's appalling. For God's sake get someone out here who can speak.'), but in fact a video game is interfering with our sound. The player agrees to stop for five minutes.

So this is what it's like, being a TV personality. Andrew and Nigel (cameraman and sound recordist: it's all first names in TV land) are reassuring. 'There are so many things that can go wrong,' they say cheerfully. Whenever I mess up, they assure me that it was the sound or the focus, for which I am pitifully grateful. But I've read *The Moon's a Balloon*, and I remember that incident David Niven describes: when as a nervous young actor he did the first take and the extras and crew burst into spontaneous, and totally insincere, applause ... just to make him relax. So I never entirely believe them.

Standing about in Venice in various attitudes, gazing into Andrew's lens as Nigel fiddles with my shirt, fixing the radio mike, I have plenty of time to mull over the differences between travel writing and travel presenting. The only thing they have in common is the subject. As a writer, you can afford to let things happen, to let a destination unfold around you. Sometimes nothing happens. At others, events happen so perfectly they seem orchestrated. You can move about unseen. You can walk, talk, smell, watch and listen. You can conduct rambling interviews with people who may tell you nothing of value to your article, but who are good company. Or go for pointless walks just to get the feel of the place.

Television can afford no such luxury. Translating the feeling of a place into visual images requires a strange combination of creativity and clockwork organization. For a start, there are quantities of people involved, both on the shoot and in the production office. Buildings must be 'filmable' at the right time of day. Interviewees, however charming, must be able to perform. Complicated permissions must be sought. Pitfalls like noise or traffic problems must be anticipated. Above all, something *must* happen in front of the camera. There is no time to waste.

Writing for television requires speed, economy and the realization that the pictures do a lot of the work for you. You soon find that a paragraph of writing does not necessarily make a fine piece of speaking. My input on the Venice film, my first, was limited by inexperience and by the fact that I was too worried about my lines to think straight, but even so, I could sense the excitement when it starts to work; the feeling of teamwork that simply doesn't exist in my other life. There is even something about performing that appeals to me at some level. When you get it right, of course.

I find myself looking at my new job with a combination of horror and delight.There are so many new things to learn, for instance, in this busy and confusing world of GVs (general views, otherwise known as 'pretties'), APs (assistant producers) and PTCs (pieces to camera), I am known as 'the talent'. I find this wildly flattering – a sure sign of ignorance – and am rather looking forward to my next film.

a What contrast does the writer describe in the first paragraph?

b What is meant by 'legging it' in line 6?

c What is meant by the phrase 'fluff my lines' in line 7?

d Why might the writer have seemed to the elderly shoppers to be behaving strangely?

e Explain in your own words what the writer thought the assistant producer was going to say about her on the phone.

f What does the writer mean by 'it's all first names in TV land' (line 16)?

g Explain in your own words what the writer is 'pitifully grateful' for (line 18).

h What does recalling David Niven's story make her think?

i Explain the phrase 'mull over' (line 23).

j What does 'others' in line 26 refer to?

k Explain what the writer means by the phrase 'do a lot of the work for you' in lines 36–37.

....

l Explain in your own words why the writer's input on the Venice film was limited.

....

....

m What is implied by the alternative name for GVs?

....

n In your own words, explain what the writer says about being known as 'the talent'?

....

....

....

o In a paragraph of 70–90 words, summarize the ways in which travel writing and making TV travel programmes differ, according to the writer.

....

....

....

....

....

....

....

....

....

....

Before you check your answers to this part of the test, go on to page 28.

ANSWERING THE QUESTIONS – GENERAL NOTES

When answering the questions in this part of the paper it is important to remember the following:

– You often do not have to write complete sentences. Sometimes it may be necessary to do so, especially when a longer answer is required, but many of the questions can be answered with a phrase, and sometimes quite a short phrase. If you write more than is required, you may make unnecessary mistakes.

– There is sometimes more than one element to answers, with a mark given for each element. Make sure that you have given a full answer and not left out anything relevant.

A DETAILED STUDY

Many of the questions in this part of the paper test detailed comprehension of parts of the text. To answer them well, it is a good idea to follow this procedure:

– locate the relevant part of the text

– decide **exactly** what is stated there

– decide whether there is **more than one aspect** to the answer; this may not be the case but make sure that you have not failed to include something required

– work out how to phrase your answer. It may be necessary to write a full sentence and the answer may be fairly complicated. However, it may be possible to answer with a fairly simple phrase or sentence. Do not feel that you have to be elaborate. You may spoil an answer that would otherwise be correct by trying to write something unnecessarily complicated.

Look at question a

What jobs done by the writer are mentioned in the first paragraph?

....

Look at question d

What do we learn about her radio mike in the second paragraph?

....

Look at question e

What does 'She's appalling' (lines 12 and 13) mean and who does it describe?

....

Look at question g

What does 'it' in line 17 refer to?
a something that can go wrong
b the solution
c her problem
d what went wrong

....

Look at question h

Do we know whether David Niven's performance was good or not?

....

Look at question n

1 Do you think that the term 'the talent' is applied to her in particular or to TV presenters in general?

....

2 In the context, 'wildly' means
a insincerely
b surprisingly
c extremely
d strangely

....

3 In this context, 'ignorance' means
a lack of knowledge
b insensitivity
c lack of intelligence
d disregard

....

Now check your answers to these questions and decide whether you wish to change any of the answers you gave in the test. If you have phrased anything you wrote in the test differently from the choices given on these pages, this does not necessarily mean that you answered incorrectly in the test.

Then check your answers to questions (a)–(n) of Section B of the test on pages 26–27.

WRITING A SUMMARY – GENERAL NOTES

When you are writing your summary, it is important to remember the following:

– You must keep to the limit on the number of words specified in the paper.

– You must not copy long phrases or sentences from the passage.

– You are not writing a composition and, since you are restricted to a relatively small number of words, it is advisable to keep the language that you use relatively simple. If you write long, elaborate sentences, you will not be able to cover all the main points in the required number of words and you may make unnecessary mistakes trying to do something you are not required to do.

– This part of the paper requires you to summarize briefly **only relevant points** in the passage relating to the aspect of it you are asked about. You may need to summarize a particular section of the passage, the passage as a whole or a number of small parts scattered around the passage. Make sure you include as many relevant points as you can in your summary without exceeding the word limit.

For the summary in this test, answer these questions.

1 Whereabouts in the passage do you think the material for your summary will come from? Explain your answer.
- **a** the passage as a whole
- **b** a section of the passage
- **c** various small parts scattered around the passage

2 Decide which of the following could be included as relevant main points in the summary. Tick the box next to each point that could be included.

TRAVEL WRITING

1 You don't have to plan things in advance. ☐
2 You can walk around a lot. ☐
3 It doesn't matter if you waste your time. ☐
4 You are on your own. ☐
5 You meet interesting people. ☐
6 Sometimes events happen perfectly. ☐

MAKING TV TRAVEL PROGRAMMES

1 Noise and traffic cause problems. ☐
2 Everything has to be planned in advance. ☐
3 Buildings are important. ☐
4 Everything you do has to be worthwhile. ☐
5 Your style of writing has to be economical. ☐
6 Lots of people are involved. ☐

Now look again at your summary and decide whether you wish to change anything.

SAMPLE SUMMARY

Now read this sample summary and answer the questions that follow it.

> As a travel writer the author has a certain independence, she can chose what to do and when and wait for things to happen and do her job without being noticed. In television, however, things such as when and what to film, the timing, organization and teamwork are very important. Also, there must be something happening in front of the cameras and what would be a nice written article is not always as good when it is spoken.

a Is anything irrelevant included or anything relevant not included? If so, what?

b Are there any language mistakes? Correct any that you think there are.

c Has any of the passage simply been copied in the summary? If so, what?

Now look again at your summary and decide whether you wish to change anything.

Then check your marks for your summary and read the assessment of this sample summary.

PAPER 4 LISTENING COMPREHENSION (about 30 mins)

PART ONE

You will hear part of a radio programme about people who have won an enormous amount of money on the national lottery in Britain. ***For questions 1–7****, choose the best answer,* ***A****,* ***B****,* ***C*** *or* ***D****.*

1 What does Hunter say about the 25 people in his book?

A Some of them disliked living abroad.
B None of them avoided changing in some way.
C Some of them had bad reactions from others.
D Few of them had had any intention of living abroad.

2 What does Hunter say about winners giving money to charity?

A The vast majority don't really intend to do so.
B Most of them never give it any thought.
C Their families often persuade them not to.
D They all prefer to give it to their families.

3 Some newspapers portrayed Mark Gardiner as

A being a mysterious figure.
B dishonest in what he told them.
C undeserving of such great wealth.
D leading a disreputable life.

4 Mark Gardiner has built up his business to

A do some good for the town he lives in.
B show he's a capable businessman.
C prove that wealth hasn't changed him.
D provide jobs for other people.

5 Hunter implies that the story in *The Mirror*

A is a distortion of the truth.
B proves that he was right in his book.
C should have said where the information came from.
D was meant to reduce the impact of his book.

6 What did Hunter discover when he met the couple in *The Mirror's* story?

A They are not as extraordinary as people might think.
B They were not the sort of people he'd expected them to be.
C They clearly weren't telling him the whole story.
D They had struggled to keep the secret from the man's mother.

7 What is Hunter's current view of that couple?

A Keeping their win secret wasn't a bad idea.
B They shouldn't have confided in him.
C The publicity will affect them badly.
D They haven't come to terms with winning.

PART TWO

You will hear a talk about old beliefs associated with houses in Britain. ***For questions 8–17****, complete the sentences.*

In Wales, if you moved house, the person transporting your furniture took **8** ________ with him.

If you visited someone you had to enter and leave **9** ________.

It was bad luck to drop your front-door key unless you **10** ________ immediately.

In sitting-rooms, people often took part in **11** ________.

A square-shaped spark with crackles meant that a letter with **12** ________ would arrive.

If a **13** ________ came from a piece of coal, it meant that a fisherman was about to come home.

It was believed that the roof would fall down if you **14** ________.

You could predict who was going to visit if you **15** ________.

If you received any kind of **16** ________, you had to give a coin in return.

It was considered bad luck to **17** ________ on a Sunday.

PART THREE

You will hear part of a radio programme, in which the children of famous fathers are interviewed. ***For questions 18–25****, decide which of them makes the statements. Write* ***G*** *for George,* ***R*** *for Ruth or* ***M*** *for Mark.*

When I was little, people accepted what I said about my father.	*18*	
My father's name denied me certain career opportunities.	*19*	
It is easier to be a famous person than the child of one.	*20*	
People have asked me to behave like my father.	*21*	
I was keen to avoid criticizing him when I wrote about my father.	*22*	
I regret some of what my book about my father contains.	*23*	
I learnt an attitude to life from my father.	*24*	
There are unlikely to be more people like my father.	*25*	

Before you check your answers to this Paper, go on to pages 33–34.

MULTIPLE-CHOICE QUESTIONS

It is important to bear in mind the following points concerning the multiple-choice questions on the Listening Paper:

- it is likely that the multiple-choice questions will focus more on the attitudes, opinions and feelings expressed on the tape than on straightforward information;
- the correct answer may depend on *inferring* from what is said and may not be based on something that is directly stated;
- the correct answer is unlikely to be the one that you would predict from common sense or general knowledge.

Listen again to Part 1 of the test on page 31, and answer the following questions by ticking the appropriate boxes. You may need to tick more than one box in each question. This will give you further practice in how to approach answering multiple-choice questions when listening and enable you to check the answers that you gave in the test. The numbers below refer to the questions in the test on page 31.

(Stop the tape after Hunter's first speech)

1 Which of the following does Hunter say about the people in his book?

A Many had said they'd leave the country if they won. ☐
B Some of them tried living abroad. ☐
C It is inevitable that they changed to some extent. ☐
D Other people started to treat them differently. ☐
E They didn't want to change when they won. ☐
F Other people got jealous when they won. ☐

(Stop the tape after Hunter's second speech)

2 Which of the following does Hunter say about winners giving money away?

A Winners don't mention giving money to charity. ☐
B Not every winner has given money to their families. ☐
C Winners don't believe in giving to charity. ☐
D Winners claim that they will give to charity when they die. ☐
E Winners' families put pressure on them. ☐
F Their families sometimes feel they should be given more. ☐

(Stop the tape after Hunter's next speech)

3 Hunter says that the press reacted to Mark Gardiner

A with annoyance at his refusal to cooperate with them. ☐
B with confusion because they could not understand him. ☐
C with a nickname meant to indicate that he was a bad person. ☐
D with disapproval because of the number of his wives and girlfriends. ☐
E with horror at the amount of money he had won. ☐
F with a desire to show that he had lied about himself. ☐

(Stop the tape after Hunter's next speech)

4 Which of the following do we learn about Mark Gardiner after he won?

A Winning gave him a chance to be a good businessman. ☐
B He wanted to use his money to help local people. ☐
C He thought he would be accused of losing control of his spending. ☐
D He wanted to make up for his previous failure in business. ☐
E He had always been fond of his home town. ☐
F If his business had failed, it wouldn't have mattered much to him. ☐

(Stop the tape after Hunter's next speech)

5 Which of these comments does Hunter make about *The Mirror's* story?

A People had doubted it was true when he put it in his book. ☐
B It has been presented in a reasonable way. ☐
C It was copied from his book. ☐
D It is a deliberate attempt to affect sales of his book. ☐
E It contains some inaccuracies. ☐
F It does not refer to his book. ☐

(Stop the tape after Hunter's next speech)

6 Which of the following does Hunter say about when he met the couple?

A There were aspects of their situation that the man concealed from him. ☐
B It had been hard for them to conceal the truth from the man's mother. ☐
C When he arrived at their house, he decided he wouldn't like them. ☐
D Their situation is typical of that of many winners. ☐
E They refused to tell him why they hadn't told the man's mother. ☐
F The man's appearance put him off. ☐

(Stop the tape after Hunter's last speech)

7 Which opinion(s) of the couple does Hunter express or imply?

A Winning is still a shock to them. ☐
B It is his fault that their story is in the newspaper. ☐
C Keeping it secret has enabled them to adapt to winning. ☐
D They will probably regret keeping their win secret. ☐
E Their personalities are likely to change now. ☐
F They wanted their story to come out one day. ☐

Now check your answers to the questions on these pages. When you have done so, decide whether you wish to change any of the answers you gave in Part 1 of the test on page 31.

Then check your answers to Part 1 of the test and then to Parts 2 and 3 on page 32.

PAPER 5 INTERVIEW

1 *Look at one or more of these photographs and answer the questions that follow them.*

1

2

3

What's happening in each picture? What's the situation?
Describe the people. What kind of people are they?
Describe the places where they are. What objects can you see in these places?
What feelings do the people appear to have?
What appears to be the relationship between the people?

Do you think that you get on well with people generally? If so, why? If not, why not?
What do you most like doing with your friends? Why do you enjoy this?
What kind of people do you find it easiest/most difficult to get on with? Why is this?
Do you consider that people in your country are generally friendly to strangers and visitors or not?
How does this compare with people in other countries, in your opinion?

2 *Read one or more of these passages and then answer the questions that follow them.*

a Alec Guinness has never had any reservations about the judgement his wife makes of his own work. 'She doesn't have to be critical. She is very very tactful and knows when comments might be injurious. But I know what she is thinking, and when she tells me I half listen, half resent it. But maybe she only drops one word about the whole performance and she is usually right.'

b There was a silence. 'We parted friends, Lena, can we not remain friends?'

'We didn't part friends.'

'Yes we did. I remember the night.'

'We parted without a fight or a scene. I certainly wasn't your friend then, nor am I now.' There was a silence.

Lena spoke again. 'So if that's all, may I wish you well. And hope that you get over this problem with your father-in-law. I'm sure you will, you're a man of great charm.'

c Happy relationships require goodwill and perseverance, and although there will always be problems if other people are bent on causing friction, there is a great deal we can do if we genuinely seek for harmony and are prepared to make a few concessions. I would never advocate peace at any price – that would undermine our self-respect – but many disagreements can only be resolved by compromise and sometimes we have to give way a little.

What kind of book do you think each passage comes from?
What relationships are described in each passage?

3 *Do one or more of these tasks. If you are working with others, discuss them together.*

a ' ..... and that's how we became friends.'

Describe how you met someone who became a good friend of yours.
What do/did you particularly like about that person?
Does/Did that person have any faults in your view? If so, describe them.
Is that person still a friend of yours? If so, describe your relationship now. If not, why did the friendship end?

b Describe an occasion on which you got very angry with someone.
What made you get so angry? How did the other person react?
Do you think now that you were right to get so angry or do you regret it?

Describe an occasion on which someone got very angry with you. Why did he/she get so angry? How did you react? Do you think now that he/she was justified?
Did you think then that he/she was justified?

c Describe an occasion on which you have been with a group of strangers. How did you feel? What did you do? Do you find it easy to talk to strangers?

In what situations do you feel tense, shy or embarrassed? How do you deal with that?
Imagine that you meet a stranger in the following situations. What would you say to them? What would you talk about?

- in the next seat on a train, plane or bus
- before a job interview
- in the next seat at the theatre or cinema
- at a party or wedding
- the person is the friend of a friend

DESCRIBING FEELINGS

You may be required in the interview to talk about your own or other people's feelings. If so, it is a good idea to be able to use more than just simple words for this.

To check or build up your vocabulary on this subject, look at the adjectives, nouns and verbs listed below. Decide which ones refer to anger, which ones refer to fear, which ones refer to happiness and which ones refer to unhappiness. Put them into the correct columns.

exasperated (adj)
bliss (noun)
disquiet (noun)
dejected (adj)
elation (noun)
fret (verb)
irate (adj)
incensed (adj)
relish (verb + noun)
indignant (adj)
sour (adj)
cut up (adj) (informal)
jubilant (adj)
glee (noun)
apprehensive (adj)
animosity (noun)
intimidated (adj)
grieve (verb)
despair (adj + noun)
anguish (noun)
despondent (adj)
trepidation (noun)
fume (verb)
disconsolate (adj)
perturbed (adj)
revel in (phrasal verb)
demoralized (adj)
chuffed (adj) (slang)
livid (adj)
unnerved (adj)

ANGER	***FEAR***	***HAPPINESS***	***UNHAPPINESS***

Now check your answers to these questions.

RELATIONSHIPS

In the interview, you may be required to talk about the relationships between people. To check or build up your vocabulary on this subject, answer the following questions about words and phrases connected with relationships.

1 If you **make conversation with** someone, what is the situation?

2 If you **see eye to eye with** someone, what is the situation?

3 Why might you **humour** someone?

4 Why might you want to **keep in with** someone?

5 If you **confide in** someone, what happens?

6 If you **have words with** someone, what happens?

7 If you describe someone as **aloof**, how do they behave?

8 If you **hit it off with** someone, what happens?

9 If you are **at loggerheads with** someone, what is the situation?

10 What is **small talk** ?

11 If you have **an affinity with** someone, how do you feel about them?

12 If you **get on with someone like a house on fire**, what is your relationship with them?

13 If there is **camaraderie** among people, what is the situation?

14 What does a **supercilious** attitude involve?

15 If you establish **a rapport with** other people, how do you get on with them?

Now check your answers to these questions.

TEST TWO

PAPER 1 READING COMPREHENSION 1 hour

SECTION A

In this section you must choose the word or phrase which best completes each sentence. On your answer sheet indicate the letter **A, B, C** *or* **D** *against the number of each item* **1** *to* **25** *for the word or phrase you choose. Give one answer only to each question.*

1 Harry doesn't .... to great fame and fortune, he just wants to make a decent living.

A crave **B** hanker **C** yearn **D** aspire

2 A lot of people are .... to the damage that is being done to the environment.

A ignorant **B** uninitiated **C** blind **D** unacquainted

3 She showed little .... of the problems we were facing.

A affinity **B** appreciation **C** regard **D** sensitivity

4 After a few weeks in the job, he .... himself to be a valuable employee.

A established **B** vindicated **C** verified **D** proved

5 This is the .... timetable for the conference – it may change later.

A conditional **B** indefinite **C** provisional **D** indeterminate

6 They worked for six .... hours without a break.

A constant **B** incessant **C** solid **D** perpetual

7 I wrote to them a fortnight ago but .... I haven't had a reply.

A as yet **B** these days **C** so long **D** just now

8 I couldn't stop myself from .... with boredom during the lecture.

A sighing **B** gasping **C** panting **D** blowing

9 Sam has always taken the .... that there is more to life than money.

A outlook **B** view **C** belief **D** opinion

10 She didn't show even a .... of emotion when the court found her guilty.

A gleam **B** wink **C** flicker **D** flash

11 The manager's future .... whether the team wins or loses this one game.

A stems from **B** counts on **C** derives from **D** rests on

12 In all ...., you'll find that you needn't have worried about this problem.

A odds **B** chances **C** probability **D** prospect

13 He shouted so much during the match that his voice was .... afterwards.

A raucous **B** grating **C** shrill **D** hoarse

14 She didn't want to .... his feelings, so she pretended to like the present he had bought her.

A harm B wound C upset D hurt

15 His whole life seemed to fall .... when he lost his job.

A apart B through C away D out

16 In my opinion, he is .... the best player in the country.

A by far B vastly C a long way D extensively

17 She was at the .... of her fame when tragedy struck.

A height B point C top D head

18 I think it's .... whether he's as good an actor as some people say he is.

A debatable B argumentative C quarrelsome D moot

19 We're not in a .... hurry so let's have another coffee.

A dashing B racing C rushing D tearing

20 We hadn't seen each other for ten years and she'd changed out of all ....

A identification B recollection C recognition D familiarity

21 He didn't understand what I was saying so I had to .... it out to him in very simple terms.

A figure B spell C clear D stand

22 We went to the end of the street together and then we .... company.

A split B parted C separated D broke

23 It doesn't .... to approach the boss when he's busy, he gets very annoyed.

A benefit B pay C advantage D profit

24 Although it was against my ...., I had to do as I was told.

A option B desire C will D preference

25 On the .... occasions when I met him, I found him quite pleasant.

A scarce B abnormal C seldom D rare

Before you check your answers to this section of the test, go on to page 41.

GRAMMATICAL STRUCTURE

Some of the questions in this part of the test require you to decide which of the four options fits grammatically. In such questions, more than one of the options fits the meaning required to complete the sentence, but only one option can be followed by the grammatical structure after the gap.

The numbers of the exercises below refer to questions 1–4 of the test on page 39, which are questions of this type.

In each of the exercises, choose which of the four options given in the test fits each gap. This may help you to eliminate some of the incorrect options in the questions they refer to and to check or learn about the grammatical structures that may follow certain words.

1 | *craved* | *yearned* | *hankered* | *aspired* |

A When he started as an actor, he .... fame and fortune.

B I've always been good at golf but I've never .... to being a professional.

C After many years of hard work, Alison .... for an easy life.

D Michael has always .... after a life of luxury.

2 | *blind* | *uninitiated* | *ignorant* | *unacquainted* |

A When she started as an actress, she was .... in the ways of show business.

B Nick seems to be completely .... to the feelings of others.

C It soon became obvious that he was .... of the rules of the game.

D Being .... with such technical language, I didn't understand the article.

3 | *regard* | *sensitivity* | *appreciation* | *affinity* |

A I feel a strong .... with him because we've had similar experiences.

B Why can't you show a bit more .... towards other people?

C Some of the tourists here have little .... for the local people.

D Try to have some .... of the pressure she's under before you criticize her.

4 | *proved* | *indicated* | *established* | *verified* |

A She has .... herself as one of the country's leading artists.

B Stuart .... himself to be one of the most dishonest people I've ever met.

C Her account of what happened was .... by the police when they checked.

D He denied the allegations and was .... in a court of law.

Now check your answers to these exercises. When you have done so, decide whether you wish to change any of your answers to questions 1–4 in the test.

Then check your answers to the test.

SECTION B

*In this section you will find after each of the passages a number of questions or unfinished statements about the passage, each with four suggested answers or ways of finishing. You must choose the one which you think fits best. On your answer sheet, indicate the letter **A**, **B**, **C** or **D** against the number of each item **26** to **40** for the answer you choose. Give **one answer only** to each question.*

FIRST PASSAGE

Musicians are a species out of the Twilight Zone with something different in their brains. This alien something manifests itself as the ability to write, read and perform music but it also takes the place of certain thought processes that normal people have. They're all marching to the beat of a different drummer.

You doubt me? I once appeared as the star comedian at a classy night spot called *The Plantation*. There were five songs in my act at the time. The bass player and drummer rehearsed the material with me but the pianist failed to turn up. Frantic phone calls followed and twenty minutes before show time the exhausted manager came to my cramped dressing room with the news that a deputy had been found. I could only hope that whatever pianist was rushing to my aid could follow my cues without preparation. At ten-thirty I was standing behind the door that led to the cabaret room, waiting to be introduced. Peering through as the waitresses traversed, I could see that no one was seated on the piano stool. Then, as the disc jockey began my introduction, a big man in overalls pushed past me into the main room. His once-white boiler suit was smeared in a dozen hues of decorator's paint from collar to ankle and he carried a canvas bag of cans and brushes which he dumped on the stage beside the piano, unzipping and stepping out of his working chrysalis to reveal the dress-suited pupa from within. Some tables applauded. The big fellow nodded in acknowledgement, sat and drowned out the conclusion of the deejay's announcement with some arpeggio sweeps of the keyboard.

I thought I heard my name, came bouncing on stage and went into my opening number. Or rather, I tried to. The player painter did something that lesser musicians would never have attempted, let alone brought off. He proceeded to transpose all five of my songs into the key of C. It's not easy to sight-read unfamiliar tunes set in F flat and E flat and play them in C. It's pretty well impossible for a really good singer to follow suit, let alone a performer of limited range like me, once described by a critic as 'vocally impaired'.

Nevertheless, with desperate misjudgement, I attempted to sing the opening song in the key imposed, failing and so switching to a lower octave, changing upwards again, then settling for a sort of declamatory recitative of my perky lyric which a moment's sober consideration would have told me would be comedy suicide. The audience must have thought I was drunk, drugged or mad. Of course I should have cut the other four numbers but in those days my act was tightly routined and my gags were going well enough to lull me into a false sense of security about taking each musical hurdle as it approached. Needless to say, I fell at each one.

I came off to bewildered applause tinged with hostility. I couldn't blame them. I felt just as bewildered and hostile as the customers who had paid good money to hear me either shrieking my parodies at them as a strangling soprano, growling them inaudibly low or yelling them like a ham actor. I resolved to cut my songs down to three in future and, in fact, I've done that ever since.

As I changed my clothes in the dressing cupboard, I asked the bass player, 'What was all that about? He played everything in the wrong key.' 'Yeah, he always does that, does Big Phil. You just have to follow him, that's all you can do with Big Phil.'

I saw the pianist on my way to my car. He was standing under a lamp, counting the cash he'd been paid. 'Excuse me a moment. Why did you play all my music in C?' 'I do that. I'm known for it.' 'But why?' 'Sounds better,' he said and walked away to his van. I imagined hiring Big Phil to paint my house white and finding him painting it black because it looked better.

26 What was the author worried about just before he went on stage?

A whether the man in the boiler suit really was the deputy pianist
B whether the deputy pianist would play too loud
C whether the audience would laugh more at the deputy pianist than at him
D whether the lack of rehearsal with the deputy pianist would spoil his act

27 What did the author discover when he started his opening song?

A He wasn't as good a singer as he had thought he was.
B The deputy pianist was unable to play well without rehearsal.
C He couldn't sing the song in the way it was being played.
D The deputy pianist was playing the wrong song by mistake.

28 One reason why the author kept the other four numbers in his act was that

A the rest of his act was being quite well received.
B he was panicking too much to think clearly.
C his act would have been too short otherwise.
D the other numbers were easier for him to sing.

29 Why were the audience both bewildered and hostile?

A because of the peculiar way in which the author delivered the songs
B because they had not come to hear so many songs
C because they thought the author was not doing his best
D because of the changes the author made to the words of the songs

30 What does the anecdote prove to the author?

A that some musicians are unpredictable
B that all musicians are weird people
C that some musicians are more adaptable than others
D that all musicians are deliberately awkward

Now check your answers to these questions.

SECOND PASSAGE

With sinking heart, I stared at Saturday's *Times*. It was no different from any of the other papers, broadsheet or tabloid. Almost the whole of the front page was devoted to a single story. 'Tears as horrific case is outlined – murder jury told of discoveries 'more terrible than words can express'.' If only. If only we really would accept that there are things more terrible than words can express. If only the words would ever cease. But having expressed ourselves too shocked to speak, we speak. Having judged a scene indescribable, we go on to try to describe it. Having found a case too dreadful to talk about, we talk about it. On and on.

And, glancing at that front page, I should like to claim that my sinking heart was sinking under the weight of dismay at the emerging facts about the murders. But it wouldn't be true. The murders are awful beyond comprehension, and that's that. No, the heart sank for a more selfish reason. It sank because I was bored. It sank because Saturday's *Times* was signalling the imminence of weeks – perhaps months – of newspaper, magazine, television and radio news which will be of little interest to me. From now on and for a long time to come, whole reams of my own and every other newspaper will be, from this reader's point of view, a blank. You see, I *really* don't want to read about it. I can't summon up much interest in the details, I simply skip.

What sort of research is conducted, I wonder, into the influence of particular stories over customer decisions to purchase a newspaper? It is doubtful whether asking customers would be the way to learn. As any editor will tell you, people are prone to declare their disgust that a newspaper should give prominence to a story, and then eagerly buy it. Indeed, the division of public opinion into those who think the press 'ought' to cover a story and those who think it 'ought not' is false. Both these sections of our readers are likely to devour the story – the one blithely, the other guiltily, both avidly.

In human nature, the propensity to be shocked at published or broadcast material, judging it offensive, undignified or harmful, is quite close to the propensity to be drawn (whether or not protesting one's horror) towards it. I often suspect that the natural censors among us are driven by an unacknowledged fear of the ruder, more violent or perverted sides of their own natures. When it comes to the privacy of the newsagent's, a circulation manager can put them in the same category as the openly prurient: they buy, they read, they relish. Then they complain.

But there is another group among us: one which I doubt circulation managers acknowledge. We are not (if we are to be honest) so much 'shocked' by the murders as uncomprehending. Since there is nothing in it for us, we step round nasty stories about crime and violence. That something is not very nice does not – for us – necessarily arouse great curiosity about it. For the next month or so, as this case unfolds on the front pages, we shall be turning straight to page two. When those 'action' movies appear late at night on our televisions, we stare at the people gunning each other down, not in horror or even disgust. We stare blankly, uncomprehending as to what viewers see in this sort of thing. The sound of gunshots is just a noise. Frankly we are not shocked: we are simply bored.

Editors, directors of programming and circulation managers, please remember us.

31 What is the writer's main subject in the first paragraph?

A the language newspapers use when covering horrific court cases
B the human habit of talking about horrific things
C the impossibility of finding the right words in some circumstances
D the shocking crimes that human beings commit

32 What does the writer emphasize in the second paragraph?

A how much this particular case differs from others
B that this particular case has changed his attitude
C that media coverage of such cases is of low quality
D how sincere his reaction to this particular case is

33 Why is it wrong to ask readers why they buy a certain newspaper?

A Their actions contradict their stated opinions.
B They find it hard to explain the appeal of a certain newspaper.
C They keep changing their minds about what a newspaper should cover.
D The analysis of such research is often inaccurate.

34 The writer believes that people who judge material offensive

A should consider an alternative point of view.
B secretly gain pleasure from such material.
C reflect a view widely held in society.
D have too much influence on public opinion.

35 The writer includes himself among people who are

A vague about moral questions.
B resentful of changes in society.
C unmoved by horrific events.
D independent in their views on violence.

Now check your answers to these questions.

THIRD PASSAGE

I drove on forty miles south to Hannibal in Missouri, and went to see the author Mark Twain's boyhood home, a trim and tidy whitewashed house with green shutters set incongruously in the middle of the downtown. It cost $2 to get in and was a disappointment. It purported to be a faithful reproduction of the original interiors, but there were wires and water sprinklers clumsily evident in every room. I also very much doubt that young Samuel Clemens' (his real name) bedroom had vinyl on the floor (the same pattern as my mother's kitchen, I was interested to note) or that his sister's bedroom had a plywood partition in it. You don't actually go in the house; you look at it through the windows. At each window there is a recorded message telling you about that room as if you were a moron: 'This is the kitchen. This is where Mrs Clemens would prepare the family's meals ... ' The whole thing is pretty shabby, which wouldn't be so awful if it were owned by some underfunded local literary society and they were doing the best they could with it. In fact, it is owned by the city of Hannibal and it draws 135,000 visitors a year. It's a little gold mine for the town.

Next door, attached to the house, was a small museum, which was better. There were cases of Twain memorabilia – first editions, one of his typewriters, photographs, some letters. There was precious little to link him to the house or the town. It is worth remembering that Twain got the hell out of both Hannibal and Missouri as soon as he could, and was always disinclined to come back. I went outside and looked around. Next door to the Twain house and museum – and I mean absolutely next to it – was the Mark Twain Drive-In Restaurant and Dinette, with cars parked in little bays and people grazing off trays attached to their windows. It really lent the scene a touch of class. I began to understand why Clemens didn't just leave town but also changed his name.

I strolled around the business district. The whole area was a dispiriting combination of auto parts stores, empty buildings and vacant lots. I had always thought that all river towns, even the poor ones, had something about them – a kind of faded elegance, a raffish air – that made them more interesting than other towns, that the river served as a conduit to the larger world and washed up a more interesting and sophisticated brand of detritus. But not Hannibal. It had obviously had better days, but even they couldn't have been all that great. The Hotel Mark Twain was boarded up. That's a sad sight – a tall building with every window plugged with plywood. Every business in town appeared to trade on Twain and his books – the Mark Twain Roofing Company, the Mark Twain Shopping Center. You could even go and be insane at the Mark Twain Mental Health Center – a possibility that would, I imagine, grow increasingly likely with every day spent in Hannibal. The whole place was sad and awful. I had been planning to stay for lunch, but the thought of having to face a Mark Twain Burger left me without any appetite for either food or Hannibal.

I walked back to the car. Every parked car along the street had a licence plate that said 'Missouri – the Show Me State'. I wondered idly if this could be short for 'Show Me the Way to Any Other State'. In any case, I crossed the Mississippi – still muddy, still strangely unimpressive – on a long, high bridge and turned my back on Missouri without regret.

36 What particularly struck the writer about Mark Twain's house?

A the fact that there was an admission charge
B the number of recorded messages there were
C how it differed from the way it was described
D how strange it looked from the outside

37 The writer implies that Mark Twain's house

A has been spoilt by the number of visitors to it.
B makes more money for the town than it deserves.
C should not be open to the public.
D would be better if it was owned by a literary society.

38 The writer felt that the museum was better because

A there were a number of facilities close to it.
B it contained some very valuable exhibits.
C it had exhibits genuinely connected with Mark Twain.
D he could understand more about Twain's early life there.

39 What had the writer thought about river towns previously?

A The presence of the river gave them an appeal.
B The business districts in them were prosperous.
C They were clean and tidy in appearance.
D They were of purely historical interest.

40 Which of the following best describes the writer's tone in the passage as a whole?

A concerned
B intrigued
C light-hearted
D harsh

Before you check your answers to these questions, go on to pages 48 and 49.

A DETAILED STUDY

The questions on these pages will help you to make sure that you have chosen the correct options for the questions on the third text, on pages 46–47.

Question 36 *Look at the first paragraph of the text and answer these questions.*

1 Does the writer comment on the fact that there was an admission charge?

....

2 Which of the following is closest in meaning to 'purported'?
a tried
b seemed
c claimed
d failed

....

3 What does 'moron' mean in the context?
a a stupid person
b a person with a bad memory
c a person who knows nothing about Mark Twain
d a deaf person

....

4 What did the writer notice about the house from the outside?

....

Question 37 *Look at the first paragraph of the text and answer these questions.*

1 What does the writer say about the city of Hannibal with regard to Mark Twain's house?

....

2 What does the writer say about the number of visitors to Mark Twain's house?

....

3 Why might something be 'shabby'?

....

4 What would be his attitude to the place if it was owned by an underfunded literary society?

....

Question 38 *Look at the second paragraph of the text and answer these questions.*

1 The sentence 'It really lent the scene a touch of class' is meant to be
a a piece of praise.
b sarcastic.
c part of a contrast.
d serious.

....

2 Did the museum give the writer an insight into Twain's early life? If so, what did he learn?

....

3 Does the writer suggest that any of the exhibits was not authentic?

....

4 What does the phrase 'precious little' mean?

....

Question 39 *Look at the third paragraph of the text and answer these questions.*

1 Why did the writer find the business district 'dispiriting'?
a because it was run down
b because it was full of buildings
c because it was so large
d because he was already in a bad mood

....

2 Does the writer say that the river helped to make river towns more interesting? If so, where?

....

3 Does the writer say that he expected to be interested in the history of Hannibal? If so, where?

....

4 In the context, if something 'fades', it
a becomes forgotten.
b is not noticed.
c gradually disappears.
d reminds one of former times.

....

Question 40 *Consider the text as a whole and answer these questions.*

1 Does the writer express a desire to find out more about the places he visits during the passage? If so, where?

....

2 Does the writer seem to be worried by anything he sees? If so, what?

....

3 Does the writer make any generous comments about the places he visits in the passage? If so, where?

....

4 Is there anything in the passage that seems intended to be humorous? If so, what?

....

Now check your answers to the questions on these pages. Then decide whether you wish to change any of the answers that you gave to the questions on the third passage, on pages 46–47.

Then check your answers to the questions in the test on the third passage.

PAPER 2 COMPOSITION 2 hours

*Write **two only** of the composition exercises. Your answers must follow exactly the instructions given. Write in pen, not pencil. You are allowed to make alterations, but make sure your work is clear and easy to read.*

1 Describe your ideal lifestyle. (About 350 words)

2 It's not easy being a teenager these days. Do you think this is true? (About 350 words)

3 Describe one of the most amusing things that has happened to you or that you have heard about. Your story may be a personal experience, something you have read or heard about or a joke. (About 350 words)

4 You have been invited to go and stay with someone you met recently, and who lives in another town or country, but you find that you cannot go. Write a letter of apology to them, giving your reasons and suggesting an alternative arrangement. (About 300 words)

Before you write your compositions, go on to pages 51 and 52.

PLANNING A COMPOSITION

One of the questions in Paper 2 requires you to **give your opinions** on a certain subject. You may be asked whether you agree with a certain statement or not. You do not have to agree or disagree completely; you can, if you wish, present contrasting points of view.

Look at question 2 on page 50 and then answer the following. This will enable you to get some ideas and make some notes that will form the plan for your composition for that question. It is advisable to practise each of the types of composition.

1 Decide which of the following you are going to do.

- ☐ agree
- ☐ disagree
- ☐ both agree and disagree

2 Depending on your answer to **1**, which of the following would you include as aspects in support of the statement?

- ☐ employment
- ☐ drugs
- ☐ education
- ☐ family life
- ☐ relationships
- ☐ morality
- ☐ entertainment
- ☐ crime
- ☐ world affairs
- ☐ other (specify below)

....

....

....

....

....

....

....

3 Depending on your answer to **1**, which of the following would you include as aspects against the statement?

- ☐ employment
- ☐ computer technology
- ☐ education
- ☐ freedom
- ☐ relationships
- ☐ morality
- ☐ entertainment
- ☐ other (specify below)

....

....

....

....

....

4 Which of the reasons you have given for or against the statement (or both for and against the statement) in the question are the most powerful? Note what will be your brief conclusion to the composition.

....

....

....

....

....

....

....

Now use these notes to write your composition. You may, of course, wish to include other points or not include some of the points noted here.

Then write one or more of the other compositions.

Now read through the following sample composition for question 2. When you have done so, answer the questions that follow it.

Adolescence always has been and always will be a very difficult time in life. You are lost somewhere between childhood and adulthood, but still, this is the time in life when you have to break free from the conformity of your peers to find yourself. Some people argue that it's more difficult to be young today than it used to be. Is this true, and in that case, why?

In modern society teenagers are pressured to mature much more quickly than one or two hundred years ago. Today, minors on a very early stage have to make decisions regarding education, often bearing upon their future careers. In the past children were expected to follow in the footsteps of their parents, that is to say, the son was supposed to take up the profession of his father, while the daughter was expected to stay at home to take care of domestic duties such as cooking and cleaning.

Furthermore, today it's much more difficult to find your place in society. As cities grow, crime increases, and the anonymity people experience grows as well. It becomes more difficult to find and cultivate your own ideals and values.

On the other hand, the adolescent of today have greater opportunities than ever before. In the past, if your father was a blacksmith or a farmer, in ten years, so would you be. Today, teenagers have the possibility to fulfil all their dreams and ambitions.

The adolescence situation today is very much unlike what it ever has been in the past. One might argue that it's more demanding being a teenager today than it used to be. I'm not sure I agree, but I'm not sure it's less arduous either. I believe it always has been difficult to pass through adolescence. It always has and always will be.

1 Does the composition actually answer the question set or does it contain irrelevant parts, 'waffle' – writing that is simply intended to fill the space but does not really say anything – or 'padding' – writing that is repetitious in order to reach the required number of words?

2 Is the composition well-organized? Is it divided into paragraphs appropriately? Explain what each paragraph contains.

3 Are appropriate linking words and phrases used for connecting sentences and paragraphs? Give examples of some that are; if some are not, correct them.

4 Does it have a good range of appropriate vocabulary or is the vocabulary used mostly too simple? Give examples and correct any inappropriate or incorrect vocabulary.

5 Is there a good range of accurate structures forming sentences that are not just simple or are the structures used mostly too basic? Give examples and correct any incorrect structures or other mistakes.

6 Is the style appropriate for this type of composition?

Now check your assessment of and corrections to this sample composition.

PAPER 3 USE OF ENGLISH 2 hours

SECTION A

1 *Fill each of the numbered blanks in the passage with* **one** *suitable word.*

What might have been

What if ...? It is interesting to speculate on the twists (1) .... turns that have shaped recent history. Would penicillin have been discovered (2) .... a microscopic organism not landed on one of Alexander Fleming's culture dishes, for instance? Every day, people in marketing departments around the world (3) .... to decisions about products that have a profound (4) .... on all our lives. The failures are soon forgotten, but that doesn't (5) .... the visionaries were wrong. More (6) .... than not, they simply didn't (7) .... their marketing right.

Take car engines. There has been (8) .... shortage of alternatives to the petrol-driven engine, but the world's automotive and petrochemical industries have made (9) .... that most of them quietly disappeared by (10) .... their commercial and political influence. A (11) .... fate befell the car tyre that would never (12) .... replacing. Polymers and rubber compounds developed (13) .... astronauts' moon boots would reputedly never have (14) .... out if they had been used to make tyres for road vehicles. But the everlasting car tyre (15) .... limited appeal for manufacturers.

Occasionally a product can (16) .... it against the odds. Sony chairman Akio Morita was strongly advised (17) .... producing a tape recorder that couldn't record. He recalls: 'Our marketing people responded (18) .... enthusiasm. They said it wouldn't (19) .... on, and it embarrassed me to be so excited about a product most others thought (20) .... be a dud.' More than 100 million Walkmans and personal cassette players have been sold worldwide.

Now check your answers to this part of the test.

2 *Finish each of the following sentences in such a way that it is as similar as possible in meaning to the sentence printed before it.*

Example: She said that he was a brilliant musician.
Answer: She described *him as a brilliant musician.*

a John and his ex-wife are still good friends.

John remains on ....

b It wasn't easy for me to decide this.

This was not a ....

c Popular opinion has it that this is a dangerous city, but that's not true.

Contrary ....

d I won't change my mind about this, whatever happens.

Come ....

e The audience didn't enjoy his performance.

His performance did not go ....

f If Anthony continues to break the law, he will get into trouble.

If Anthony persists ....

g As far as I know, there's no reason for James to be so unhappy.

To the ....

h The idea no longer interests her.

She has gone ....

Now check your answers to this part of the test.

---

3 *Fill each of the blanks with a suitable word or phrase.*

Example: She had difficulty making up her mind which one to buy.

a The building had got into .... total disrepair after years of neglect.

b What Louise lacks in natural ability, she more .... in determination.

c I don't .... me a big favour, could you?

d We were still in .... things ready for the party when the first guests arrived.

e I think we can .... read that we all want this problem to be resolved.

f Usually I panic and she stays calm but on that occasion it was .... round.

Before you check your answers to this part of the test, go on to page 55.

FILL IN THE MISSING PHRASE

Look again at Part 3 of this test on page 54, and then for each question, decide which of the following choices could be the first word of the missing phrase. Only one of the choices can be the first word. You may wish to change some of the answers you gave in the test when you have made your choice or choices. However, if the first word of the answer that you gave there is not included among the choices here, your answer is not necessarily incorrect.

a **1** the
2 some
3 a
4 poor
5 its

b **1** can
2 than
3 has
4 of
5 does

c **1** reckon
2 guess
3 suppose
4 assume
5 believe

d **1** the
2 our
3 some
4 that
5 time

e **1** have
2 let
3 hold
4 accept
5 take

f **1** her
2 the
3 as
4 on
5 opposite

Now check your answers to these questions and to Part 3 of the test.

Then go on to Part 4 of the test on page 56.

4 *For each of the sentences below, write a new sentence as similar as possible in meaning to the original sentence, but using the word given. This word* ***must not be altered*** *in any way.*

Example: She paid no attention to his warning.
notice
Answer: *She took no notice of his warning.*

a I couldn't lend him any money because I didn't have enough myself.
position

....

b You wouldn't gain anything from taking that course.
while

....

c Bad publicity badly affected sales figures.
detrimental

....

d The crime was almost certainly committed by professional thieves.
doubt

....

e If we don't tackle this problem now, it will get worse.
either

....

f Since there wasn't a better alternative, I accepted the job.
absence

....

g When he won the gold medal, his delight was obvious.
mistaking

....

h She is determined to become a doctor.
heart

....

Before you check your answers to this part of the test, go on to page 57.

REWRITE THE SENTENCES

Look again at Part 4 of this test on page 56, and then decide in which of the following ways your answer to each of the questions there could begin. Sometimes only one of the choices is possible and sometimes more than one choice is possible. You may wish to change some of the answers you gave in the test when you have made your choice or choices. However, if the answer that you gave there does not begin with any of the choices here, this does not necessarily mean that it is wrong.

a **1** It wasn't my position ....
2 I wasn't in a position ....
3 My position wasn't ....
4 The position wasn't ....
5 It was the position ....

b **1** You wouldn't ....
2 There wouldn't ....
3 Taking that course wouldn't ....
4 It wouldn't ....
5 That course wouldn't ....

c **1** Bad publicity had ....
2 The sales figures had ....
3 Sales figures were ....
4 Bad publicity was ....
5 It was ....

d **1** There is ....
2 It is ....
3 No ....
4 There can be ....
5 It holds ....

e **1** We can either ....
2 Either we ....
3 If we don't either ....
4 Unless either ....
5 Either that ....

f **1** As an ....
2 In the ....
3 For a ....
4 On the ....
5 With an ....

g **1** There was ....
2 It couldn't ....
3 His delight ....
4 It was obvious ....
5 The gold medal was ....

h **1** She has ....
2 Her heart ....
3 To become ....
4 As a doctor ....
5 For her ....

Now check your answers to these questions and to Part 4 of the test.

SECTION B

Read the following passage, then answer the questions which follow it.

Reading aloud

A few years ago I did my first reading. It was at the Edinburgh Festival, under a tent. Things went pretty well until I got to a place near the middle of the last paragraph, where I began to feel that I was going to cry. I wouldn't have minded crying, or at least pausing to swallow down a discreet silent sob, if what I'd been reading had been in any obvious way sad. But the sentence that was giving me difficulty was a description of a woman enclosing a breakfast muffin in bakery tissue, placing it in a small bag, and sprinkling it with coffee stirrers and sugar packets and pre-proportioned pats of butter. Where was the pathos? And yet by the time I delivered the words 'plastic stirrers' to the audience, I was in serious trouble, and I noticed a listening head or two look up with sudden curiosity: Hah, this is interesting, he is going to weep openly and copiously for us now.

Why that sentence, though? Why did that image of a succession of small white shapes, more stirrers and sugar packets and butter pats than I needed, and in that sense semi-decorative rather than functional, grab at my grief lapels? There were a number of reasons.

I'd had a slight disagreement with my editor over the phrase 'tissue-protected muffin'. She'd held that it should be 'paper-wrapped muffin' and I'd said I didn't think so. The next day I'd stopped in a bakery and spotted a box of the little squares in question and seen the words 'bakery tissue' in capital letters on the side; and, exulting, I'd called my editor the next day and said 'It's tissue, it's tissue,' and as a compromise it became a 'tissue-wrapped muffin'. But now, reading it aloud in Scotland, I could turn it into a 'tissue-protected muffin' all over again. And that might have been enough to make me cry.

But it wasn't just that. It was also that this tiny piece of a paragraph had never been one that I'd thought of proudly when I thought over my book after it was published. I'd forgotten it, after writing it down, and now that my orating tongue forced me to pay attention to it I was amazed and moved that it had hung on in there for all those years, unrewarded but unimpaired, and it had become the tearjerker moment that would force me, out of pity for its very unmemorableness, to dissolve in grief right in the midst of all my intended ironies. That was a big part of it.

Contrition too. Contrition made its contribution, for these audience members didn't know how much pure mean-spirited contempt I had felt back in my rejection-letter days for writers who 'gave readings', how self-congratulatory I'd thought it was to repudiate the divine economy of the published page and to require people to gather to hear a reticent man or woman reiterate what had long since been set in type.

And yet, far from feeling dismissive and contemptuous before my turn came, I'd been simply and sincerely nervous, exceedingly nervous, and now I was almost finished, and I hadn't done anything too humiliating, and the audience had innocently listened, unaware of my prior disapproval, and they had even tolerantly laughed once or twice – and all this was too much. Evidently I was going to cry.

And then, as the unthinkable almost happened, I recognized that if I did break down now, the intensity of my feeling, in this supposedly comic context, would leave the charitable listeners puzzled about my overall mental well-being. It would be this that they would take home with them, rather than any particular fragment from what I'd read that they liked, and whenever I tried to right something light thereafter I would remember my moment of shame on the orange couch and to counteract it I'd have to invent something bleak and brooding and wholly out of character. I couldn't let it happen; I couldn't let reading aloud distort my future output. That was frightening enough, finally, to stabilize the nutation in my Adam's apple, and I just barely got through to the last word.

a What does the writer imply about 'pausing to swallow down a discreet silent sob' (lines 3–4)?

....

....

b What does the writer mean when he says 'I was in serious trouble' (line 8)?

....

....

c What was the writer's opinion of the sentence that made him want to cry?

....

....

....

d What does the writer mean by the phrase 'grab at my grief lapels' (line 13)?

....

....

e Why was the writer 'exulting' in the bakery?

....

....

f What does 'it' in line 18 refer to?

....

....

g What does the writer mean by the phrase 'unrewarded but unimpaired' (line 24)?

....

....

h What does the writer mean when he says that he was 'right in the midst of all my intended ironies' (line 26)?

....

....

i What does the writer say had caused his contempt for writers who gave public readings?

....

....

j Explain in your own words the writer's objections to readings.

k In what sense had the audience 'innocently listened' (line 34)?

l What is meant by the phrase 'the unthinkable' (line 37)?

m What does 'this' in line 39 refer to?

n What does the writer say about the effect that crying then would have had on his subsequent writing?

o In a paragraph of 70–90 words, summarize the reasons the writer gives for why he felt like crying.

Before you check your answers to this part of the test, go on to pages 61 and 62.

For general guidance on the questions for this part of the test, see Answering The Questions – General Notes on page 28.

EXPLAIN THE MEANING

In some questions in this part of the paper, you are asked to explain the meanings of certain phrases. These questions normally begin "What is meant by the phrase...?", "Explain the meaning of the phrase ...?.", "What does the writer mean by ..." and a reference to the line in which the phrase occurs.

These questions ask you to explain in your own words the meaning of a particular phrase, either in general terms or in the particular context of the text. There may be more than one part to be explained in this type of question.

This is not intended to be purely a test of your vocabulary. Even if you do not know the phrase or parts of it, you may be able to work it out from the context.

Look at question b

In the context, 'in serious trouble' is most likely to mean

a making the audience very annoyed.
b becoming unable to stop myself from crying.
c becoming extremely confused.
d crying too much to continue.

....

Look at question d

1 If you 'grab at' something, you

a move towards it unnoticed.
b take hold of it suddenly.
c push it hard.
d draw attention to it.

....

2 'Grief' is a feeling of

a embarrassment.
b self-confidence.
c indifference.
d great unhappiness.

....

Look at question g

1 In the context, 'unrewarded' is most likely to mean

a not noticed by others.
b not remembered.
c not satisfactory.
d not valued highly.

....

2 If something is 'unimpaired', it is

a still the same.
b not valued highly enough.
c inoffensive.
d of some significance.

....

Look at question k

In the context, 'innocently' means

a without realizing something.
b not having done anything wrong.
c without being critical.
d not caring about something.

....

Look at question l

If something is 'unthinkable', it is

a too hard to understand.
b never considered.
c too awful to think about.
d impossible to foresee.

....

EXPLAIN THE REFERENCE

Some questions in this section require you to explain what something in the passage refers to. This reference is to something mentioned earlier in the text, perhaps in the same sentence or paragraph or perhaps even earlier. The questions test whether you have understood the relationship between things that are mentioned in the passage and to answer them you must locate exactly what is referred to.

Look at question f

In line 18, 'it' refers to
a the story.
b the phrase describing the muffin.
c the sentence about the muffin.
d the muffin.

....

Look at question m

In line 39, 'this' is most likely to refer to
a the writer's mental state.
b the part that made him cry.
c being charitable towards him.
d being puzzled about his mental state.

....

Now check your answers to these questions and decide whether you wish to change any of the answers you gave in the test. If you have phrased anything you wrote in the test differently from the choices given on these pages, this does not necessarily mean that you answered incorrectly in the test.

Then check your answers to questions a–n of Section B of the test on pages 59–60.

WRITING A SUMMARY

For general guidance on writing the summary for this part of the test, see Writing a Summary – General Notes on page 29.

For the summary in this test, answer these questions.

1 Whereabouts in the passage do you think the material for your summary will come from? Explain your answer.

....

2 Decide which of the following could be included as relevant main points in the summary. Tick the box next to each point that could be included.

1 the situation described in the sentence ☐

2 his disagreement with his editor ☐

3 the fact that he could read the original phrase ☐

4 the memory of going to the bakery ☐

5 the fact that the sentence was not remarkable ☐

6 his regret for his previous contempt for readings ☐

7 the rejection letters he had received ☐

8 the fact he hadn't done anything embarrassing ☐

9 the good response he'd had from the audience ☐

10 his general mental state ☐

Now look again at your summary and decide whether you wish to change anything.

PAPER 4 LISTENING COMPREHENSION (about 30 mins)

PART ONE

You will hear part of a radio programme about the Innu, a group of North American Indians.
***For questions 1–10**, complete the sentences.*

In a few months, Labrador will become an enormous **1** ______.

The Innu have had few rivals for **2** ______.

Europeans consider the area to be both **3** ______.

The Government started developing the Innu's **4** ______.

In the past, the Innu led a **5** ______ way of life.

In the summer, they would make **6** ______ *and* ______ at the coast.

Lejeune found that one of the worst things you could say to an Innu was **7** ______.

There was no **8** ______ at a social gathering.

Lejeune often disapproves of the Innu's **9** ______ *and* ______.

The Innu see hunting as a **10** ______.

PART TWO

You will hear a discussion on the radio about the decision to set up a rock music college in the UK.
***For questions 11–17**, decide which of the speakers expresses the views. Write **J** for Jane, **P** for Paul or **B** for both of them.*

It is a good idea to invest money in rock music.	*11*	
Rock music should not be defined as culture.	*12*	
Good music makes people feel better.	*13*	
The general attitude to rock music is wrong.	*14*	
It is important to consider the effect that rock music has on young people.	*15*	
People have to get used to new types of music.	*16*	
Rock music is an alternative to formal musical training.	*17*	

PART THREE

You will hear a radio item about solo performers. ***For questions 18–25****, choose the best answer,* ***A****,* ***B****,* ***C*** *or* ***D****.*

18 What do we learn about the presenter from her introduction?

A She was unsuccessful as a solo performer.
B She has often wondered why people perform solo.
C She regrets having been a solo performer.
D She admires people who perform solo.

19 What does Guy find particularly difficult?

A concealing from audiences how tired he is
B varying the form of his performance
C getting the audience to participate
D being able to carry on until the end of the play

20 Guy's main motivation for performing solo is to

A keep himself in work for a while.
B revive the art of story-telling.
C develop a unique style of acting.
D play a lot of different characters.

21 When Stu is doing his act, he

A is unsure whether he will make the audience laugh.
B prefers certain types of audiences to others.
C comes into close contact with the audience.
D chooses his material while he is performing.

22 Stu doesn't work with other people because

A he kept falling out with them.
B they weren't as motivated as him.
C it got in the way of what he wanted to achieve.
D he felt he was taking on too much responsibility.

23 What does Stu say about getting encores?

A It doesn't happen so frequently to him any more.
B He has started to take it for granted.
C It no longer reflects how good a performer is.
D He is no longer sure how to react to it.

24 Clare says that before she started performing solo, she was

A nervous.
B self-confident.
C pessimistic.
D brilliant.

25 Clare uses Glenn Gould as an example of

A how difficult performing solo can be.
B how much solo musicians differ from solo actors.
C how self-contained solo performers can be.
D how much audiences enjoy solo performances.

Before you check your answers to this Paper, go on to page 65.

COMPLETE THE SENTENCES OR NOTES

It is important to bear in mind the following points concerning questions which require you to write a word or short phrase:

- you will normally be required to write only words and phrases which you actually hear on the tape; however, the sentence or note you have to complete will not simply be a repetition of what you hear on the tape, as this is not a dictation exercise;
- if you write something quite different from what you hear, you may lose the mark even though you have understood that part of the tape perfectly; stick to what you hear;
- if you don't know what to write for one question, do not spend too long thinking about it; you may miss the answers to subsequent questions which you may have got quite easily if you had kept up with the tape.

Listen again to Part 1 of the test on page 63, and answer the following questions. This will give you clues as to the answers to each question if you were unable to get all the answers and to check the answers that you gave in the test. The numbers below refer to the questions in the test on page 63.

1 The gap should be filled by a word or phrase meaning
A a cold climate.
B a bare area.
C a frozen mass.

2 The gap should be filled by a word or phrase meaning
A the country people inhabit.
B an undiscovered area.
C a place where people settle.

3 The gap should be filled by words meaning
A unattractive.
B unfamiliar.
C unchanged.

4 The gap should be filled by a word or phrase meaning
A places where natives live.
B areas where animals are killed for food.
C ancient regions.

5 The gap should be filled by a word or phrase meaning
A harmonious.
B unchanged for a long time.
C wandering from place to place.

6 The gap should be filled by words meaning
A boats and objects for moving them.
B homes and furniture.
C meals and tools.

7 The gap should be filled by a quote meant to describe
A greed.
B friendliness.
C envy.

8 The gap should be filled by a word or phrase referring to
A a sequence of events.
B social rank.
C confusion.

9 The gap should be filled by words used pejoratively of people who are
A unknown.
B suffering.
C primitive.

10 The gap should be filled by a word or phrase meaning
A source of pleasure.
B a religious activity.
C a routine.

Now check your answers to the questions on this page. When you have done so, decide whether you wish to change any of the answers you gave in Part 1 of the test on page 63

Then check your answers to Part 1 of the test and then to Parts 2 and 3 on pages 63–64.

PAPER 5 INTERVIEW

1 *Look at one or more of these photographs and answer the questions that follow them.*

1

2

3

What's happening in each picture?
What dangers are involved in what the person is doing?
What skills are involved in what the person is doing?
How do you think each photograph was taken?

Why do you think people do these things? What appeals to them?
Which of these activities, or what similar activities, are popular in your country?
Describe something you have done that you found extremely exciting.
What do you do for exercise? What do you find enjoyable about it? If you don't do any exercise, why not?

2 *Read one or more of these passages and then answer the questions that follow them.*

a Discussing risk, the argument goes circular very quickly. Why do something with a risk attached? Because it is exhilirating. Why do something exhilirating? Because it's a buzz, it's fun. Why is it a buzz? Because your body releases adrenalin, because it perceives a risk. Is taking a small risk for a big buzz worth the trouble? Too right it is: I have not stared death in the face but there is a simple value in doing something new, in overcoming a fear, in feeling and saying that you've done it.

b You've got to have a head for heights in this sport! Sky surfers throw themselves out of planes or hot air balloons at around 3,500m – with a snowboard strapped to their feet. They surf at speeds of around 200 kph, cruising along in the slipstream of the plane. It's just like surfing on water! Total extremists put on a dizzy display of somersaults and spins before pulling the ripcord to open their parachute and drifting down to safety.

c As we rounded the first curve in the river, laughing at our bravado in taking on such an adventure, there was suddenly a huge splash beside the canoe. Surprised, wet and not sure how to fend off what had to be a huge crocodile, we both stared at the water with paddles raised, not knowing what to expect. There was another splash, and a cheeky pink nose and squinty little eyes popped up out of the river. We had just met our first Amazonas dolphin, having a bit of fun at our expense

What is the purpose of each passage?
What feelings are referred to in each passage?

3 *Do one or more of these tasks. If you are working with others, discuss them together.*

a What's the most risky thing you've ever done? Why did you do it? Describe the circumstances and what you did.
How did you feel before, during and after this? Are you glad you did it now or would you never consider doing it again?
Is there anything that you haven't done because you didn't have the courage? What put you off? Are you glad now that you didn't do it or do you regret not doing it? Give reasons.

b Which of the following have you done? Describe the experience.
If you have not done any of them, which appeal to you and which would you certainly not like to do? Give reasons.

- drive a racing car
- climb a mountain
- jump out of an aeroplane
- run a marathon
- windsurfing
- do a bungee jump
- fly an aeroplane
- hang-gliding
- surfing
- fly in a hot-air balloon
- canoeing
- abseiling

c 'It's not worth the risk.'

Describe anything in life that you think this is true of. Explain why.

DESCRIBING MOVEMENT AND POSITION

In the interview, you may be required to describe people's movements or positions. To check or build up your vocabulary on this subject, look at the verbs below and decide whether they refer to walking, sitting/lying, moving quickly or moving across water or air. Tick the appropriate boxes.

VERB	WALKING	SITTING /LYING	MOVING QUICKLY	MOVING ACROSS
slump				
stagger				
tear				
wander				
race				
slouch				
meander				
scurry				
recline				
trudge				
stroll				
float				
dash				
stride				
lounge				
saunter				
drift				
trot				
march				
slide				
amble				
sprint				
glide				
dawdle				
pace				
dart				
bolt				
waft				
scamper				
perch				

Now check your answers to these questions.

TALKING ABOUT PASSAGES

In the interview, you may be asked about the purpose or style of a passage or passages.

Look again at the three passages on page 67 and answer these questions.

1 Which of the three passages is mainly informational?

2 What does that passage aim to explain?

3 What is emphasized in that passage?

4 Which of the passages has a persuasive purpose?

5 Which phrase in that passage indicates agreement with a point of view?

6 What point of view is agreed with?

7 Which of the passages is mainly narrative?

8 What changes of emotion are mentioned in that passage?

9 What causes this change of emotion?

Now check your answers to these questions.

TEST THREE

PAPER 1 READING COMPREHENSION 1 hour

SECTION A

*In this section you must choose the word or phrase which best completes each sentence. On your answer sheet indicate the letter **A**, **B**, **C** or **D** against the number of each item **1** to **25** for the word or phrase you choose. Give one answer only to each question.*

1 They were .... from their apartment because they hadn't paid the rent.

A evicted **B** deposed **C** expelled **D** discarded

2 I bought them a gift as a .... of thanks for all the help they had given me.

A hint **B** gesture **C** signal **D** symbol

3 A lot of the photos came out .... because I wasn't sure how to use the camera properly.

A blurred **B** distorted **C** warped **D** smudged

4 I didn't know the words to the song, so I could only .... the tune while the others sang.

A whine **B** hiss **C** mutter **D** hum

5 It was three days before the storm .... and life began to return to normal.

A abated **B** dwindled **C** slackened **D** alleviated

6 It's quite out of .... for Paul to behave so terribly.

A temperament **B** personality **C** nature **D** character

7 To forget her problems, she .... herself with her work.

A devoted **B** occupied **C** immersed **D** dedicated

8 It was obvious that his .... intention was to cause an argument.

A pure **B** sheer **C** sole **D** mere

9 I took .... with him on a number of his comments, which I thought unfair.

A challenge **B** offence **C** exception **D** issue

10 Despite all the evidence, he wouldn't admit that he was in the ....

A fault **B** error **C** wrong **D** slip

11 If you pay for both of us now, I'll settle .... when we get home.

A for **B** on **C** up **D** in

12 The hotel didn't .... the description given in the brochure.

A fit **B** conform **C** tally **D** correspond

13 Jane didn't take .... to your suggestion that she was mean with her money.

A pleasantly **B** kindly **C** cheerfully **D** agreeably

14 I'm expecting to contact them by phone but .... that, I'll write to them.

A leaving **B** excluding **C** omitting **D** failing

15 He .... this city down so much that I don't know why he doesn't leave.

A holds **B** pulls **C** talks **D** runs

16 He is held in high .... by everyone who works with him.

A reputation **B** respect **C** regard **D** renown

17 .... he caught his plane; he hasn't phoned to say anything went wrong.

A Presumably **B** Supposedly **C** Assuming **D** Granted

18 I thought I had made it .... that I didn't wish to discuss this matter.

A distinct **B** plain **C** frank **D** straight

19 It never .... my mind that such a terrible thing would happen.

A struck **B** dawned **C** ocurred **D** entered

20 It was a bad mistake but it had no .... on the outcome of the match.

A bearing **B** relevance **C** significance **D** repercussion

21 From now on, staff meetings will be held on a .... basis, once a month.

A persistent **B** commonplace **C** standard **D** regular

22 We took such a great .... to the place that we decided to go and live there.

A affection **B** fondness **C** liking **D** attraction

23 In the .... of demand for tickets, it has been decided that an extra performance will be staged.

A view **B** light **C** consideration **D** grounds

24 She works very hard and finds it difficult to .... when she gets home.

A give in **B** switch off **C** let out **D** wind up

25 I was worried but their reassurances put my mind at ....

A rest **B** comfort **C** calm **D** relief

Before you check your answers to this section of the test, go on to page 71.

THE RIGHT WORD

Some of the questions in this part of the test require you to choose the only word with the right meaning in the context of the sentence. Such questions do not involve completing a collocation or deciding on the grounds of grammatical structure; they focus purely on the meaning of each option.

The numbers of the exercises below refer to questions 1–5 of the test on page 69, which are questions of this type.

In each of the exercises, choose which of the four options given in the test fits each gap. This may help you to eliminate some of the incorrect options in the questions they refer to and to check or learn the meanings of various words.

1 | *discarded* | *expelled* | *deposed* | *evicted* |

A The party leader was .... by a rebellion among dissatisfied colleagues.

B Her visa expired and eventually she was .... from the country.

C After one game, he was .... and never played international football again.

D After a dispute with the owners, she was .... from the flat.

2 | *hint* | *gesture* | *signal* | *symbol* |

A They see their enormous house as a .... of their success.

B On a pre-arranged ...., the troops went into action.

C My invitation was meant as a .... of friendship to them.

D Tom dropped a .... that he wanted a watch for his birthday.

3 | *blurred* | *distorted* | *warped* | *smudged* |

A There's something wrong with the speakers – the sound is very ....

B The paper got wet and some of the writing on it got ....

C He started to suffer from headaches and .... vision.

D Because of the heat, the door is .... and won't close properly.

4 | *muttered* | *hissed* | *hummed* | *whined* |

A He .... along to a song on the radio as he worked.

B She .... something about feeling ill, but I didn't hear exactly what she said.

C The children .... throughout the journey because they were bored.

D The audience booed and .... to show their disapproval.

5 | *abated* | *slackened* | *dwindled* | *alleviated* |

A I read a magazine in the waiting room, which .... my boredom a bit.

B When the storm ...., it was possible to survey the damage.

C Audiences ...., until eventually the show had to close.

D They ran very fast at the start of the race but after a while the pace ....

Now check your answers to these exercises. When you have done so, decide whether you wish to change any of your answers to questions 1–5 in the test.

Then check your answers to the test.

SECTION B

In this section you will find after each of the passages a number of questions or unfinished statements about the passage, each with four suggested answers or ways of finishing. You must choose the one which you think fits best. On your answer sheet, indicate the letter ***A***, ***B***, ***C*** *or* ***D*** *against the number of each item* ***26*** *to* ***40*** *for the answer you choose. Give* ***one answer only*** *to each question.*

FIRST PASSAGE

Many rich people aspire to own islands, but an island in the Venetian lagoon, within sight and easy reach of the city, yet perfectly private, verdant and isolated, is a privilege reserved for very few. Ivan Durridge got his chance when the Englishwoman, old and ailing, sold it for a small fortune. Expecting some ostentatious pleasure pavilion, Zen had been surprised by what awaited him. The floor of the artificial island was now covered in trees, shrubs and plants artfully arranged to form a dense, seemingly natural garden. In its midst stood the guardhouse, a long low structure of military severity which had been skilfully transformed into a residence retaining the essential characteristics of the original while suggesting something of the rustic pleasures of the country cottage. Zen wandered idly about the property, inspired less by the sense that there was anything to be discovered than by the beauty of the spot. He was standing on the lawn in front of the house, looking up at the ragged blue patch of sky visible through the encircling foliage, when a cry disturbed his reverie.

'Hey!' Zen had grown so accustomed to the peace and quiet that he stared violently. The thought that he might not be alone on the island had never occurred to him. He looked round. At the corner of the house stood an elderly man dressed in baggy dark overalls. 'What are you doing here?' he demanded gruffly.

Zen lit a cigarette with elaborate nonchalance. 'Well?' the man demanded, walking across the lawn towards him. 'This is private property.'

'Police.' The man's expression of mute hostility did not change. His face was marked with a series of concentric wrinkles, like ripples on water.

'And you are ...?' barked Zen. 'Calderan, Franco.' 'What are you doing here?' 'Doing? I live here I'm the gardener and caretaker.'

Zen sniffed sceptically, as though this were a transparent fiction. 'Where were you the day your employer disappeared?' The man frowned. 'I've already made my statement.' 'So make it again,' snapped Zen. 'Or are you afraid the two accounts won't tally? Maybe you've forgotten whatever pack of lies you made up the first time?' 'I told them the truth. It was Tuesday, my day off. I rowed over to Alberoni and caught the bus to go and see my sister and her family, same as every week. They can vouch for me.'

Zen's sneer indicated the value he ascribed to alibis which depended on the corroboration of the suspect's relations. 'Why are you lying? Who are you trying to protect?'

Zen broke off, appalled at himself. Why the hell was he browbeating this old man? But he had been a policeman too long not to try and make Calderan sweat a little in return for his surly welcome. 'I'm not protecting anyone. Everyone knew that I went to see my sister on Tuesdays, and have done these thirty years.'

He took a step forward, confronting Zen openly. 'Anyway, what are you doing coming out here and raking all this over again? I've been through it all often enough already. Or haven't you bothered to read what I told your colleagues?'

Calderan's eyes narrowed as a new suspicion struck him. 'You say you're from the police? Let me see your identification.'

Zen had obliged, and after some further acrimonious exchanges he had been able to depart in a relatively dignified manner. But the experience had merely had the effect of making his private investigation of the Durridge affair seem even more of a mockery. The case had already been fully investigated, and at a time when clues and memories were still fresh. What hope had he of solving the mystery now, three months after the event?

26 What surprised Zen about the island?

A It was more pleasant than he had expected.
B It had been artificially created.
C It had a guardhouse.
D It contained little for him to look at.

27 Zen wanted Calderan to think that he was

A dynamic.
B shrewd.
C impulsive.
D unorthodox.

28 Why did Zen pursue his questioning of Calderan?

A He knew that Calderan was lying.
B Calderan had been unfriendly to him.
C He liked making suspects uncomfortable.
D Calderan's story contradicted his previous one.

29 Which of the following best describes Calderan's attitude in the passage?

A secretive
B baffled
C fearful
D indignant

30 After speaking to Calderan, Zen felt that

A he had missed a vital clue.
B his visit had been futile.
C he had asked the wrong questions.
D his visit would cause him trouble.

Before you check your answers to these questions, go on to pages 74 and 75.

A DETAILED STUDY

The questions on these pages will help you to make sure that you have chosen the correct options for the questions on the first text, on pages 72–73.

Question 26 *Look at the first paragraph of the text and answer these questions.*

1 Had Zen expected to see a guardhouse on the island? Tick the box.
yes ☐
no ☐
we aren't told ☐

....

2 Had the island been artificially created?

....

3 Did Zen wander around because he expected to make a discovery there?

....

4 Are there any words or phrases that suggest Zen found the place pleasant? If so, note them.

....

Question 27 *Look at lines 13–30 of the text and answer these questions.*

1 Zen 'sniffed sceptically' to indicate that
a his methods were different from those of most policemen.
b he had decided on a more active approach to the case.
c he could perceive that Calderan wasn't telling the truth.
d he tended to jump to conclusions when questioning people.

....

2 Zen's 'sneer' showed that
a he had suddenly changed his mind about Calderan.
b he was too experienced to believe stories like Calderan's.
c he was keen to make rapid progress with the case.
d he was not typical of most policemen.

....

Question 28 *Look at lines 31–34 of the text and answer these questions.*

1 If you 'browbeat' someone, is it your intention to make them feel uncomfortable?

....

2 Zen was 'appalled at himself' because
a he had not intended to upset Calderan.
b he had misunderstood something Calderan said.
c he had no reason to accuse Calderan of lying.
d he had been rude to Calderan when he first spoke to him.

....

3 Which of the following is closest in meaning to 'surly'?
a uneasy
b suspicious
c hostile
d self-conscious

....

4 Did Calderan stick to his original story about what he had done on that Tuesday?

....

Question 29 *Look at the parts of the text describing Calderan and what he says and answer these questions. Give evidence from the text for each of your answers.*

1 Does Calderan seem to be telling the truth?

....

2 Does Calderan have difficulty understanding Zen's questions?

....

3 Does Calderan appear to be afraid of Zen?

....

4 Does Calderan indicate that he feels he is being treated unfairly?

....

Question 30 *Look at the last paragraph of the text and answer these questions.*

1 In the context, which of the following is closest in meaning to 'a mockery'?
a a mistake
b a nuisance
c a waste of time
d a mystery

....

2 Was it now more or less likely that Zen would find clues?

....

3 Did Zen feel that there was something he had failed to notice?

....

4 Is there any reference to the repercussions of his visit? If so, where?

....

Now check your answers to the questions on these pages. Then decide whether you wish to change any of the answers that you gave to the questions on the first passage, on pages 72–73.

Then check your answers to the questions in the test on the first passage.

SECOND PASSAGE

The first 200 pages were an author's dream. PJ Proby was surging through his disreputable early career like a river in full spate. His ghost-writer found him charming, loquacious and sober. 'The words flowed easily, I couldn't get them down fast enough,' says Rosemary Kingsland. Her two-year contract to record the manic life of the ageing rock legend started to go wrong in the fourth month of interviews, and it is a lesson to those of us who deride ghost-writing as a matter of simultaneously turning on the flattery and the tape-recorder.

Proby decided his story was worth a £1 million advance; Kingsland tried to inject a note of realism. From then on, the sessions became turbulent. 'I discovered he is prone to terrible mood swings,' she says. It was not just that he expected his story to be as hefty as *Gone With The Wind*. Kingsland boldly explained that she did not write by the kilo, and trusted that the original 400,000 words could, in time, be trimmed to the modest 120,000 demanded by the publishers without upsetting him. Even his unusual request for a £1 million advance did not unduly bother her: the agent could sort that one out (£15,000 was offered, to be split between them). It was when relations reached the shouting, table-thumping stage that the ghost realized she had better make herself invisible. 'It is difficult to remember what these tirades were all about,' she says. 'We would start to talk and he would suddenly explode like a volcano. On one occasion, I thought he would throttle me. I ran away.'

But not for long. Rosemary Kingsland decided to stand her ground. 'At least if I kept quiet and sat tight, I'd get the book.' Can it be worth the tension? She is bracing herself for another encounter, well aware that PJ thinks he could have done it all better himself, if only he'd had the time. 'I only use a ghost-writer because I'm too lazy to put pen to paper,' he announced. 'I don't know that he'll *ever* approve of the manuscript,' Rosemary Kingsland sighs. 'I've spent a year on this book and it's been quite traumatic. I don't think I'll ever be a ghost again.'

There were almost peaceful interludes. PJ would spend weeks at Kingsland's cottage in Wales, ruminating and listening to music in his bedroom when not required to talk about himself, and enjoying being waited on. 'He wasn't a *bad* house guest,' she concedes. 'But he did rather behave like the master of the plantation. There would still be these unexpected outbursts when we worked or had dinner. He couldn't bear to sit at a dinner table with the family. When things got too much for me, I'd take him back to London.'

Proby, 56, lives among a profusion of wooden statuary and potted plants in an Edwardian house in Barnet, on the leafy outskirts of London, where Kingsland's work as part-time mother-confessor, psychologist and interviewer has continued its bumpy course. He admits in a forthcoming TV programme that he is not easy-going. 'Yes, I'm a difficult character. I love it,' he drawls. 'Only I don't call it difficult. I call it colourful.' Their routine has been to meet on Mondays at his place, but when she arrives at the appointed time, she cannot be sure what mood PJ will be in, or even if he will be there at all.

31 The writer of the article suggests in the first paragraph that
A some people have a low opinion of ghost-writers.
B Rosemary Kingsland's experience of ghost-writing is untypical.
C the life stories of some people are not worth writing.
D being a ghost-writer is a fairly simple job.

32 What has Rosemary Kingsland found particularly difficult about PJ Proby?
A his unwillingness to discuss certain subjects
B his unrealistic financial expectations
C his unpredictable behaviour
D his idea about the length of the book

33 Why has Rosemary Kingsland persisted with writing the book?
A She thinks she is the best person to write it.
B She wants to prove PJ Proby wrong.
C She thinks it will be a great book.
D She wants something to show for her trouble.

34 What spoilt the 'peaceful interludes' with PJ Proby?
A He was only prepared to talk about himself.
B Rosemary Kingsland couldn't stand him as a house guest for too long.
C Rosemary Kingsland's family objected to PJ Proby's presence.
D He resented spending so much time on his own.

35 PJ Proby describes himself as
A interesting.
B troubled.
C misunderstood.
D unique.

Now check your answers to these questions.

THIRD PASSAGE

Booklovers' Corner occupied two rooms – a large one filled with the second-hand books and a small one containing a lending library of novels. There were several minor sidelines, including a small stock of used typewriters, and some calendars. The shop also sold stamps to collectors, but this business held little interest for Orwell. 'Stamp-collectors are a strange, silent, fish-like breed,' he commented later, adding that the oddest aspect of the breed was its sex – as far as he could tell, they were all male. 'Women, apparently, fail to see the peculiar charm of gumming bits of coloured paper into albums.' Interestingly, the image of Orwell which remained most vivid in a colleague's memory from these days was that of a tall, imposing figure standing in the centre of the shop looking down at a small boy buying stamps.

All types of customer frequented the place, 'from baronets to bus-conductors', to quote Orwell's description in his essay 'Bookshop Memories', which appeared in November 1936. By all accounts he did his job well, but he was more than a little annoyed by some of the customers, especially the ones who came in looking for a book whose cover they could remember as being a certain colour but whose title and author they had completely forgotten. 'Many of the people who came to us,' he wrote, 'were of the kind who would be a nuisance anywhere but have special opportunities in a bookshop'. He was astonished at the number of people who would order special books or ask for certain volumes to be put aside for them, and then never return. He speculated that half the people who made such requests never came back to pick up the books. He was bothered not only by the fact they caused him unnecessary trouble, but that so many of them apparently never intended to return. He concluded that merely ordering the books was satisfaction enough for them because 'it gave them ... the illusion that they were spending real money.'

But dealing with a wide range of customers taught him some sobering things about the book market. It gave him real insights into readers' tastes, and reminded him that publishing was a business, not a philanthropic endeavour. Books were a commodity, a manufactured item consumed by people with diverse tastes, and though he wanted to think of books as something precious and profound, he saw how easily they could be reduced to serving the particular appetites of certain consumers, produced in quantity and devoured rapidly, like so many sausages. He saw this plainly in the insatiable appetite for detective fiction. One subscriber to the shop's lending library read at least four or five detective novels each week, and appeared never to take out the same book twice. 'Apparently the whole of that frightful torrent of trash (the pages read every year would, I calculated, cover nearly three-quarters of an acre) was stored for ever in his memory. He took no notice of titles or authors' names, but he could tell by merely glancing into a book whether he had 'had it already'.' All authors like to imagine that their work will be treasured by their readers, but clearly some books are merely 'had', tasted once and tossed aside.

36 What contradiction is alluded to in the first paragraph?
A Orwell disliked stamp collectors but sometimes took an interest in them.
B Orwell was unfriendly but sometimes befriended children.
C Orwell disliked women but sometimes sympathised with them.
D Orwell was cautious but sometimes jumped to conclusions.

37 What do we learn about Orwell's time as a shop assistant in the second paragraph?
A He would sometimes lose his temper with customers.
B It led to him changing his view of human nature.
C His employers had no reason to complain about him.
D He was surprised by the variety of people who came in.

38 Orwell noticed how many people ordered books
A in a way that the shop's staff found irritating.
B as a way of pretending to the staff that they were rich.
C because they felt they ought to.
D because they enjoyed doing so.

39 One of the 'sobering things' that Orwell realized when working in the shop was
A how unpredictable people could be.
B how successfully poor books were marketed.
C that books were no different from other products.
D that writing books would not make him rich.

40 Why did Orwell mention the amount of paper used for detective novels?
A to demonstrate how popular they were
B to show how much he could remember
C to emphasize his dislike of them
D to suggest that they were too long

Now check your answers to these questions.

PAPER 2 COMPOSITION 2 hours

*Write **two only** of the composition exercises. Your answers must follow exactly the instructions given. Write in pen, not pencil. You are allowed to make alterations, but make sure your work is clear and easy to read.*

1 Describe a place that holds particularly fond memories for you. (About 350 words)

2 'It's a shame that national cultures are being replaced by an international culture.' Do you agree with this statement? (About 350 words)

3 Write an account of attending an event which left a lasting impression on you. (About 350 words)

4 Write a report for a local newspaper about the entertainment available in your town, city or area, commenting on good and bad aspects and making recommendations. (About 300 words)

Before you write your compositions, go on to pages 79 and 80.

PLANNING A COMPOSITION

One of the questions in Paper 2 requires you to **write a narrative or story**. You may be able to write about a real event or you may need to use your imagination to make up your answer.

Look at question 3 on page 78 and then answer the following. This will enable you to get some ideas and make some notes that will form the plan for your composition for that question. It is advisable to practise each of the types of composition.

1 Decide which of the following events you are going to describe.

- ☐ a concert
- ☐ a play
- ☐ a party
- ☐ a festival
- ☐ a demonstration/protest
- ☐ a wedding
- ☐ a sports event
- ☐ other (specify below)

....

2 Note briefly why you attended it. Explain briefly why you were or were not keen to attend it.

....

....

....

....

....

3 Note briefly your journey to the event.

....

....

....

....

....

4 Note briefly what happened during the event.

....

....

....

....

....

....

....

....

....

....

5 Note briefly why the event impressed you.

....

....

....

....

....

....

....

....

....

....

Now use these notes to write your composition. You may, of course, wish to include other points or not include some of the points noted here.

Then write one or more of the other compositions.

Now read through the following sample composition for question 3. When you have done so, answer the questions that follow it.

When I was fifteen years old, I moved with my family from Brazil to Portugal because of my father's work. It was a shock for me and I felt as homesick as one can feel in an imposed sort of 'exile'. A couple of months after my arrival a Formula One Grand Prix took place there and my father invited me to go, together with my brother and sister.

We got there early and, suspecting that I might feel bored, I took a bag full of pens, pencils and paper to write letters with me. But as soon as the people started to arrive wearing T-shirts bearing drivers' names and waving their countries' flags I forgot about the letters. I began to feel something different going on. Before the actual race another one took place and I used this time to read the catalogue I got about the cars and pilots and the current situation of the championship.

When I finished my reading and everything was ready for the 'big race' to begin I was surrounded by a 'multi-national' crowd and my attention was grabbed by the people dressed in green and yellow or wrapped in our country's flag. I realized that I wasn't the only 'alien' in a strange land and that made me feel better.

The race began and all the hopes of a Brazilian victory were on Ayrton Senna's and Nelson Piquet's hands. We were sitting on a good place but, nonetheless, we had to wait until the drivers completed another lap to see them again. None of the Brazilian drivers did that well – the best of them was Senna who managed to go from a fifth to a second place – and their performance didn't leave a lasting impression.

What did leave a lasting impression was what happened when the cars passed in front of us. Everyone would stand up and I could only see the cars between the sea of waving flags. I didn't care about the noise – the loudest I ever heard – or the summer heat, all that mattered was that feeling of being part of what was going on there, a part of the race itself. The feeling was so strong that I followed that championship through the television to the end – and Senna won – and still follow it.

1 Does the composition actually answer the question set or does it contain irrelevant parts, 'waffle' – writing that is simply intended to fill the space but does not really say anything – or 'padding' – writing that is repetitious in order to reach the required number of words?

2 Is the composition well-organized? Is it divided into paragraphs appropriately? Explain what each paragraph contains.

3 Are appropriate linking words and phrases used for connecting sentences and paragraphs? Give examples of some that are; if some are not, correct them.

4 Does it have a good range of appropriate vocabulary or is the vocabulary used mostly too simple? Give examples and correct any inappropriate or incorrect vocabulary.

5 Is there a good range of accurate structures forming sentences that are not just simple or are the structures used mostly too basic? Give examples and correct any incorrect structures or other mistakes.

6 Is the style appropriate for this type of composition?

Now check your assessment of and corrections to this sample composition.

PAPER 3 USE OF ENGLISH 2 hours

SECTION A

1 *Fill each of the numbered blanks in the passage with **one** suitable word.*

CHARM

On the last Friday of every month, there is an 'organized coincidence' of cyclists in London. (1) .... assembled, these cyclists begin a slow, good-natured excursion around their city, reclaiming it, (2) .... only temporarily, from the traffic.

These events are organized by a group known as CHARM, which (3) .... for Cyclists Have A Right to Move. One of its founders explains the thinking (4) .... it. 'The point is not to annoy motorists (5) .... to show everyone that there is a better way to get (6) .... Once people see how much fun cycling can be, and how much safer and more pleasant it (7) .... their streets – well, it just (8) .... them thinking.'

More than 1,000 riders attended the last ride, and CHARM (9) .... the numbers to grow, at (10) .... until October, when darkness will (11) .... some off. The result is that the cyclists create a vacuum in front of them in (12) .... people walk safely and hand out leaflets.

But (13) .... some motorists do get annoyed (14) .... faced with this slow-moving swarm of cyclists? 'We make a (15) .... of explaining to them what we're doing, and the vast (16) .... are sympathetic. First and (17) ...., we're not trying to cause trouble. A couple of hours a month of slowing the traffic is just our (18) .... of pointing out to people

(19) .... a hideous mess the roads are in all the (20) .... of the time.'

Before you check your answers to this part of the test, go on to page 82.

FILL IN THE MISSING WORD

Look again at Part 1 of this test on page 81 and then for each question, decide which of the four choices below best expresses the meaning of the part of the text in which the gap appears. You may wish to change some of the answers you gave in the test after you have done this.

1 A then they assemble
B after they have assembled
C by assembling
D in order to assemble

2 A and they only reclaim it for a short time
B they may reclaim it more than temporarily
C although it is true they only reclaim it temporarily
D in this way they reclaim it for a short time

3 A CHARM is the initials of Cyclists Have a Right to Move
B CHARM is a new name for Cyclists Have a Right to Move
C CHARM is an organization founded by cyclists
D CHARM supports the rights of cyclists

4 A the reason for the idea
B how much thought went into the idea
C what people think of the idea
D opposition to the idea

5 A we don't want to annoy motorists so we show them ....
B so that we don't annoy motorists we show them ....
C instead of annoying motorists, we show them ....
D we don't want to annoy motorists, we want to show them ....

6 A to have good relationships
B to get into good physical condition
C to arrive somewhere
D to go from place to place

7 A their streets are now safer and more pleasant
B they believe their streets are safer and more pleasant
C their streets become safer and more pleasant because of it
D they want their streets to be safer and more pleasant

8 A it alters the way they think
B it conforms with the way they think
C it causes them to consider the matter
D it allows them to consider the matter

9 A CHARM would like the numbers to grow
B CHARM thinks the numbers are likely to grow
C CHARM is sure the numbers will grow
D CHARM has calculated how much the numbers will grow

10 A the numbers may not grow when October comes
B the numbers will grow by a particular amount until October
C the numbers may not grow much by October
D the numbers will be at their highest in October

11 A the darkness will make it impossible for some to go
B the darkness will make some not want to go
C some will leave when it gets dark
D some will get bored when it gets dark

12 A so that people can walk in the vacuum
B the vacuum suddenly appears
C people walk in the vacuum
D the vacuum is very large

13 A it's a fact that some motorists get annoyed
B don't some motorists get annoyed?
C that's why some motorists get annoyed
D why don't motorists get annoyed?

14 A that they are often faced
B and confront
C and come into contact with
D on being faced

15 A we are keen to explain
B we frequently explain
C we succeed in explaining
D we are careful to explain

16 A almost all
B a lot
C more than half
D every one

17 A on top of that
B more than anything else
C in the beginning
D as a first reason

18 A this is what we show people
B this is the reason for showing people
C this is how we show people
D this makes it possible to show people

19 A why the roads are bad
B that the roads don't need to be bad
C with emphasis
D how bad the roads are

20 A recently
B when we're not slowing the traffic
C at the busiest periods
D before it's too late

Now check your answers to these questions and to Part 1 of the test on page 81. Then go on to Part 2 of the test on page 83.

2 *Finish each of the following sentences in such a way that it is as similar as possible in meaning to the sentence printed before it.*

Example: She said that he was a brilliant musician.
Answer: She described *him as a brilliant musician.*

a We must think about ways of improving the transport system.

Thought must ....

b In my opinion, he is the best pianist in the whole country.

In my opinion, there is ....

c You're asking these questions because you didn't listen to what I told you earlier.

If ....

d Although I didn't want to pay such a high price, I had no choice.

Reluctant ....

e Only a few minutes remained when the winning goal was scored.

There wasn't ....

f It was the challenge more than the money that appealed to me about the job.

It wasn't so ....

g I'm not to blame for your financial problems.

You can't hold ....

h I certainly won't be promoted this year.

There is no question ....

Before you check your answers to this part of the test, go on to page 84.

COMPLETE THE SENTENCES

Look again at Part 2 of this test on page 83, and then for each question, decide which of the four choices below is correct. You may wish to change some of the answers you gave in the test as you do so. However, if the answer that you gave in the test is not among the choices here, this does not necessarily mean that it is wrong.

a 1 Thought must we give about ways of improving the transport system.
2 Thought must be had for ways of improving the transport system.
3 Thought must be given to ways of improving the transport system.
4 Thought must be taken on ways of improving the transport system.

b 1 In my opinion, there is nobody who is better pianist than him in the whole country.
2 In my opinion, there is no better pianist than him in the whole country.
3 In my opinion, there is no such good pianist than him in the whole country.
4 In my opinion, there is nobody so good a pianist as him in the whole country.

c 1 If you'd listened to what I told you earlier, you wouldn't be asking these questions.
2 If you listened to what I told you earlier, you wouldn't have asked these questions.
3 If you'd listened to what I told you earlier, you wouldn't have asked these questions.
4 If you were listening to what I told you earlier, you wouldn't ask these questions.

d 1 Reluctant was I to pay such a high price, I had no choice.
2 Reluctant that I was to pay such a high price, I had no choice.
3 Reluctant for paying such a high price I was, I had no choice.
4 Reluctant though I was to pay such a high price, I had no choice.

e 1 There wasn't many minutes left when the winning goal was scored.
2 There wasn't much time remained when the winning goal was scored.
3 There wasn't long remaining when the winning goal was scored.
4 There wasn't long time remaining when the winning goal was scored.

f 1 It wasn't so much the money as the challenge that appealed to me about the job.
2 It wasn't so as to earn money than a challenge that appealed to me about the job.
3 It wasn't so much money as challenge that appealed to me about the job.
4 It wasn't so financial as challenging that appealed to me about the job.

g 1 You can't hold out blame to me for your financial problems.
2 You can't hold me responsible for your financial problems.
3 You can't hold me the responsible for your financial problems.
4 You can't hold me as to blame for your financial problems.

h 1 There is no question that I will be promoted this year.
2 There is no question of me being promoted this year.
3 There is no question to promote me this year.
4 There is no question for me to be promoted this year.

Now check your answers to these questions and to Part 2 of the test.

Then go on to Part 3 of the test on page 85.

3 *Fill each of the blanks with a suitable word or phrase.*

Example: She had difficulty *making up her* mind which one to buy.

a I don't feel very well – I think I'm coming .... flu.

b Needless ...., Harry turned up late yet again.

c So stunned .... all by the news that none of us knew what to say.

d The whole holiday was a disaster .... finish.

e It is by .... certain that I'll be able to give you a lift, so don't rely on it.

f She has been working too hard and is badly in .... a break.

Now check your answers to this part of the test.

---

4 *For each of the sentences below, write a new sentence as similar as possible in meaning to the original sentence, but using the word given. This word* **must not be altered** *in any way.*

Example: She paid no attention to his warning.
notice
Answer: *She took no notice of his warning.*

a Are you suggesting that I'm dishonest?
questioning

....

b He was shouting as loud as he could.
top

....

c The forthcoming biography of him will make him seem an arrogant and selfish man.
portrayed

....

d I am aware of the fact that Rebecca is upset about something.
escaped

....

e Her latest novel isn't as good as her previous one.
par

....

f This is the first time I've tried cooking this dish.
attempt

....

g I don't dislike Ronnie, but he annoys me sometimes.
just

....

h There is an enormous variety of tourist attractions in this part of the country.
manner

....

Now check your answers to this part of the test.

SECTION B

Read the following passage, then answer the questions which follow it.

The human face of genius

Pity the poor science writer. Richard Feynman, the most brilliant and influential scientist of our time, once said that if you want to appreciate science, it is necessary to understand the language it speaks in. That language is, of course, mathematics, which, Feynman noted, is hard for many people.

Tough luck. 'All the intellectual arguments that you can make will not communicate to deaf ears what the experience of music really is,' he went on. 'In the same way, all the intellectual arguments in the world will not convey an understanding of science to those of 'the other culture'.'

Let's call this Myth No 1: that science is a place apart; alien, the preserve of specialists, incomprehensible to the lay culture. If you don't have a ticket, you can't get in.

Myth No 2 is more subtle. It is that the principal task of the science writer is to popularize, to translate knowledge from one language (mathematics) to another (in this case, English), however imperfectly.

Myth No 3 is a cousin of the others: that the science writer must fall back on metaphor and poetry, like puffs of gauze, whereas the scientist builds with numbers and equations, like steel rods.

Like all good myths, they rest on half-truths. Mathematics *is* the language that nature speaks in, and much of science *has* grown distant from our common-sense understanding. Certainly, a science writer is haunted by the spectre of compromise, the feeling of having to filter a lush panorama through a flawed lens.

Yet how absurd it is to speak of science as something apart from our culture, from the fabric of ideas, traditions, language and devices that surround us. If anything, in this century of the atomic bomb and the computer, of relativity and uncertainty and chaos, we are more deeply and knowledgeably embedded in a scientific world than ever before. We may quiver at the sight of an equation, but we know how powerfully science changes our lives. We have seen our world, as our ancestors never could, through the eyes of microbes and galaxies.

Perhaps because I came to science writing by accident, I have never believed that it is right to set out merely to *translate* science. It seems more useful to behave as any other writer does: to report news, if one is a news reporter, and to write history if one is a historian. Let the explanation follow behind.

When I wrote *Chaos*, an account of the recent revolution in scientists' understanding of complex systems, my intention – at least my primary intention – was not to explain the ideas, as one might hold a finished *objet d'art* up to the light. It was to tell the dramatic story of how a few people, at first mavericks in their fields, managed to transform the way scientists and the rest of us think about the world.

Science as we learn it in school is cut and dried. Not so in real life. Scientists make false steps, miscommunicate with colleagues, endure confusion. My goal was to let this science emerge as it had for these pioneers: gradually, in uncertain steps.

In *Genius*, I tried to write Feynman's biography as one would write the life of a politician, a painter, a cleric, or any other specialist in a discipline with its own jargon and tribal customs. I believe that we have come to expect less from scientists' biographies than from those of others. We have tended to settle either for gross popularizations (Feynman's own anecdotal memoirs omitted the science that in reality he breathed from morning to night), or for stitched-together collections of technical explication; not biography at all.

Feynman's life in science encompassed far more than his profound contributions to quantum electrodynamics and other specific problems. I found myself drawn into the rapidly changing place of technology in the 20th century's public life; the philosophy of scientific explanation, in a time so dominated by uncertainty; the role of visualization in new scientific ideas; and the nature of genius itself.

a In what way do Feynman's remarks in the first paragraph support the statement 'Pity the poor science writer'?

....

....

b What comparison did Feynman draw between music and science?

....

c Explain what is meant in the context by the sentence 'If you don't have a ticket, you can't get in.' (line 10)

....

d What does the phrase 'however imperfectly' (lines 12–13) imply?

....

e What comparison between science writing and the work of scientists is implied by the phrases 'puffs of gauze' (line 15) and 'steel rods' (lines 15–16)?

....

....

f Explain in your own words what a science writer is said to be 'haunted by' (line 19).

....

g According to the writer, why is it absurd to regard science as being 'apart from our culture' (line 21)?

....

h Why might we 'quiver at the sight of an equation' (lines 24–25)?

....

i Explain briefly the writer's approach when he wrote *Chaos*.

....

....

j What is meant by the phrase 'mavericks in their fields' (line 34)?

....

k Explain the phrase 'cut and dried' (line 36).

....

l According to the writer, what is wrong with most biographies of scientists?

....

....

m What was misleading about Feynman's memoirs?

....

n Explain briefly the writer's approach to writing Feynman's biography.

....

o In a paragraph of 70–90 words, summarize what the writer sees as common misconceptions about both science and science writing.

....

....

....

....

....

....

....

....

....

....

....

....

Before you check your answers to this part of the test, go on to page 89.

For general guidance on the questions for this part of the test, see Answering the Questions – General Notes on page 28.

A DETAILED STUDY

(see page 28 for guidance on this type of question)

Look at question a

1 What is meant by the sentence 'Pity the poor science writer'?

....

2 What problem concerning mathematics is described in the first paragraph?

....

Look at questions b and c

What is meant in this context by 'the lay culture' (line 10)?

....

Look at question f

1 A 'lush panorama' (lines 19–20) would present
a a distant object.
b a wide view.
c a confusing picture.
d small details.

....

2 If something is 'flawed', it is
a the wrong size.
b covered.
c hidden.
d faulty.

....

Look at question g

What is the computer used as an example of in line 23?

....

Look at question i

Why might one 'hold a finished *objet d'art* up to the light' (line 33)?

....

Look at question l

How many categories of scientists' biographies are mentioned?

....

Look at question m

If a book is anecdotal, it contains
a well-known facts.
b amusing stories.
c controversial opinions.
d brief descriptions.

....

EXPLAIN THE MEANING

(see page 61 for guidance on this type of question)

Look at question j

A 'maverick' is most likely to be someone who
a holds unorthodox views.
b fails on a grand scale.
c makes important discoveries.
d seeks to influence others.

....

Look at question k

The opposite of 'cut and dried' is most likely to be
a unsuccessful and misunderstood.
b interesting.
c unclear and complicated.
d simplified.

....

Now check your answers to these questions. When you have done so, decide whether you wish to change any of the answers you gave in the test. If you have phrased anything you wrote in the test differently from the choices given on these pages, this does not necessarily mean that you answered incorrectly in the test. Then check your answers to questions a–n of the test on pages 87–88.

WRITING A SUMMARY

(For general guidance on writing a summary for this part of the test, see Writing a Summary – General Notes on page 29.)

When planning your summary, it is a good idea to decide which part or parts of the text are relevant to it. Decide which of the highlighted parts of the text below are relevant to your summary.

Pity the poor science writer. Richard Feynman,
the most brilliant and influential scientist of our
time, once said: 'If you want to appreciate nature,
A it is necessary to understand the language she
speaks in.' The language is, of course,
mathematics, which, Feynman noted, is 'hard for
some people.'

Tough luck. 'All the intellectual arguments that
you can make will not communicate to deaf ears
what the experience of music really is,' he went
on. 'In the same way, all the intellectual
arguments in the world will not convey an
B understanding of nature to those of 'the other
culture'.'

Let's call this Myth No 1: that science is a
place apart; alien, the preserve of specialists,
C incomprehensible to the lay culture. If you don't
have a ticket, you can't get in. Myth No 2 is more
subtle. It is that the principal task of the science
D writer is to popularise, to translate knowledge from
one language (mathematics) to another (in this
case, English), however imperfectly.

Myth No 3 is a cousin of the others: that the
science writer must fall back on metaphor and
E poetry, like puffs of gauze, whereas the scientist
builds with numbers and equations, like steel
rods.

Like all good myths, they rest on half-truths.
F Mathematics is the language that nature speaks
in, and much of science has grown distant from
our common-sense understanding. Certainly, a
science writer is haunted by the spectre of
compromise, the feeling of having to filter a lush
panorama through a flawed lens.

Yet how absurd it is to speak of science as
something apart from our culture, from the fabric
G of ideas, traditions, language and devices that
surround us. If anything, in this century of the
atomic bomb and the computer, of relativity and
uncertainty and chaos, we are more deeply and
knowledgeably embedded in a scientific world
than ever before. We may quiver at the sight of
an equation, but we know how powerfully science
changes our lives. We have seen our world, as
our ancestors never could, through the eyes of
microbes and galaxies.

Perhaps because I came to science writing by
accident, I have never believed that it is right to
set out merely to *translate* science. It seems more H
useful to behave as any other writer does: to
report news, if one is a news reporter, and to
write history if one is a historian. Let the
explanation follow behind.

When I wrote *Chaos*, an account of the recent
revolution in scientists' understanding of complex
systems, my intention – at least my primary
intention – was not explain the ideas, as one
might hold a finished *objet d'art* up to the light. It
was to tell the dramatic story of how a few people,
at first mavericks in their fields, managed to
transform the way scientists and the rest of us
think about the world.

Science as we learn it in school is cut and
dried. Not so in real life. Scientists make false
steps, miscommunicate with colleagues, endure J
confusion. My goal was to let this science emerge
as it had for these pioneers: gradually, in
uncertain steps.

In *Genius*, I tried to write Feynman's biography
as one would write the life of a politician, a
painter, a cleric, or any other specialist in a
discipline with its own jargon and tribal customs. I
believe that we have come to expect less from
scientists' biographies than from those of others.
We have tended to settle either for gross
popularisations (Feynman's own anecdotal
memoirs omitted the science that in reality he
breathed from morning to night), or for stitched-
together collections of technical explication; not
biography at all.

Feynman's life in science encompassed far
more than his profound contributions to quantum
electrodynamics and other specific problems.
I found myself drawn into the rapidly changing L
place of technology in the 20th century's public
life; the philosophy of scientific explanation, in a
time so dominated by uncertainty; the role of
visualisation in new scientific ideas; and the
nature of genius itself.

Now look again at your summary and decide whether you wish to change anything.

SAMPLE SUMMARY

Now read this sample summary and answer the questions that follow it.

'If you want to appreciate science, you have to understand the language it speaks' which is mathematics. The writer put this statement into three different myths. The first one is that science is only for specialist people and not for the layman. The second one is that the principal task of the science writer is to translate knowledge from one language (mathematics) to another (English) and finally, science writer must fall back on metaphor and poetry which it has nothing to do with science. Furthermore, people believe that science is something apart from our culture when actually we live in a scientific world more than ever. In addition, writers, when writing a biography often forget to write about science instead they would either write anecdotal memoirs or use technical explanation.

a Is anything irrelevant included or anything relevant not included? If so, what?

b Are there any language mistakes? Correct any that you think there are.

c Has any of the passage simply been copied in the summary? If so, what?

Now look again at your summary and decide whether you wish to change anything.

Then check your marks for your summary and read the assessment of this sample summary.

PAPER 4 LISTENING COMPREHENSION (about 30 mins)

PART ONE

You will hear part of a radio programme about traffic wardens, whose job is to stop people from parking illegally and give them a ticket if they do. **For questions 1–9**, *decide which of the two speakers makes the statements. Write* **K** *for Keith,* **J** *for Julia or* **N** *for neither of them.*

I sometimes pretend that some insults are not familiar to me.	1	
I sometimes give someone a ticket even though I hadn't intended to.	2	
I sometimes decide not to give someone a ticket after I have started writing it.	3	
It is reasonable to give shopkeepers special consideration.	4	
It is understandable that some traffic wardens behave aggressively.	5	
I have found it necessary to criticize a colleague.	6	
I gave special treatment to a certain person.	7	
I dislike drivers who ignore my authority.	8	
I warn angry drivers about the consequences of shouting at me.	9	

PART TWO

You will hear a talk about Mrs Beeton, an English woman who wrote some extremely popular cookery books in the 19th century. **For questions 10–19**, *complete the sentences.*

As a character, Mrs Beeton was **10** __________.

She took up writing because she felt a **11** __________ after marrying.

One of her most famous books was called *The Book of* **12** __________.

It contained recipes and a large number of **13** __________.

Her husband's monthly publication was called *The* **14** __________.

Mrs Beeton said that she wrote her books so that **15** __________ could be prevented.

Many said that she was successful because of the **16** __________ in her books.

She also included **17** __________ concerning such matters as gossip.

Her books appealed to people who felt they did not have the necessary **18** __________.

She thought her books benefited the poor by giving them information about **19** __________.

PART THREE

You will hear part of a radio programme about birth order. ***For questions 20–25****, choose the best answer,* ***A****,* ***B****,* ***C*** *or* ***D****.*

20 Frank's research has shown him that first-born children

A resent the role they play in the family.
B tend to disapprove of younger siblings.
C are keen to please their parents.
D are jealous of younger siblings.

21 Sophie believes that she rebelled against her mother because

A she was not the first-born child.
B her mother was unconventional.
C she was encouraged to do so.
D it was an inevitable part of growing up.

22 Sophie says that her older sister was more conventional than her because

A she had some bad experiences as a child.
B she was worried about Sophie.
C of the particular circumstances of their family.
D of their parents' anxieties when her sister was born.

23 Sophie thinks that her nickname as a child illustrates

A that she was something of an exception to Frank's theory.
B how peculiar her upbringing was.
C how unusual her personality was when she was a child.
D that she was misunderstood as a child.

24 What does Sophie say about Frank's model?

A She has trouble understanding what it involves.
B She knows people who don't conform to it.
C It doesn't take account of older people.
D It is only true under certain circumstances.

25 Frank says that the younger children of unconventional parents

A don't want to be unconventional themselves.
B don't get on well with the first-born child.
C are much more difficult to analyse.
D tend to disapprove of their parents.

Before you check your answers to this Paper, go on to page 94.

MATCHING

Matching questions may require you to do any of the following:

- decide which of **three speakers** makes each of the statements, expresses each of the opinions, attitudes, feelings, etc;
- decide which of **two speakers** makes each of the statements, expresses each of the opinions, attitudes, feelings, etc., or whether **neither** speaker does;
- decide which of **two speakers** makes each of the statements, expresses each of the opinions, attitudes, feelings, etc., or whether **both** speakers do;
- decide which of **three topics** each of the statements applies to;
- decide which of **two topics** each of the statements applies to, or whether each statement applies to **neither topic** or **both topics**.

Listen again to Part 1 of the test on page 92, and write **K** *for what Keith says,* **J** *for what Julia says,* **N** *if neither of them says it or* **B** *if both of them says it. This will help you to practise doing this type of task and to check the answers that you gave in the test. The numbers below refer to the questions in the test on page 92.*

1 *(Stop the tape after Keith says 'said to you, you know')*

A There are some insults I haven't heard before. ☐
B I ask about some insults. ☐
C There are some insults I object to more than others. ☐
D Some insults don't make much sense to me. ☐
E I don't let insults upset me. ☐
F There are some insults I decide to use myself. ☐

2 and 3 *(Stop the tape when Keith says 'it's still the same, yeah')*

A I sometimes change my mind about giving a ticket. ☐
B Drivers assume that I am giving them a ticket. ☐
C I give a ticket if a driver lies to me. ☐
D I am actually writing something else in my book. ☐
E It can be too late to change your mind about giving a ticket. ☐
F I am kinder to people if they are upset about getting a ticket. ☐

4 and 5 *(Stop the tape when Julia says 'liaison with people')*

A The job has got harder than it used to be. ☐
B Some traffic wardens give the rest a bad name. ☐
C Some traffic wardens are particularly hard on shops. ☐
D Some traffic wardens are too keen to use their power. ☐
E There is a limit to how much you should compromise. ☐
F Some traffic wardens give people orders. ☐

6 and 7 *(Stop the tape when Keith says 'move it quick')*

A Some traffic wardens pick on certain people. ☐
B I allowed someone to park illegally. ☐
C People who keep breaking the law annoy traffic wardens. ☐
D I stopped giving someone tickets. ☐
E Traffic wardens shouldn't pick on people. ☐
F I informed someone he was about to get a ticket. ☐

8 and 9 *(Stop the tape at the end)*

A I refuse to talk to drivers who shout at me. ☐
B I let people park illegally for a certain length of time. ☐
C I might let off people who shout at me. ☐
D Some drivers park illegally regardless of traffic wardens. ☐
E I threaten drivers with a bigger fine if they argue. ☐
F It's easy to get people to stop arguing with you. ☐

Now check your answers to the questions on these pages. When you have done so, decide whether you wish to change any of the answers you gave in Part 1 of the test on page 92

Then check your answers to Part 1 of the test and then to Parts 2 and 3 on pages 92–93.

PAPER 5 INTERVIEW

1 *Look at one or more of these photographs and answer the questions that follow them.*

1

2

3

What's happening in each picture? What's the situation?
Describe the people. What feelings do they seem to have?
What kind of people do you think they are?
Describe the faces and facial expressions of the people.
Where do you think each picture was taken?

During what period of their lives do you think people are at their happiest? Why?
What do you think is the most difficult period in people's lives? Why?
What do you think you will be doing when you are ten years older?
What do you think you will be like as a person when you are ten years older?

2 *Read one or more of these passages and then answer the questions that follow them.*

a As I grew older, my picture of where I lived grew wider and more complicated. The expanding of one's vision is usually enough in itself to generate a feeling that everything is falling apart. Nevertheless one had a sense of constancy even at the time, and looking back on it I can see that my whole childhood was remarkable for the amount of entertainment on flow. All you had to do was turn the tap and bend your pursed lips to the bubbler.

b Many years ago I made a resolution to stay at the age of forty-two for the rest of my life. That is a proper moment at which to petrify. One is young enough to be sprightly, yet old enough to be solid. I have many years' experience of being forty-two, and I see no reason to improve on it. Life begins at forty-two, and there it stays. There are, of course, minor drawbacks. It is hard to get a pension. The appalling lapses of memory that beset one are less easily explained away. These are small disadvantages.

c It's rather like the old story about the man who wanted to know the meaning of life, and climbed a Himalayan mountain to ask the guru sitting on top. 'Master, what is the meaning of life?' 'The meaning of life, my child, is chicken soup.' 'Chicken soup? I come all this way, climb this mountain, and you tell me the meaning of life is chicken soup.' The old man was quite taken aback. 'You mean it isn't chicken soup?'

What is the purpose of each passage?
What is the tone of each passage?
What point is the writer making in each passage?

3 *Do one or more of these tasks. If you are working with others, discuss them together.*

a What is your earliest memory of childhood?
Is it a pleasant or unpleasant memory? Give reasons.
What is your favourite childhood memory? Why is it so special to you?
In what ways do you think you are still the same and in what ways do you think you have changed since you were a small child?

b What is your idea of a successful future for yourself? What kind of lifestyle would it involve?
Do you think you will achieve it?
Have you achieved any of your aims yet? If so, which? How did you achieve them?
If not, what do you think has prevented you from achieving them?
Do you have any unconventional aims in life? If so, what are they? Will you try to achieve them?
If so, how will you go about it? If not, why not?

c 'The elderly should be respected, not discarded.'

Do you agree with this statement? If so, why? If not, why not?
What is the general attitude towards elderly people in your country? How are they treated?
Do you approve or disapprove of this attitude? Has it changed?
Describe an elderly person you have particularly liked or disliked. Why do/did you like or dislike that person? What influence has he/she had on you?

DESCRIBING PERSONAL CHARACTERISTICS

In the interview, you may talk about your own or other people's personalities. To check or build up your vocabulary on this subject, look at the adjectives listed on this page. Decide which ones are generally used to express approval of someone and which ones are generally used to express disapproval. Put them into the correct columns.

callous
spineless
amiable
cordial
genial
grumpy
pompous
obnoxious
compassionate
headstrong
impetuous
jovial
courteous
pretentious
overbearing
dignified
tough
self-possessed
complacent
discreet
cold
malicious
surly
soft
ruthless

moody
self-reliant
morose
underhand
level-headed
conceited
offhand
vile
self-assured
squeamish
decent
vindictive
snobbish
obliging
principled
hard
bigoted
loyal
fickle
obsequious
tactless
magnanimous
self-righteous
gutsy
affable

APPROVAL	DISAPPROVAL

Now check your answers to these questions.

TEST FOUR

PAPER 1 READING COMPREHENSION 1 hour

SECTION A

In this section you must choose the word or phrase which best completes each sentence. On your answer sheet indicate the letter **A**, **B**, **C** *or* **D** *against the number of each item* **1** *to* **25** *for the word or phrase you choose. Give one answer only to each question.*

1 The weather wasn't very good but, ... , it was a good holiday.

A as a rule **B** all in all **C** over and above **D** at the most

2 By the .... of it, the economy will improve over the next few months.

A face **B** impression **C** evidence **D** look

3 Working there was good for me, ... I gained a lot of valuable experience.

A as far as **B** in that **C** as for **D** in terms of

4 His amazing natural skills set him .... from most other players.

A aside **B** off **C** apart **D** out

5 He was thrilled at living in a new country but the fascination soon .... off.

A faded **B** wore **C** died **D** let

6 I've applied, but I don't .... much hope of getting the job.

A keep at **B** hold out **C** bear up **D** stand by

7 Harriet has now arrived late for work three days in a ....

A line **B** sequence **C** series **D** row

8 He refused to .... on why he took such an unexpected decision.

A elaborate **B** amplify **C** account **D** clarify

9 She .... disputed his version of what had happened.

A hotly **B** intensely **C** harshly **D** acutely

10 Rose has always had a .... interest in matters to do with the environment.

A fierce **B** sharp **C** grave **D** keen

11 As he accepted the award, his voice .... with emotion.

A quivered **B** flinched **C** cringed **D** winced

12 All the others were experts and I was out of my .... in the conversation.

A level **B** depth **C** limit **D** range

13 If you're ever in this area again, don't .... to come and stay with us.

A hesitate **B** dither **C** pause **D** linger

14 There was a huge .... of applause when the star of the show appeared.

A bout **B** stint **C** round **D** spate

15 I'm sure there's a definite .... of envy in her nasty comments about you.

A factor **B** ingredient **C** component **D** element

16 In the .... of just two days, her whole life changed.

A interval **B** space **C** spell **D** duration

17 Tim and Alan have never got on well and there is a lot of .... feeling between them.

A cross **B** adverse **C** ill **D** vile

18 He was so .... in his career that he neglected his friends and family.

A obsessed **B** preoccupied **C** riveted **D** engrossed

19 I'll have to call a .... to this discussion, as we have a lot of work to do.

A halt **B** stoppage **C** close **D** standstill

20 It was a rather .... day, with dark clouds everywhere.

A gloomy **B** despondent **C** downcast **D** glum

21 She was .... to tears by the kind things that were said about her.

A touched **B** inspired **C** moved **D** aroused

22 It took him a long time to come to .... with the fact that he was never going to be a great author.

A acceptance **B** terms **C** understanding **D** allowances

23 The thieves took .... when they heard a police car approaching.

A retreat **B** flight **C** escape **D** getaway

24 Afterwards, when I .... on the events of that day, I could hardly believe what had happened.

A contemplated **B** reviewed **C** reflected **D** weighed

25 They tried to .... on their children the importance of a good education.

A impress **B** instil **C** highlight **D** underline

Before you check your answers to this section of the test, go on to pages 100 and 101.

CONNECTORS ADVERBIALS

A few questions in this part of the test require you to select words or phrases or to complete phrases which:

link parts of a sentence; or

have an adverbial function in a sentence.

The numbers of the exercises below refer to questions 1–3 of the test on page 98, which are questions of this type.

In each of the exercises, choose which of the four options given in the test fits each gap. This may help you to eliminate some of the incorrect options in the questions they refer to and to check or learn a variety of connectors and adverbial phrases.

1 *at the most* *all in all* *as a rule* *over and above*

A I've got a few financial problems, but .... I'm quite happy at the moment.

B It's unusual for Jake to be late because .... he's very punctual.

C Our journey tomorrow should take two hours ....

D .... her normal duties, she has to do extra work quite often.

2 *evidence* *impression* *look* *face*

A He gives the .... of being someone who worries a lot.

B On the .... of it, everything about their lives was normal.

C On the .... of his recent work, he's become a valuable employee.

D By the .... of it, nothing's going to persuade her to change her mind.

3 *as for* *in that* *as far as* *in terms of*

A .... I'm aware, they're still living at the same address.

B This is probably the best car you could buy, ... value for money.

C I quite like Mandy but .... her husband, I must say I'm not keen.

D My flat's in a convenient place, ... it's not far from where I work.

PHRASAL VERBS

A few questions in this part of the test require you to choose or complete phrasal verbs. The options may be complete phrasal verbs or parts of them.
The numbers of the exercises below refer to questions 4–6 of the test on page 98, which are questions of this type.

In each of the exercises, choose which of the four options given in the test fits each gap. This may help you to eliminate some of the incorrect options in the questions they refer to and to check or learn a number of phrasal verbs.

4 | *aside* | *off* | *apart* | *out* |

A She decided to set some money .... for emergencies.

B I set .... my objections very clearly in a letter.

C What sets Mike .... from everyone else is his incredible sense of humour.

D Sarah cries a lot and any romantic film can set her ....

5 | *faded* | *died* | *wore* | *let* |

A When the applause .... down, he started his speech.

B It was a busy day at work and the pressure didn't .... up for a moment.

C I watched the boat as it .... away into the distance.

D After a while, my enthusiasm for the sport .... off.

6 | *stand by* | *hold out* | *keep at* | *bear up* |

A The doctors didn't .... much hope for him but he recovered.

B I .... everything I told you – it was all true.

C She manages to .... well, despite all the problems in her life.

D I'm going to .... this game until I've mastered it.

Now check your answers to these exercises. When you have done so, decide whether you wish to change any of your answers to questions 1–6 in the test.

Then check your answers to the test.

SECTION B

*In this section you will find after each of the passages a number of questions or unfinished statements about the passage, each with four suggested answers or ways of finishing. You must choose the one which you think fits best. On your answer sheet, indicate the letter **A**, **B**, **C** or **D** against the number of each item **26** to **40** for the answer you choose. Give **one answer only** to each question.*

FIRST PASSAGE

It was like love, my fascination for those huge, noisy machines that were already near the end of their golden age. They moved with such magnificent purpose. They were alive, they had steam, smoke and the smell of minerals; they burned energy without concealment, and you could see their fire. They raced against themselves, losing more heat than they used, running by burning their own cargo of coal; but there was something very human about the need to keep the fire going by hand, shovelling and watching, never for a second being able to forget responsibility for the journey and the work. Their waste didn't have to be buried in lead-lined coffins, it was exhaled as carbon, sulphur and nitrogen, or swept and scattered as ash, the unburnt particles of coal settling gently on our clothes and hair.

Some things that humans make transcend their function; instruments can be magical. That explosive, rhythmic sound we call puffing says more to us about getting under way, about departure, than a petrol-driven snarl can ever do; perhaps it has something close to the beat of our pulse. Even if we were using up and heating the earth too much, and no-one knew that at the time, it would have been worth making an exception for steam engines. They were beautiful machines; the most beautiful machines produced in the industrial revolution.

The honest power of a steam engine is overwhelming – most of its important parts are on display. You see the great cylinder with cranks and mechanisms outside it, you see the ingenious connection of levers and rods to the enormous wheels and you have already understood that this combination of things will work, and you might even see how. Unlike a motor car or a nuclear ship, there's no secrecy about a steam engine's force. What engineers call the 'motion', the linked shafts and pistons and wheels that drive the engine, is as fascinating as the movement of a watch. And almost as jewel-like, for the couplings and connecting rods were often still chipped and filed smooth by hammer and chisel, after they came off the milling machine. Hands still made parts of these engines, and it is no surprise that drivers spoke of them as individuals. But essentially, the engine was a boiler held in heavy frames on a set of steel wheels.

The simplicity of it fascinated me. Coal burnt in a furnace surrounded by water created steam; steam confined in a cylinder pushed a piston, and linked to wheels by rods that turned the straight thrust of the piston into rotatory motion, the engine moved and worked. The idea that hordes of people and commodities could be carried at such shakingly powerful speeds by a sort of articulated kettle, in which the water could never be allowed to fall below the top of the furnace or there would be an explosion, seemed amazing to me. What made it all so different from today's electric railways, which run at set speeds, was the need to be aware at every moment of the perilous balance of fire and water, which also gave the possibility of going a little faster if the engineman was good, or of disaster if he was incompetent.

Like everything else we make – like firearms, for example – the simple idea could be endlessly refined, developed and decorated. I discovered trains in their heyday, when steam under pressure had achieved astonishing things. Libraries of books were written on the improvement of Watt's basic idea. More sophisticated valve gears gave more subtle control of pressure; steam could be superheated to get more pressure out of it; more yards could be added to the labyrinth of copper firetubes inside the boiler to give a bigger heating area, and therefore more heat and steam. But it was the way it all worked together that mattered, in the poetry of great engines, their appearance, speed and mystique.

26 One of the attractions of steam engines mentioned in the first paragraph is

A their connection with a previous period of history.
B the speed at which they were capable of travelling.
C the fact they needed people to make sure they ran properly.
D the smell of the waste that they produced.

27 The author says that it would be wrong to criticize steam engines for

A the way they changed people's lives.
B damaging the environment.
C being less useful than cars.
D the amount of noise they made.

28 The author thinks that drivers spoke of steam engines as individuals because

A some of them seemed to have human characteristics.
B it was possible to see their function from their appearance.
C they were not wholly manufactured by machines.
D not all of them were constructed on the same principle.

29 What aspect of steam engines does the writer emphasize in the fourth paragraph?

A how much they depended on the skill of the engineman
B how much they were capable of transporting
C that there were relatively few disasters involving them
D that they were much more complicated than they looked

30 What does the author emphasize about steam engines in the passage as a whole?

A how much they developed over the years
B how much they differed from other machines
C how much beauty he found in them
D how much they remind him of his boyhood

Now check your answers to these questions.

SECOND PASSAGE

You can't blame the movies for having a centenary, but there's no escaping the embarrassment or the vulgarity of the celebration. It's too close to having to attend the birthday party of a 100-year-old person. This is a remarkable achievement, you say; yet you cringe at the absence of vitality and the agony on an ancient face trying to remember who you are. So many things at 100 are past their prime, or grisly imitations of youth.

Now you're going to suppose that I'm tongue-in-cheek or playing devil's advocate. Really, I'm not. Just because someone spends 30 years thinking and writing about movies doesn't mean his mind is made up. It's thinking and writing I depend on, and movies just happen to be my most available pretext. I could have been a golfer, or a yachtsman. So, in the spirit of that thinking, let me suggest why we might have been better off if the inventors of the movies had been gardeners or golfers.

There have been so many movies, and so many more versions of movies on TV. We haven't seen them all, but 'story' has become a part of our air. We all of us know, deep down (and are dispirited by), the notion that there are only seven, nine or thirteen basic story forms in fiction. The number varies, but day after day the same stale mythic outlines are served up. So myth has gone dead on us, too. The wellsprings of imaginative life have been rendered sweet and synthetic. The excess of material has become wearying and unreliable. In 30 years, movies turned the western from a resonant metaphor into a stupid distortion of the real history of America. The genres of American film have taught us to be cynical about our own legends. And so narrative tradition has been befouled.

As narrative suspense breaks down, the complex involvement of a reader's sensibility in prolonged story – a novel – is less and less likely. Films are quicker; they require less imaginative work; the 'world' is immediately there, a given, pretty as a picture; the seductiveness of the spied-on fantasy is so much more beguiling than the developing powers of private insight and questioning called for in reading. That's a fancy way of reiterating the cliché: 'no one reads any more'. Kids spend between four and eight hours a day with the TV on, looking at the broken pieces of stories, remoting themselves from one strand to another. Concentration, attention, introspection, learning coherent linguistic response, all suffer. I am not saying that children, or teenagers, relish this life. On the contrary, many seem bitter and vengeful about it, and often employ its catchphrases and attitudes to undermine other attempts at parental or educational advice. It is as if they know they have been belittled and betrayed by film and TV – after all, in many cases those things have cheated them of the company of their parents.

31 The writer says in the first paragraph that the centenary of the movies

A is not worth celebrating at all.
B draws attention to how poor they have become.
C is being given too much publicity.
D reminds him of events in his own life.

32 What does the writer emphasize in the second paragraph?

A that his article is meant to be light-hearted
B that his attitude to movies has changed over the years
C that he has decided to write a controversial article
D that he has never been sure of his views on movies

33 The writer uses westerns as an example of films that

A depict actual events inaccurately.
B keep repeating the same basic story.
C no longer appeal to people in general.
D were never based on real situations.

34 According to the writer, films today discourage people from

A being optimistic about life.
B trying to improve their lives.
C making correct moral decisions.
D thinking for themselves.

35 The writer believes that children and teenagers today

A resent the effects that watching TV and films have on them.
B get a view of life from films and TV that is too depressing.
C prefer films and TV programmes that adults don't want them to watch.
D hold adults responsible for the things they see in films and on TV.

Before you check your answers to these questions, go on to page 105.

A DETAILED STUDY

The questions on these pages will help you to make sure that you have chosen the correct options for the questions on the second text, on pages 104.

Question 31 *Look at the first paragraph of the text and answer these questions.*

1 Does the writer say that he has attended someone's 100th birthday party?

....

2 Which of the following is closest in meaning to 'grisly'?
a predictable
b laboured
c awful
d unsuccesful

....

3 Does the writer say that there should be no celebration of the centenary of the movies? If so, where?

....

4 Which of the following is closest in meaning in the context to 'escaping'?
a excusing
b preventing
c keeping away from
d failing to notice

....

Question 32 *Look at the second paragraph of the text and answer these questions.*

1 Which word or phrase refers to not being serious?

....

2 What is your intention if you are 'playing devil's advocate'?
a to be amusing
b to provoke discussion
c to emphasize a point of view
d to express uncertainty

....

3 Why does the writer mention being a golfer or a yachtsman?

....

4 Does the writer imply that he has been writing about movies for 30 years?

....

Question 33 *Look at the third paragraph of the text and answer these questions.*

1 Which word or phrase does the writer intend westerns to illustrate?
a sweet and synthetic
b stale
c cynical
d unreliable

....

2 Does the writer refer to the popularity of westerns? If so, where?

....

3 Explain in your own words what the writer's objection to modern westerns is.

....

4 Does the writer suggest that all films repeat the same basic stories? If so, where?

....

Question 34 *Look at the last paragraph of the text and answer these questions.*

1 Does the writer mention the moral issues raised by films or novels? If so, where?

....

2 Does the writer mention ways in which viewers could improve their lives? If so, where?

....

3 Does the writer say that films today are depressing? If so, where?

....

4 Does the writer suggest that novels require effort on the part of the reader? If so, where?

....

Question 35 *Look at the last paragraph of the text and answer these questions.*

1 Does the writer mention attempts by adults to prevent children and teenagers from watching certain films and TV programmes? If so, where?

....

2 What is 'this life' that children and teenagers are 'bitter and vengeful' about?

....

3 Why, according to the writer, do children and teenagers feel 'betrayed'?

....

4 Explain in your own words what the writer says about the 'catchphrases and attitudes' of films and TV programmes.

....

Now check your answers to the questions on these pages. Then decide whether you wish to change any of the answers that you gave to the questions on the second passage, on page 104.

Then check your answers to the questions in the test on the second passage.

THIRD PASSAGE

Kanzi is a pygmy chimpanzee. When he was two and a half he was separated briefly from his mother (who had already begun her own language training) and he suddenly, without any coaxing at all, began to use her board and the symbols on it to request food and activities and announce what he was about to do. In *one day* he showed that he had learned signs his mother had failed to learn. His trainers decided that from that point on Kanzi should be trained to use symbols, but that his training would reflect the casual, spontaneous learning he had already demonstrated. Kanzi has never been required to use symbols to get anything – if he does use them it is because he has seen someone else using them, in much the same way (it's thought) a child learns to speak.

Kanzi is quite different from all other chimpanzees that have been taught to use symbols to express their thoughts. For one thing, he understands spoken English. Kanzi's trainers have even tested him with words produced by a speech synthesizer, one that produces a sound for every letter of the alphabet and comes out with a very weird, flat, clipped, montonous kind of speech, only two-thirds of which is understandable by adult humans. Kanzi understands about two-thirds of it as well, meaning that the emotional content, unintentional stresses on words and any of the other cues that might have tipped him to the meaning of the words spoken by his trainers cannot explain his understanding of speech.

There is also evidence that he can comprehend grammatically complicated commands, as long as they're precise. So if there's an orange sitting in front of Kanzi, and he's told, 'Go to the sitting room and get the orange,' he hesitates (is he thinking 'which orange'?). But if the sentence is rearranged: 'Get the orange that's in the sitting room,' he has no trouble, even though there's that complicated (for a chimp) phrase in the middle, 'that's in the.' In fact at age eight Kanzi was better at understanding such sentences than a two-year-old girl who was being asked the same sorts of questions. However even a brilliant performance by Kanzi is going to be treated with caution by the sceptics, and there has already been some doubt cast on exactly what the symbols on the board mean to Kanzi. It has been argued that because Kanzi switches from one meaning to another for a given symbol, depending on the context, the symbols cannot mean the same thing to him as a word means to a child. For instance, Kanzi will use 'juice' to refer to the 'drink', the place where he gets the drink, or the act of going to that place. But when tested for his vocabulary, he links the symbol 'juice' with the picture of a glass of juice. Critics use this evidence to claim that Kanzi just uses the symbol as a means of solving different problems in different circumstances and has no idea that it means 'juice' all the time. This sounds like a tricky argument, because children do what appears to be the same sort of thing, like pointing to the chair and saying 'Daddy'. But the critics say that children rarely use a word for two different *kinds* of things, like using 'table' to mean both the thing in the kitchen and breakfast, whereas Kanzi does.

36 What approach have Kanzi's trainers taken to him?
A a constantly changing one
B one that does not follow a strict pattern
C a specially devised one
D one that gives him rewards for his efforts

37 What does the experiment with the speech synthesizer suggest?
A The way words are stressed plays a vital part in the understanding of them.
B Chimpanzees are better at understanding certain types of sound than others.
C Kanzi is really capable of understanding speech in English.
D Kanzi is unable to understand speech that has an emotional content.

38 What does the example of the orange suggest, according to the writer?
A Certain tasks are more appealing to Kanzi than others.
B Kanzi is unable to make any sense of certain instructions.
C Researchers often make mistakes in this kind of research.
D Kanzi understands the meaning of sentences from their structures.

39 People who are doubtful about Kanzi's language ability believe that
A he gives the same word too many meanings.
B it is wrong to compare his ability with that of a child.
C the symbols have been created to make him seem intelligent.
D children connect objects with places more accurately than he does.

40 What is the writer's purpose in the passage?
A to present a balanced view of the experiments with Kanzi
B to promote the notion that chimpanzees are intelligent
C to cast doubt on the conclusions drawn by Kanzi's trainers
D to point out the similarities between chimpanzees and children

Now check your answers to these questions.

PAPER 2 COMPOSITION 2 hours

*Write **two only** of the composition exercises. Your answers must follow exactly the instructions given. Write in pen, not pencil. You are allowed to make alterations, but make sure your work is clear and easy to read.*

1 Describe a famous performer. Why do you think he or she has become famous? You may choose someone you like or someone you dislike. (About 350 words)

2 'Work is by no means the most important thing in life.' Do you agree with this statement? (About 350 words)

3 Write a story which you believe has a moral lesson. What is the moral? Your story may be something that actually happened or it may be imaginary. (About 350 words)

4 You are considering going to work for a while in a foreign country. Write a letter of enquiry to a potential employer. Include relevant information about yourself, the reasons for your enquiry and your ambitions, and ask for advice as to how you should proceed. (About 300 words)

Before you write your compositions, go on to pages 108 and 109.

PLANNING A COMPOSITION

One of the questions in Paper 2 requires you to **do some formal writing.** You may be required to write a formal letter or a report, for example. You will normally be required to write a little less for this question than the others (300 instead of 350 words). However, to answer this question well, you will have to demonstrate the ability to use language appropriate for such formal writing.

Look at question 4 on page 107 and then answer the following. This will enable you to get some ideas and make some notes that will form the plan for your composition for that question. It is advisable to practise each of the types of composition.

1 Decide which job you wish to do.

....

2 Note what you would like to ask about whether your qualifications are appropriate or which qualifications you should get.

....

....

....

....

....

....

3 Note what you must ask about visas and work permits.

....

....

....

....

....

....

4 Give your personal details briefly.

....

....

....

....

5 Briefly explain the reasons for your enquiry, your aims and your ambitions.

....

....

....

....

....

....

6 Briefly ask what steps you are recommended to take.

....

....

....

....

....

....

Now use these notes to write your composition. You may, of course, wish to include other points or not include some of the points noted here.

Then write one or more of the other compositions.

Now read through the following sample composition for question 4. When you have done so, answer the questions that follow it.

Dear Sir,
I am writing regarding an article in a Swedish newspaper that stated that Harrods were currently looking for management trainees from different countries in Europe. Since it would be a golden opportunity for me to join the team at such a successful and respected enterprise as Harrods, I couldn't wait to contact you. As I haven't seen a formal job ad, I would just like to give you some brief information about myself and my qualifications, along with some enquiries.

I am 22 years old and I have recently finished my degree in business administration at the University of Stockholm in Sweden. I majored in marketing, but apart from that, I particularly enjoyed studying finance. My working experience consists of two years of part time work as a manager assistant at Faltman Malmen, an advertising agency in Sweden.

Apart from being a very ambitious and motivated person I always have a positive approach to my work. I have no problems with working under stress or to deadlines and I work equally as good as a part of a team, as I do on my own initiatives. Moreover, I do not think I would have any problems with using English as a corporate language even though it is not my native tongue.

I would be very grateful if you would inform me about what is required for the job as management trainee and whether or not my qualifications messures up. If my qualifications are suitable, please let me know what I should do in terms of a formal application, and if not, please keep my information on file in case of future vacancies which are more suitable. However, I am certain that I could be of great value to you and I would be utterly delighted to get the opportunity to become a part of the team at Harrods.

Looking forward to hearing from you
Yours faithfully,

1 Does the composition actually answer the question set or does it contain irrelevant parts, 'waffle' – writing that is simply intended to fill the space but does not really say anything – or 'padding' – writing that is repetitious in order to reach the required number of words?

2 Is the composition well-organized? Is it divided into paragraphs appropriately? Explain what each paragraph contains.

3 Are appropriate linking words and phrases used for connecting sentences and paragraphs? Give examples of some that are; if some are not, correct them.

4 Does it have a good range of appropriate vocabulary or is the vocabulary used mostly too simple? Give examples and correct any inappropriate or incorrect vocabulary.

5 Is there a good range of accurate structures forming sentences that are not just simple or are the structures used mostly too basic? Give examples and correct any incorrect structures or other mistakes.

6 Is the style appropriate for this type of composition?

Now check your assessment of and corrections to this sample composition.

PAPER 3 USE OF ENGLISH 2 hours

SECTION A

1 *Fill each of the numbered blanks in the passage with* **one** *suitable word.*

HELPING THE POLICE WITH THEIR ENQUIRIES

Scientific aids to the British police were slow (1) .... coming for the first 150 years of its history. When Sir Edward Henry was (2) .... as Commissioner of the Metropolitan Police in 1903, he brought from India a novel system (3) .... identifying people from their finger prints, and it (4) .... to be (5) .... the most significant developments in crime investigation. However, even as (6) .... as the 1970s, a search of the national fingerprint collection took days, (7) .... not weeks.

In the early days of policing, policeman had a rattle for (8) .... the alarm and 'gallopers' on horseback (9) .... ride from one police station to (10) .... with urgent messages. However, by 1857 (11) .... was a telegraph system connecting every police station in London (12) .... in 1922 wireless was installed in patrol cars.

In the 1950s the government became concerned about rising crime. (13) .... so, it was (14) .... from impossible for a police car to complete an eight-hour tour in a rough area (15) .... getting a single assignment.

Even in 1960, police reporting for night (16) .... would be required to produce pieces of black cotton, which were used for stretching (17) .... doorways, and matches for inserting in door frames. The disturbance of any of those could mean that there had (18) .... a break-in. The policeman had very little, (19) .... than his cotton, his matches, his whistle and his truncheon, (20) .... which to fight crime.

Now check your answers to this part of the test.

2 *Finish each of the following sentences in such a way that it is as similar as possible in meaning to the sentence printed before it.*

Example: She said that he was a brilliant musician.

Answer: She described *him as a brilliant musician.*

a I'll sort this problem out for you.

Leave it ....

b It would be much better for you to ask someone who really knows about the law.

You'd be far ....

c When I made my suggestion, he laughed.

He greeted ....

d Considering how young he is, he has achieved a lot.

If you bear his ....

e She didn't know it but her family had reported her missing.

Unbeknown ....

f Why is it so funny that I want to learn the saxophone?

What's so ....

g I told her that she had good taste in music.

I complimented ....

h What makes him succeed in being popular with everyone he meets?

How does he contrive ....

Now check your answers to this part of the test.

---

3 *Fill each of the blanks with a suitable word or phrase.*

Example: She had difficulty *making up her* mind which one to buy.

a Their policies are so unpopular that they don't stand .... elected.

b We rushed to the airport and arrived with very .... spare before our flight.

c My home town is pretty .... same as it was when I was growing up there.

d I felt that, if I persevered, ... later I would succeed.

e If he's always that rude to his staff, it's no .... such a low opinion of him.

f With .... next June, new tax regulations will apply.

Before you check your answers to this part of the test, go on to page 112.

FILL IN THE MISSING PHRASE

Look again at Part 3 of this test on page 111, and then for each question, decide which of the four choices below best expresses the meaning of the sentence or the missing part of the sentence. You may wish to change some of the answers you gave in the test after you have done this.

a **1** They don't expect to win the election.
2 They aren't going to win the election.
3 It would be bad if they won the election.
4 They aren't going to enter the election.

b **1** We arrived just as our flight took off.
2 We arrived for our flight in a very nervous state.
3 We didn't have much time left before our flight.
4 We needn't have rushed to the airport.

c **1** It's very similar to when I grew up there.
2 It's just as nice as when I grew up there.
3 It hasn't changed at all.
4 It reminds me of when I was young.

d **1** It would take me a long time to succeed.
2 It would not be long before I succeeded.
3 I would succeed at some point.
4 I may succeed and I may not.

e **1** It's not surprising his staff don't like him.
2 It's possible that his staff dislike him.
3 He doesn't realize that his staff don't like him.
4 His staff have changed their opinion of him.

f **1** There are many tax regulations planned for next June.
2 There may be new tax regulations next June.
3 The new tax regulations next June will be a problem.
4 New tax regulations come into operation next June.

Now check your answers to these questions and to Part 3 of the test.

Then go on to Part 4 of the test on page 113.

4 *For each of the sentences below, write a new sentence as similar as possible in meaning to the original sentence, but using the word given. This word* ***must not be altered*** *in any way.*

Example: She paid no attention to his warning.
notice
Answer: *She took no notice of his warning.*

a These pictures don't show the true beauty of the place.
justice

....

b Hilary knows almost everything about the history of this town.
hardly

....

c Eventually, the time came when he couldn't stand the job any longer.
reached

....

d His Italian has improved so much that he's virtually fluent now.
degree

....

e Anita is not at all afraid about travelling abroad on her own.
holds

....

f She is no longer hoping to become a star.
lost

....

g One day he's going to get himself into serious trouble.
matter

....

h Over the next few years, the business became more and more successful.
strength

....

Before you check your answers to this part of the test, go on to page 114.

REWRITE THE SENTENCES

Look again at Part 4 of this test on page 113, and then for each question, decide which of the four choices given below is correct and has the same meaning as the given sentences. You may wish to change some of the answers you gave in the test as you do so. However, if the answer that you gave there is not among the choices here, this does not necessarily mean that it is wrong.

a **1** These pictures don't do justice to the beauty of the place.
2 The beauty of the place isn't of justice by these pictures.
3 These pictures aren't a justice for the beauty of the place.
4 There isn't justice for the beauty of the place in these pictures.

b **1** Hilary has hardly nothing she doesn't know about the history of this town.
2 Hardly all the history of this town Hilary knows.
3 There is hardly anything Hilary doesn't know about the history of this town.
4 Hardly everything about the history of this town Hilary knows.

c **1** Eventually, there was reached his point when he couldn't stand the job any longer.
2 Eventually, he reached the point when he couldn't stand the job any longer.
3 Eventually, he reached to a time when he couldn't stand the job any longer.
4 Eventually, the time reached when he couldn't stand the job any longer.

d **1** He has come to a degree of Italian that is virtually fluent.
2 His Italian has improved to such a degree that he's virtually fluent.
3 The degree of his Italian has improved so that he's virtually fluent.
4 He is virtually fluent to a degree of Italian.

e **1** Anita holds not frightening to travel abroad on her own.
2 There holds no fear for Anita travelling abroad on her own.
3 Travelling abroad on her own holds no fear for Anita.
4 There holds nothing to be afraid of for Anita travelling abroad on her own.

f **1** Her hope to become a star is lost.
2 She lost hope for becoming a star.
3 Her hope is lost to become a star.
4 She has lost hope of becoming a star.

g **1** No matter when, he's going to get himself into serious trouble.
2 As a matter of fact, he's going to get himself into serious trouble.
3 The matter will be that he'll get himself into serious trouble.
4 It's a matter of time before he gets himself into serious trouble.

h **1** The business got up strength over the next few years.
2 The business went from strength to strength over the next few years.
3 More and more strength happened for the business over the next few years.
4 The next few years increased strength to the business.

Now check your answers to these questions and to Part 4 of the test.

SECTION B

Read the following passage, then answer the questions which follow it.

Time to take the bull by the horns

Turn to any guide book and it is clear where one can find Africa's wildlife. It is in the great national parks. The spectacle takes place in parks, it appears, because there the perennial conflict between man and animal has been resolved, mostly by removing the former. Behind these enduring images and ideas, however, there are complexities that a new generation of ecologists and managers is trying to unravel, often while under fire from campaigners who prefer the older stereotypes.

As Daniel B Botkin writes in his new book, we risk being blinded by a view that sees nature as being stable and harmonious and man always malign. Botkin notes that by the 1970s, Tsavo – one of Kenya's national parks – was overpopulated by elephants, which had turned the place into a near desert. They had for years been managed on the premise that wildlife would establish a balance of its own. But, Botkin writes, 'even Tsavo, large as it is, is too small to sustain an elephant population 'naturally''. In times of drought-stress, elephants could no longer migrate to areas where they might survive.

Botkin stresses that man's hand can be benign, and even, in a crowded world, vital. In Africa's case, the management of parks needs to take account of the fact that most of the continent's animals are not within them. Well over 70 per cent of Kenya's wildlife lives outside the parks. The animals' neighbours, on the whole, loathe the beasts. Most weeks, a Kenyan is killed by an elephant somewhere in the country. Animals, especially – but by no means exclusively – elephants, destroy crops on a big scale.

Dr David Western, director of the Kenya Wildlife Service, is engaged in a fascinating battle. In Kenya, he must persuade poor farmers that they can profit from the presence of wildlife. Abroad, he must explain to conservationists that peasants should be allowed sometimes to kill, or sell licences to kill, lovely wildlife.

'The trouble is,' he says, 'we've disenfranchized the landowner. We've said: 'The animals have rights and you don't'.' Local people have received a few advantages from being near wildlife parks – there have been goodwill gestures such as school-building. 'What we are achieving now is quite different. It is recognizing the landowner as a legitimate voice in decision-making,' says Dr Western.

'Tourists don't like fences,' is one of Dr Western's maxims. Yet the success of anti-poaching measures has created a new need for fences, to keep the growing number of animals in, rather than poachers out. If the new arrangements defuse the animosity of local farmers towards wildlife, fences will be far less necessary to keep animals in the parks. And when wildlife outside the parks is profitable to locals, they will be less likely to poach, or condone poaching, inside or outside parks.

Dr Western's vision is of big areas of countryside in which cattle and wild animals engage in a very ancient ritual of land-sharing. 'The diversity of Africa's savannah depends on space,' he says. 'When we created parks, we banished cattle and pushed in elephants. Then poaching further concentrated elephants in parks as they retreated there.'

Dr Western says he is often told by local landowners, large and small: 'Yes, bring the elephants out of the parks, provided you let the tourists come with them.' If this approach succeeds, tourists will be able to enjoy the sensation of being in working countryside: cattlemen and park rangers, livestock and wildlife, will be seen to co-exist in a dance in which nature and man are not antagonistic.

But hearts and minds will have to be won over, especially abroad. Many conservationists dislike the hunting and culling that will be a part of the mix of incomes in many areas. This may change. Dr Western and others are trying to convince the world that they are no longer merely defending animals in parks that can never really work, but instead have a strategy for hugely extending the opportunities for wildlife across vast tracts of countryside. In exchange, they feel they are right to stress that the African people must benefit too, even at the risk of upsetting Westerners for whom the issue is one of armchair admiration rather than everyday survival.

a According to the writer, why do tourists like the great national parks of Africa?

b What does the writer say about campaigners in the first paragraph?

c What mistake was made in Tsavo national park and what wrong idea led to it?

d What were the results of this mistake?

e Explain briefly the problematic situation described in the third paragraph?

f What does Dr Western aim to convince two groups of people of?

g What is meant by the phrase 'goodwill gestures' in line 26?

h Explain briefly the reason for 'a new need for fences' (line 30).

i Explain the phrase 'defuse the animosity of' (line 31).

j What does Dr Western believe to have been the disadvantage of creating parks in Kenya?

k Why does the writer use the word 'dance' in line 42?

l Explain the phrase 'hearts and minds will have to be won over' (line 44).

m What does 'This' in line 45 refer to?

....

n Why does the writer use the word 'armchair' in line 50?

....

....

o In a paragraph of 70–90 words, summarize Dr Western's intentions concerning wildlife and local people in Kenya.

....

....

....

....

....

....

....

....

....

....

....

....

Before you check your answers to this part of the test, go on to pages 118 and 119.

For general guidance on answering the questions for this part of the test, see Answering the Questions – General Notes on page 28.

A DETAILED STUDY

(see page 28 for guidance on this type of question)

Look at question b

Does the writer say that some ideas about national parks in Africa are false?

....

Look at question c

What word in the second paragraph means 'assumption' or 'belief'?

....

....

Look at question d

What might cause 'drought-stress'?

....

Look at question e

Who are 'the animal's neighbours' in the third paragraph?

....

Look at question f

How many types of people must Dr Western negotiate with?

....

....

Look at question h

What do poachers do?

....

....

Look at question j

What did cattle and wild animals used to do that they don't do now, according to Dr Western?

....

....

Look at question n

What view of the 'Westerners' in the final paragraph is conveyed?

a They are unsympathetic towards the Africans.
b They are justified in their objections.
c They take an unsentimental view of the situation.
d They are not personally involved in the problem.

....

EXPLAIN THE MEANING

(see page 61 for guidance on this type of question)

Look at question g

If you do something out of 'goodwill', you do it
a to express gratitude for services.
b to demonstrate honourable intentions.
c to compensate for an unpleasant act.
d to clear up a misunderstanding.

....

Look at question i

1 In this context, if you 'defuse' something, you
- **a** make it less mysterious.
- **b** bring it to people's attention.
- **c** justify it to other people.
- **d** cause it to be reduced.

....

2 If you feel 'animosity', you are
- **a** bewildered.
- **b** scared.
- **c** hostile.
- **d** disinterested.

....

Look at question k

The word 'dance' in this context suggests
- **a** entertainment.
- **b** organization.
- **c** change.
- **d** partnership.

....

Look at question l

1 In line 44, 'hearts and minds' is most likely to mean
- **a** people who often change their minds.
- **b** people who are too sensitive.
- **c** people who may not agree.
- **d** people who don't know about the subject.

....

2 In line 44, 'won over' is most likely to mean
- **a** persuaded.
- **b** defeated.
- **c** recruited.
- **d** flattered.

....

EXPLAIN THE REFERENCE

(see page 62 for guidance on this type of question)

Look at question m

In line 45, 'This' refers to
- **a** Dr Western's policy.
- **b** opposition to hunting and culling.
- **c** the mix of incomes in many areas.
- **d** the practice of hunting and culling.

....

Now check your answers to these questions. When you have done so, decide whether you wish to change any of the answers you gave in the test. If you have phrased anything you wrote in the test differently from the choices given on these pages, this does not necessarily mean that you have answered incorrectly in the test.

Then check your answers to questions a–n of the test on pages 116–117.

SAMPLE SUMMARY

Now read this sample summary and answer the questions that follow it.

> Dr Western's vision is of big areas in the countryside of Africa where peasants and wildlife will be able to live harmonically and benefit from eachother. In order for that to become reality, he is trying to close parks, since there can't be a balance in animals lives when they are put in there. He's also trying to convince Africans that such a situation is possible to exist successfully. Finally, he's working on an approach according to which, though animals will be free, tourists will not be afraid, and concequently peasants won't dislike animals.

a Is anything irrelevant included or anything relevant not included? If so, what?

b Are there any language mistakes? Correct any that you think there are.

c Has any of the passage simply been copied in the summary? If so, what?

Now look again at your summary and decide whether you wish to change anything.

Then check your marks for your summary and read the assessment of this sample summary.

PAPER 4 LISTENING COMPREHENSION (about 30 mins)

PART ONE

You will hear an interview with a well-known person in the classical music world. ***For questions 1–7,*** *choose the best answer,* ***A, B, C*** *or* ***D.***

1 When asked about the fact that he is versatile, Previn

A stresses that he is a conductor first and foremost.
B says that he feels he ought to do more playing.
C jokes that it may be an act of revenge.
D says that it was a response to getting bored.

2 What does he say about the choices he made when he was very young?

A Some of them were mistakes.
B They have led to his current position.
C Some of them were difficult to make.
D He made them according to a strict plan.

3 What does he imply about film music?

A that it is underrated
B that it is not serious music
C that it requires discipline
D that few people write it for long

4 While working as a composer of film music, Previn says that he

A tried to find someone to teach him about chamber music.
B had trouble finding opportunities to play chamber music.
C developed an interest in composing chamber music.
D was lucky to learn a lot about chamber music.

5 The 'rehearsal orchestra' was formed so that

A children could hear symphonies being played live.
B the studio musicians could play more demanding music.
C the studio musicians could improve the quality of their playing.
D Hollywood composers and conductors could practise conducting.

6 What does Previn say about young musicians diversifying?

A If they do so, they won't regret it.
B It's unusual for apprentice conductors to do it.
C Only the most talented should consider doing it.
D It comes naturally to the young.

7 Previn says that if you want to be a conductor, you must

A not react badly to failure.
B learn to deal with uncooperative musicians.
C not expect too much too soon.
D take into account what musicians tell you.

PART TWO

You will hear a radio talk given by someone from the United States who spent some time living in Britain. He talks about the sports of the two countries – baseball and cricket. **For questions 8–15**, *decide which of the sports he is referring to. Write* **B** *for Baseball,* **C** *for Cricket or* **E** *for each of them.*

There was an attempt to recreate the atmosphere of this game in the other country.	8	
Signs are left when the game has been played.	9	
It is believed that this game is a strange form of the other.	10	
What happens at the end of this game can cause disbelief.	11	
People have a powerful image of the places where this game is played.	12	
This game is considered more elegant than others.	13	
Spectators at this game appear to be disinterested in the game.	14	
Followers of this game think that it should be more widespread.	15	

PART THREE

You will hear part of a radio programme about Marconi and the history of radio. **For questions 16–25**, *complete the sentences.*

Marconi was in **16** ________ in Italy when he did his experiments.

The Italian government rejected his idea because they thought they could simply **17** ________.

At customs in England, his equipment was **18** ________.

His first public demonstration is described as being extremely **19** ________.

Before his transmission across the Atlantic, he knew that signals could go **20** ________.

To get the aerial wire into the air it had to be **21** ________.

After singing *Home Sweet Home*, Dame Nellie Melba **22** ________.

After a while, the Marconi company manufactured the first **23** ________.

Other companies objected to Marconi's **24** ________.

Most of what was broadcast by the British Broadcasting Company was **25** ________.

Before you check your answers to this Paper, go on to pages 123, 124 and 125.

MULTIPLE-CHOICE QUESTIONS

For advice on the multiple-choice questions on the Listening Paper, see page 33.
Listen again to Part 1 of the test on page 121, and answer the following questions by ticking the appropriate boxes. You may need to tick more than one box in each question. The numbers below refer to the questions in the test on page 121.

(Stop the tape after Previn says 'the piano more')

1 What does he say about his different musical activities?
A He conducts at more concerts than he plays in. ☐
B He intends to do more playing. ☐
C A lot of pianists have started conducting. ☐
D Varying his activities stops him getting bored. ☐

(Stop the tape after Previn says 'away from that')

2 What does he say about himself when he was very young?
A He didn't always have a single career path. ☐
B He always had clear ideas about his future. ☐
C He was afraid to make career changes. ☐
D It is clear now what decisions he made then. ☐

(Stop the tape after Previn says 'enough')

3 What can be inferred from his comments on when he composed film music?
A He felt that it should be more prominent in films. ☐
B It wasn't the kind of music he was trained for. ☐
C It is hard to make a long career out of it. ☐
D His discipline was useful to him. ☐

(Stop the tape after Previn says 'extraordinary')

4 What does he say about his involvement in chamber music in Los Angeles?
A A famous violinist was kind to him on the subject. ☐
B There were few musicians who would play with him. ☐
C He learnt about composing it. ☐
D He performed a lot of it. ☐

(Stop the tape after Previn says 'during those days')

5 What do we learn about the 'rehearsal orchestra'?
A Some Hollywood composers and conductors conducted it. ☐
B It was formed by studio musicians for their own entertainment. ☐
C It enabled studio musicians to learn new pieces and techniques. ☐
D It was a way of taking classical music to schoolchildren. ☐

(Stop the tape after Previn says 'practise at home')

6 What does he say about young musicians?
A They shouldn't specialize too much. ☐
B Few of them are talented enough to specialize. ☐
C Those who want to conduct tend to be single-minded. ☐
D In general they are open-minded. ☐

(Stop the tape at the end)

7 What does he say about apprentice conductors?
A Musicians often give them advice. ☐
B Musicians often disagree with their instructions. ☐
C They should be prepared to do any kind of conducting. ☐
D They should realize how hard it is to be a good conductor. ☐

Now check your answers to these questions. When you have done so, decide whether you wish to change any of the answers you gave in Part 1 of the test on page 121.

Then check your answers to Part 1 of the test.

MATCHING QUESTIONS

For advice on the matching tasks on the Listening Paper, see page 94.

Listen again to Part 2 of the test on page 122, and answer the following questions by writing T for True or F for False in the appropriate boxes, according to what the speaker says. The numbers below refer to the questions in the test on page 122.

8 and 9 *(Stop the tape when he says 'with much success')*

A Cricket has been shown on TV in America. ☐
B A baseball game in London attracted small crowds. ☐
C Cricket was meant as a substitute for baseball in America for a time. ☐
D A baseball game in London was accompanied by other entertainment. ☐
E Americans watch cricket being played in America with confusion. ☐
F Cricket has been staged in America as it is staged in Britain. ☐
G They are both played in the other country mostly by people living abroad. ☐
H It is possible to see when cricket has been played in a park. ☐

10 and 11 *(Stop the tape when he says 'either side winning')*

A British people use baseball phrases incorrectly. ☐
B Americans find cricket a curious game. ☐
C Americans think that cricket should be more like baseball. ☐
D British people compare baseball and cricket. ☐
E Americans cannot see the purpose of a game of cricket. ☐
F British people accept that cricket can seem pointless. ☐
G Americans get excited at the end of a game of baseball. ☐
H British people think that a game of baseball is rather short. ☐

12 and 13 *(Stop the tape when he says 'despite the clock')*

A Cricket and baseball are both played mostly in the countryside. ☐
B British people find village commons very appealing. ☐
C Americans have a particular image of a baseball pitch. ☐
D Cricket has a more romantic image than baseball. ☐
E Baseball and cricket matches both last for a long time. ☐
F There are other sports which last for as long as cricket and baseball. ☐
G There seems to be no hurry in a game of cricket. ☐
H Other games proceed more quickly than baseball. ☐

14 *(Stop the tape when he says 'good play')*

A Cricket fans never respond to the play. ☐
B Baseball fans get excited during a game. ☐
C Cricket fans concentrate hard on the play. ☐
D Baseball fans make a lot of noise. ☐

15 *(Stop the tape at the end)*

A English people have a special feeling towards cricket. ☐
B Baseball has important associations for American people. ☐
C The popularity of cricket has not spread throughout Britain. ☐
D Americans think that baseball has a good effect on people. ☐

Now check your answers to these questions. When you have done so, decide whether you wish to change any of the answers you gave in Part 2 of the test on page 122.

Then check your answers to Part 2 of the test.

COMPLETE THE SENTENCES OR NOTES

For advice on filling the gaps on the Listening Paper, see page 65.
Listen again to Part 3 of the test on page 122, and answer the following questions. The numbers below refer to the questions in the test on page 122.

16 The gap should be filled by a word or phrase meaning
A a building outside a house
B a room at the top of a building
C the area of a building below ground

17 The gap should be filled by a word or phrase meaning
A buy more supplies.
B install more wires.
C get better equipment.

18 The gap should be filled by a word or phrase meaning
A took it away.
B took it apart.
C took it out.

19 The gap should be filled a word or phrase meaning
A significant.
B unpredictable.
C ambitious.

20 The gap should be filled by a word or phrase meaning
A across an ocean.
B to another country.
C into the distance.

21 The gap should be filled by a phrase meaning
A lifted in an object that flies.
B supported by a solid structure.
C fixed by a heavy object.

22 The gap should be filled by a phrase describing
A a mistake.
B a formal action.
C a discovery.

23 The gap should be filled by a word or phrase referring to something
A mass-produced.
B complicated.
C modified.

24 The gap should be filled by a word or phrase meaning
A methods of selling.
B domination of a market.
C refusal to cooperate.

25 The gap should be filled by a word or phrase meaning
A meant to amuse.
B unlikely to shock.
C easy to understand.

Now check your answers to these questions. When you have done so, decide whether you wish to change any of the answers you gave in Part 3 of the test on page 122.

Then check your answers to Part 3 of the test.

PAPER 5 INTERVIEW

1 *Look at one or more of these photographs and answer the questions that follow them.*

1

2

3

What's happening in each picture? What's the situation?
Describe the people. What feelings do they appear to have?
Where do you think each picture was taken?
What other objects can you see in the picture?
Why do you think each picture was taken? What message do they convey?

What do you think is the appeal of video games?
Do you think they are harmless entertainment or are there any problems associated with them?
Are you able to use a computer? If so, how and when did you learn?
What benefit does this have for you? If not, do you think this puts you at any disadvantage?
Why is it important for people to be able to use a computer?

2 *Read one or more of these passages and then answer the questions that follow them.*

a Playing computer games, it is said, rots a child's mind quicker than drugs. With persistent looped music and repetitive screen displays, it may be a slower process, but it is just as addictive. Add to that the violent, male-dominated imagery and there seems to be a huge potential for harm. But computer games are a number one demand. And a good thing too. Computer games are the nursery slopes of computer literacy.

b As education aids, computers are in a league of their own. Now frequently taking preference over traditional learning aids (such as reference books), they are getting more powerful all the time. As with any technology, there are drawbacks and some people view computers as a mixed blessing. But as long as you take a sensible approach with your children and their computer usage, the pros will far outdo the cons.

c But is the way we live now really so much better? Among my generation, there is a creeping suspicion that many of the inventions acclaimed as lightening life's burdens may not be quite what they seem; that, paradoxically, they could be adding to our workload or subtly destroying things we hold dear.

What is the purpose of each passage?
What point of view is expressed in each passage?

3 *Do one or more of these tasks. If you are working with others, discuss them together.*

a 'The computer is taking over our lives.'

Do you agree with this statement? Give reasons why or why not.
In what ways have computers affected your own life?
In what ways have computers affected the lives of people in general?
Do you feel that the effects have been good, bad or both good and bad? Give reasons.

b 'In ten years from now, we'll all be able to ......'

Predict a technological development of the future.
Will you welcome this development? If so, why? If not, why not?
In terms of technological advances, in what ways do you think life in ten years' time will be different from now? Do you think life will be made better or not? Give reasons.

c 'I wish there was a machine that could ....'

What would you like machines to be able to do that they can't at present? Why?
What effect would such machines have on your life and on the lives of others?

DESCRIBING FACIAL EXPRESSIONS

*When talking about the pictures, you may need to describe the facial expressions of the people in them. To check or build up your vocabulary for doing so, look at the following and decide whether they refer to facial expressions that indicate pleasure or displeasure. Write **P** if you* think they indicate pleasure and **D** if you think they indicate displeasure.

glum (adj) ____
grin (verb + noun) ____
glare (verb + noun) ____
grim (adj) ____
sulky (adj) ____
wince (verb) ____
gloomy (adj) ____
scowl (adj) ____
sullen (adj) ____
grimace (verb + noun) ____
smirk (verb + noun) ____
frown (verb + noun) ____

Now check your answers to these questions.

DESCRIBING VOCAL SOUNDS

*When describing people in the pictures, you may need to talk about the sounds they seem to be making. Look at the following, which can all be used both as verbs and as nouns, and decide whether they can be used to refer to vocal sounds that indicate pleasure or displeasure. Write **P*** if you think they may indicate pleasure, **D** if you think they may indicate displeasure and **P/D** if you think they may indicate both pleasure and displeasure.

jeer ____
snap ____
moan ____
chuckle ____
roar ____
sob ____
scream ____
grumble ____
groan ____
snigger ____
curse ____
giggle ____
sigh ____
sneer ____

Now check your answers to these questions.

TALKING ABOUT PASSAGES

When talking about the passages, you may be asked about the opinions expressed in them.

Look again at the three passages on page 127 and answer these questions.

1 Which one of the passages tries to present an objective point of view?

2 Which phrases in that passage refer to advantages and which to disadvantages?

3 Which verb in that passage means 'exceed'?

4 Which one of the passages is entirely concerned with refuting an allegation?

5 What allegation is refuted in that passage?

6 What phrase is used in that passage to refute the allegation most clearly?

7 Which one of the passages assumes that a certain belief is generally held?

8 In what way is it emphasized in that passage that this view is false?

9 What do we learn about the writer of that passage?

Now check your answers to these questions.

KEY AND EXPLANATION

TEST 1

p6–9 PAPER 1 SECTION A

FURTHER PRACTICE AND GUIDANCE (p8-9)

1	A proliferated	B escalated
	C amassed	D enhanced
2	A severely	B amply
	C profusely	D heavily
3	A contain	B restrict
	C inhibit	D reserve
4	A air	B utter
	C divulge	D vent
5	A effort	B pains
	C endeavours	D trouble
6	A refresh	B renew
	C reinstate	D revive
7	A progress	B step
	C pace	D track
8	A dampened	B eroded
	C receded	D belittled
9	A lay	B pay
	C put	D attach
10	A conspicuous	B blatant
	C pronounced	D salient

PAPER 1 SECTION A (TEST)

Note that all explanations in this part refer to the meaning or use of each option most closely related to the question, not necessarily to the only meaning or use of each option.

One mark per question (Total: 25)

1 B: If something **escalates**, it becomes both bigger and worse.
A: If someone *amasses* something, they collect a very large amount of it.
C: If something *proliferates*, it increases enormously in number.
D: If something *enhances* something, it makes it increase in quality or level so that it becomes more impressive.
All the options are connected with the idea of 'growing' but only B can be used to express the idea of 'growing and therefore getting worse'.

2 C: If you **rely/depend heavily** *on* someone or something, you rely or depend on them very much.
A: If you *apologize profusely*, you apologize at length and sincerely, rather than with one simple statement.
B: If you are *amply rewarded* for something, you gain big rewards from it.
D: *Severely* = very much, when describing bad situations, actions, events or feelings (*severely disabled/punished/injured/depressed*).
All the options can be used to mean 'to a very great extent' but only C can be used with the verb 'rely'.

3 D: If you **contain a feeling**, you succeed in preventing yourself from expressing it.
A: If you *restrict yourself to* something, you limit yourself to that, you don't exceed it.
B: If something *inhibits you*, it prevents you from having the confidence to say or do something.
C: If you *reserve judgement*, you decide not to give an opinion, perhaps until you have been able to consider the matter or until you learn more about it.
All the options are connected with the idea of 'not expressing feelings' but only D can be used with the word 'feelings' or with a noun describing a feeling.

4 D: If you **air views/opinions**, you express them openly; if you *air grievances*, you say that you are very unhappy about something which you feel to be unfair or unjustified and which affects you personally.
A: If you *divulge* something previously secret or unknown, you reveal it or allow it to be known.
B: If you *vent anger/frustration*, you express it openly.
C: If you *utter something*, you say it or make a sound with your voice.
All the options are connected with the idea of 'expressing' but only D can be used with the noun 'views'.

5 C: If you are **at pains to do** something, you take great care and try hard to make sure that you do it.
A: If you *make an effort to do* something, you try to do it.
B: If you *take a lot of trouble to do* something, you make a lot of effort and take a lot of care in order to do it.
D: *Your best endeavours* are the greatest efforts you can make, trying as hard as you can.
All the options can be used to form phrases connected with the idea of 'trying' but only C can be used with 'at'.

6 A: If something is **revived**, it improves and returns to a good condition or level after a period of doing badly.
B: If you *renew your acquaintance* with someone/something, you have contact with them again after a period without any contact.
C: If you *refresh someone's memory*, you remind them of something they have forgotten.
D: If someone is *reinstated*, they are put back into a position they had held before but had then been removed from.
All the options are connected with the idea of something happening again or returning but only A can be used with a noun describing something that can go from success to failure and then back to success.

7 A: If you **keep pace with** something, you are able to follow it even though it changes, develops or moves quickly.
B: If you *keep track of something*, you keep up to date with changes or developments in it.
C: If you *follow the progress of* something, you continue to be informed about developments in it.
D: If you *keep in step with* something, you make sure that you respond to the way it develops by doing the same.
All the options can be used to form phrases connected with the idea of remaining up to date with something but only A can be used both after 'keep' and before 'with'.

8 B: If something **dampens your spirits/enthusiasm**, it causes you to stop being very happy/lively/enthusiastic.
A: If a *fear recedes*, it begins to disappear; if the *prospect* of something *recedes*, it becomes less likely.
C: If something *erodes your confidence*, it causes you to lose confidence gradually.
D: If you *belittle* something, you say or act as if it has much less value or importance than it really has.
All the options are connected with the idea of 'reducing' but only B can be used with 'enthusiasm'.

9 B: If you **attach importance to** something, you consider it important.
A: If you *put emphasis on* something, you emphasize it.
C: If you *lay blame on* someone, you blame them for something.
D: If you *pay heed to* something, you take notice of it, you don't ignore it.
All the options can be used in phrases where they have the meaning 'put'; only B can be used with 'importance'.

10 A: If an action or statement is described as **blatant**, it is bad or dishonest and nobody could fail to realize that this is the case.
B: The *salient points/features* of something are the most important and most noticeable ones.
C: If someone or something is *conspicuous*, it is very easy to notice them because they stand out in their surroundings.

D: If someone has a characteristic that is *pronounced*, that characteristic is very noticeable.
All the options are connected with the idea of 'something being obvious or standing out to anyone observing it' but only A can be used to describe 'a lie'.

11 D: If you **read something into** what someone says, you believe something serious or complicated was meant or implied by what they said.
A: What you *draw from* something is what you decide as a result of experiencing or thinking about it (*Little can be drawn from the evidence./ What conclusions did you draw from the experience?*)
B: *See* can be used with the meaning 'understand' (*Do you see what I'm saying?*); if you can *see into the future*, you can predict what will happen.
C: The way that you *take* something that is said to you is the way that you react to it or how you interpret it (*He takes criticism badly./ She took my remark as an insult.*)

12 B: If you **reconcile yourself to something/doing something**, you accept that it is the case or that you have to do it, even though you are unhappy about this.
A: If you *acknowledge something/ that ...*, you accept or say that you accept that it exists or is the case. (*His contribution to the company's success has never been acknowledged. /She wouldn't acknowledge that I had been right all along.*)
C: If you *concede that* something is the case, you admit it. (*I have to concede that this was my mistake.*)
D: If you *allow that* something is the case, you accept it (*Even if you allow that he'd been badly treated, there was no excuse for the way he behaved.*)

13 A: If something **outweighs** something else, the first thing is more important than the second.
B: If someone *monopolizes* something, they use or take so much that others can't have it, or they dominate it. (*My brother monopolizes the TV when he's at home./ Harry tends to monopolize conversations.*)
C: If a place is *overrun with/by* something, too many of something go or are there (*a town overrun with tourists*).
D: If something *surpasses* something, it is better than it or exceeds it (*a success record unlikely to be surpassed*).

14 B: If you **sulk**, you refuse to speak because you are annoyed.
A: If you *ponder* something, you think very carefully about it (*ponder a situation before making a decision*).
C: If you tell someone to *hush*, you tell them to be quiet. (*Hush I'm trying to listen to this programme.*)
D: If you *muse on/over/upon* something, you think very carefully about it and the consequences of it. (*Afterwards, I mused on the events of that day.*)

15 B: If you did something **there and then** (or do something here and now), you did it immediately rather than waiting until later.
A: If you do something *in one go*, you do all of it at the same time. (*We cleaned the whole apartment in one go.*)
C: If you do something *at a stroke*, you complete it with a single, brief action (*You can't change your whole life at a stroke.*)
D: If you do something *on and off*, you do it from time to time, not continuously. (*I've been reading this book on and off for months.*)

16 B: If a feeling is **mutual**, it is shared by both people mentioned.
A: *respective* = connected with or belonging to each of the individual people or things previously mentioned. (*We discussed the problems in our respective jobs.*)
C: *joint* = done together with another person or other people (*a joint enterprise*).
D: *collective* = shared by or relating to a group of people (*collective responsibility*).

17 A: If you **assure yourself** that something is the case, you make sure that it is the case so that you are not worried about it.
B: If you *confirm something/that...*, you check and make sure that it is definite or that it is definitely the case (*confirm an appointment/confirm that tickets have been booked*).
C: If you *ascertain something/that...*, you make enquiries and are then sure about something (*I haven't been able to ascertain exactly what happened/ascertain that a rumour is true*).
D: If you *guarantee something/that...* , you make it certain or promise that it is certain (*a qualification that guarantees a good job/ I guarantee that this won't happen again*).

18 C: If you **come by** something, you find or get it, often by chance.
A: How something *comes about* is what causes it to happen or exist. (*How did such a peculiar situation come about?*)
B: If you *come in for* something such as criticism, you do something that causes you to receive it. (*After coming in for a lot of criticism from the fans, he was dropped from the team.*)
D: If you *come out with* something, you say it, often unexpectedly. (*Suddenly she came out with the most unpleasant remarks about me.*)

19 A: **Of late** = recently
B: *For now* = for the time being, temporarily (*This job is fine for now, but I don't want to do it for years.*)
C: *In a while* = some time from now, after an unspecified period (*I'll be back in a while.*)
D: *Shortly* = soon, not long from now (*I'll phone you back shortly.*)

20 D: If you are **indifferent** to something, you have no particular feelings about it, you don't care about it.
A: If you do something in a *casual* way, you do it without much thought or without taking it seriously (*make a casual remark/ have a casual conversation*).
B: If you are *disinterested*, you are not personally involved in a situation and can therefore be objective or neutral about it (*a disinterested observer*).
C: If you are *detached*, you are not involved or decide not to get involved in a situation and so your feelings are not affected. (*It's hard to remain detached about such tragic events.*)

21 C: If you are **under no illusions** about something, you know and fully accept the reality of it.
A: If you *have fantasies* about something, you have thoughts about something good that are unrealistic because it is very unlikely to happen (*have fantasies about becoming a millionaire*).
B: If you *have daydreams*, you stop concentrating on what you are doing and start thinking about pleasant things. (*She often has daydreams when she's supposed to be working.*)
C: A *deception* is a dishonest act or statement that is intended to deceive. (*His constant deceptions make it hard to trust him at all.*)

22 C: If you **sprawl** somewhere, you fall or lie there with your arms and legs stretched out.
A: If you *slouch*, you sit or stand with your shoulders and head bent forward or down in a way that is considered bad. (*Don't slouch .You look half asleep.*)
B: If you *lounge* somewhere, you sit or lie in a lazy, untidy manner (*lounge in front of the TV*).
C: If something *droops*, it bends or hangs forward, often as a result of weakness or tiredness (*drooping shoulders*).

23 D: If something **bears out** something, it indicates or proves that it is true.
A: If you *pull off* something, you succeed in doing something difficult or adventurous. (*He has tried to write an unconventional novel but he hasn't quite pulled it off.*)
B: If something *checks out*, it proves to be correct when it is checked. (*The evidence he gave to the police didn't check out.*)

C: If you *show off* something, you make sure that people notice it because you want to impress them. (*She showed off her engagement ring.*)

24 B: If you **hazard a guess**, you guess but you know when doing so that you might well be wrong.
A: If you *speculate as to/on* something, you make a guess or prediction about it, even though you have no real evidence to base this on (*speculate as to what the result will be*).
C: If you *advance a theory/idea*, you propose it and say that you believe in it (*advance new scientific theories*).
D: If you *envisage that* something will happen or *envisage something happening*, you imagine or expect that it will happen. (*I never envisaged such a wonderful thing happening to me.*)

25 C: **In accordance with** = in agreement with, conforming to, complying with.
A: *Assent to* something is formal agreement with or approval of it. (*Parliament yesterday gave its assent to the new law.*)
B: *Obedience to someone or something* is the act of obeying orders, doing what you are told to do (*obedience to your parents/authority*).
D: A *concession* is an agreement not to keep demanding or insisting on something when you are negotiating or discussing something. (*We both made concessions and finally we reached a compromise.*)

p10–16 PAPER 1 SECTION B

Two marks per question (Total: 30)

FIRST PASSAGE

26 D: (lines 1–9)
Some of Rachel's secretaries had been *a positive asset* (a great advantage, something very useful) but others had been *a liability* (a real disadvantage, something useless that causes you trouble). Rachel thought that Felicity probably *fell into the latter category* (would be a liability). Rachel also didn't feel that Felicity looked like *a model of efficiency* (an extremely efficient person).
A: Rachel was put off by Felicity's appearance but she *smiled warmly at her because one couldn't help smiling at her*, which indicates that she thought she might like her as a person.
B: Felicity is compared to other secretaries Rachel had had but they are not compared in terms of appearance.
C: Rachel considers Felicity to be *untidy*, she notices her *garish* (brightly coloured and horrible) clothes and thinks she looks *scatty* (eccentric and/or tending to forget things) but there is no suggestion that Felicity doesn't care what she looks like.

27 B: (lines 10–14)
When she saw Rachel, Felicity felt that she wanted *to be like that* – to look like her and be *dead sophisticated* (very sophisticated) like her. However, she thought *Some hope*, which means 'There is no hope of that'.
A: Felicity *marvelled at what she saw* (was extremely impressed by Rachel when she first saw her). She envied her in many ways – because of her figure, her face, her hair, her sophistication, her *knockout smile* (a very charming smile) and her expensive shoes – but there is no suggestion that she was afraid of her.
C: Felicity is very impressed when she sees Rachel but there is no reference to her having had any particular expectations before they met.
D: Felicity felt that Rachel's appearance and manner were impressive and that she would like to be like her but there is no reference to whether Felicity thought Rachel would be good at her job or not.

28 B: (lines 20–37)
Rachel asks Felicity if she wants to be given some work *to be getting on with* (so that she can keep busy until some more important work can be done) and says that she assumes that Felicity likes *to keep busy*. Felicity looks surprised at this (her eyes *widened*) and she *murmured* (said quietly) that this was true but in fact it wasn't true. She thought *Oh dear this one seemed a bit keen* (unfortunately this person seemed rather enthusiastic). It had been *a doddle* (a very easy thing to do) working for Mr O'Connell but Rachel was *quite a different proposition* (a very different matter to be dealt with) because she expected her to be busy all the time. Felicity realized that she would have to *become amazingly efficient*.
A: When Felicity tells Rachel that Mr Lamb wouldn't like her calling Rachel by her first name because he's *a real one for form* (a person who is very keen on doing things according to the rules of formality), and that he would not call Rachel by her first name, Rachel replies that she hopes not (she hopes he won't call her anything but Miss Dean) and that *office managers are a breed apart* (they are a different species from other people, the implication of the phrase being that they are strange in some way). Rachel also laughs with Felicity when she says she doesn't want to think about office managers. All of this indicates that Rachel was not impressed by Mr Lamb.
C: Rachel tells Felicity to address her informally but there is no suggestion that she intends to change the atmosphere in the office as a whole. She accepts that Mr Lamb is typical of office managers and does not seem to intend to change the way he is.
D: It will take Rachel a little time to settle in – files from her old firm are due to arrive, and she is not sure what work to do on her first day. The first job, the standard letter is not *very exciting*, but has to be done. She is unimpressed but not alarmed by Mr Lamb. There is no suggestion, though, that she has any regrets about the new job.

29 A: (lines 38–42)
Rachel sees Felicity's *blank expression* (the expression on her face indicates that she hasn't understood the word *protocol*, which means a system of rules concerning the correct formal behaviour when people are dealing with each other). Therefore she explains the word in simple terms (*a way of doing it*).
B: Rachel explains that getting files from her old company is a sensitive issue. Even though there are *no hard feelings* about her leaving the company (they are not annoyed about it), they are unlikely to *fall over themselves* (go to a lot of trouble) *to pass things on* (to send the files). Felicity's only response is to murmur (say quietly) *'Right'*. which means that she has understood. There is no suggestion that Felicity suspects Rachel of doing anything dishonest.
C: Rachel explains that she has left one firm, *taking quite a bit of business with me* (taking clients of the old firm to become clients of the new one) and that therefore she can't expect the old firm to hurry up sending the files to her. However, she does not say that she feels she has acted badly in any way with regard to the old firm, only that she should follow the protocol when dealing with them.
D: When Felicity says *'Right'*, this means only that she has understood the situation; it does not mean that she has any opinion on whether it is an important issue or not.

30 D: (see the passage as a whole) In lines 17-18, Mr Lamb accuses Felicity of *wasting enough time this morning chatting your way round the building* (going round the building having social conversations with people rather than working). In line 44, Felicity plans to *have a little natter* (a conversation about unimportant matters) with Moira in accounts but since *there was nothing to be got on with* (nothing to work on), Mr Lamb couldn't really *have a go at her* (tell her off, criticize her), which implies that he could normally be expected to tell her off when she was talking to

someone and not working. At the beginning he tells her in *cold and meaningful tones* (in an unfriendly way that is meant to indicate that he knows why she is late) that they have been waiting for her for ten minutes. Mr Lamb seems to regard Felicity as lazy and unreliable.
A: We know that Mr Lamb is rather formal (lines 20–24) and that he tries to be strict with Felicity. She doesn't like this but there is no suggestion that she thinks some of his power should be taken away from him – she seems to accept that he is a powerful person.
B: We know that Felicity feels badly treated by Mr Lamb, but there is no mention of the way he treats anyone else in the office.
C: We know that Mr Lamb has a low opinion of Felicity, but she doesn't like him and there is no suggestion that she has any desire to impress him.

SECOND PASSAGE

FURTHER PRACTICE AND GUIDANCE (p10–15)

For explanations, see the explanations to the questions in the test that follow.

Question 31

1 yes **2** no **3** no **4** c

Question 32

1 no **2** c **3** no
4 the fact that it was a completely male-dominated event, that it involved only men and things associated with being a man

Question 33

1 no **2** no **3** no
4 abuse (rude things said in anger); hated; outrage (great anger); sullen (silently angry); discontent; bitter

Question 34

1 the idea that entertainment could come from suffering or that suffering could be entertaining
2 to have a good time
3 yes (lines 26–27) **4** no
5 yes, the crowd at the football match

Question 35

1 it might have been influenced by his experiences at football matches
2 taking certain things too seriously
3 with anger
4 no

SECOND PASSAGE (TEST)

31 B: (see first paragraph)
He doesn't recall much about the game because the only thing he really saw was *a bewildering chain of incomprehensible incidents* (a confusing series of events that he was totally unable to understand). He refers to *that first afternoon*, so we know it was his first time at a football match and he didn't understand what was going on because it was all new to him.
A: Even though he knows that his recollection of the details of the goal may be *one of those tricks of the memory* (an inaccurate recollection), he refers to it as *the only goal* and he does not suggest that any more goals were scored. However, he does not suggest that the fact that there was only one goal has made him forget most of what happened that afternoon.
C: He says that *everyone around me stood and shouted*, and although he clearly didn't understand why they did this, he does not suggest that this made him nervous, nor that it prevented him from watching what was going on.
D: He says that it is possible that he did the same (*If I did the same*) and if he did so, he assumes that it was (*it must have been*) just after the rest of the crowd, an action that he would have found embarrasssing. However, even if he did copy the others, and he is not sure that he did, he does not say that the desire to do so had any effect on his being able to remember what happened in the game.

32 D: (see second paragraph)
One of his *more reliable* and *more meaningful* memories is of *looking at the crowd more than at the players* and he comments on how many heads he could see from where he was sitting. He clearly felt that it was a very large number because he says that only sports fans, rock stars and politicians can see such large crowds. When his father told him that the number of people in the stadium was nearly as great as the population of his town, he was *suitably awed* (extremely impressed, as was appropriate when given such information).
A: He doesn't say that he began to feel his town was small, only that he was astonished that there were nearly as many people in the stadium as in his town, which implies that he thought that this was a large number. Furthermore, he mentions no feelings about the town he lived in.
B: He heard *foul language* and he had heard the words before, even though he had not heard adults using them so loudly, but he doesn't say he had used them himself.
C: He remembers *the overwhelming maleness of it all*, but although he was clearly fascinated by this, he doesn't say he wanted to be like the men he saw.

33 C: (see third paragraph)
He says that he later discovered on visits to other grounds that what he observed that day was typical of all crowds at football matches: that all football fans are naturally in a state of *bitter disappointment, no matter the score* (they feel just as bad or angry whether their team is winning or losing).
A: The fan quoted is annoyed because he thinks Holt is a poor player. He shouts that Holt is paid £100 a week (a lot of money when this match took place) and jokes that because Holt is *a disgrace* (unacceptably bad), he should be paid the same amount for having to suffer watching him play. The writer does not suggest that the crowd felt the players in general were paid too much or that they should be paid as much – he says that one player was considered so bad that he didn't deserve such high wages.
B: The crowd's mood didn't change constantly, it was one of anger all the time – they were angry at the start (they *hated being there; within minutes of the kick-off there was real anger*), they steadily got angrier (*anger turned into outrage* – loud declarations of anger) and then they became silently angry (*sullen, silent discontent*).
D: The writer describes someone shouting at a player and this may well be an example of many similar things shouted at the players, but he doesn't say whether he thought such comments were fair or unfair and doesn't seem to have an opinion on that.

34 A: (see fourth paragraph)
He says of the public entertainments he had been to before *But that was different*, because the audiences he had *hitherto* (until then) been part of *had paid to have a good time*. This is in contrast to the crowd at the football match, who seemed to expect to hate it when they went to a match and whose natural state was to be angry throughout the match. He describes football matches as *Entertainment as pain*, whereas other audiences simply expected to enjoy themselves.
B: *Entertainment as pain* was *something I'd been waiting for*, which means that the idea of it and the experience appealed to him. At other entertainments, audiences generally enjoyed themselves, since he seldom saw *faces contorted* (twisted out of their normal shape) *by rage or despair or frustration*, as he saw at the football match. He therefore implies that he preferred the crowd at the football match to these audiences – they saw entertainment as pain and he liked that idea.
C: He had occasionally seen *a fidgety child* (a child moving about in his/her

seat because of boredom) or *a yawning adult* (an adult opening the mouth wide and then closing it because of being bored or tired) but he does not say that he had acted in such a way.
D: He obviously observed the crowd at the football match very closely but it seems that he had also observed the audiences at other entertainments closely. He says that *one might spot* (one might see when trying to see/looking for) *a fidgety child or a yawning adult.*

35 B: (see last paragraph)
He says that he has been accused of *taking the things I love... too seriously* and seems to accept this accusation (*and I do feel a kind of anger...*). He gets annoyed by what he considers bad records and if someone is *lukewarm* (not very enthusiastic) about a book he is keen on.
A: He says that it may be that the angry men in the football crowd *taught me how to get angry in this way* and that sometimes he is angry as a critic but he does not suggest that he thinks he is not very good as a critic.
C: He seems to accept the accusation of taking things too seriously. This is the only accusation mentioned and he does not defend himself against it.
D: He says that it might not be *too fanciful* (too unrealistic) to suggest that *it* (this refers to the idea of *entertertainment as pain*) was *an idea that shaped my life.* He feels the influence of the crowd that day when he is working as a critic – he wants to shout *YOU'RE A DISGRACE, X* (X refers to the author of the book he is reviewing), just like the man in the crowd shouted at Holt. However, he does not suggest that he thinks the influence the crowd has had on him is too great or a bad thing.

THIRD PASSAGE

36 A: (see first paragraph)
The writer says that people *never know how to edit their own lives* (when interviewed they don't know which parts of their lives are worth including in the interview and which are not); they don't understand *what it is about them that makes a good story* (what will interest readers about them); and they don't realize that the journalist will have to cut what they've said because if they *go on* (talk boringly) for two hours, it will be far too long to print *verbatim* (exactly as it was said). They therefore don't appreciate what the journalist requires from them in order to produce a good article.
B: Interviewees are *obsessed with minutiae* (far too concerned about minor, insignificant details) and don't realize what is interesting about them, but there is no suggestion that they are unwilling to discuss things that journalists ask them about.
C: Interviewees *go on* for a long time and the writer certainly seems to find them boring but that is not the reason why one-to-one interviews are so difficult; the real reason is that interviewees don't know what journalists want from them.
D: Interviewees *have no comprehension that five minutes' talk comes out at a thousand words* – they don't understand the relationship between the length of speech and how long it is when put on paper – but this doesn't imply that they talk nonsense.

37 B: (see second paragraph)
The writer tells people not to *skip down the page* (go further down the page and ignore some of the article) *to find something you haven't heard a million times before* (to find something that hasn't been said or written a great many times before) because his article is *not another slap in the face of the genre* (not one more of many criticisms of TV chat shows as a type of programme). He therefore implies that readers will think he is going to say something that has been said many times before but says this is not so.
A: He makes a comment about journalists – that their *most common failure* is that they want the people they are interviewing to like them – and he says that this desire is *at the heart of* (the main cause of) *the dreadful fiasco* (the terrible, ridiculous disaster) that TV chat shows have become. However, he doesn't imply that he is going to go on to make a complex comparison between journalism and TV chat shows, he says that he is going to offer *constructive criticism* (criticism that is intended to help someone improve) of TV chat shows.
C: He implies that a lot has been said and written about TV chat shows but he doesn't say that he has previously written anything about them himself.
D: He implies that readers may expect him to repeat things that have already been said about journalists and/or chat shows, but he doesn't suggest that they aren't interested in these subjects themselves.

38 A: (see third paragraph)
The writer says that the *editorial supposition* (what is assumed by those in charge of the programmes) is that viewers will be *eternally enthralled* (permanently fascinated) *by the electric propinquity* (by the exciting feeling of being near to) *fame.* The hosts want to see themselves as *allowing the public to eavesdrop on mutual celebrity and warmth* (letting them listen to a private and friendly conversation between famous people, among whom they include themselves).
B: The writer says that *news-driven interviewers* (those who do interviews on political current affairs programmes) are generally *pretty good* because they *behave and ask questions like journalists* (like 'proper', professional people, this implies). He compares them with TV chat-show hosts, who he believes *want to see themselves as celebrities* (famous people). However, he doesn't say that programme makers believe that news-driven journalists would make poor chat-show hosts.
C: The writer says of chat shows that *the questions are supposed to be as interesting as the answers*, by which he means that the host is supposed to say things that are as interesting as what the guests say. He does not say that the role of chat show hosts is seen by programme makers as making dull guests seem more interesting.
D: Programme makers see chat shows as different from political current affairs programmes but the writer says that this is a *self-imposed, artificial division* (a division created by the programme makers themselves rather than by any outside force such as viewers, and not a true distinction). This implies that the opinions of viewers have not been sought or considered. There is, therefore, no suggestion by the writer that viewers prefer chat shows to any other kind of programme.

39 C: (see fourth paragraph)
In the 1960s and 1970s, according to the writer, *celebrity came with its own cachet* (famous people were considered very special and admired) but *not any more.* The *population increase in fame and notoriety* (the enormous increase in the number of people who are famous) *has devalued the currency* (made it much less special to be famous). Celebrity has become *ubiquitous* (it can be found everywhere) now.
A: The writer says that there never was *a golden age of chat shows* (a great period of really good chat shows) and that the hosts today are just as *ingratiating* (talking and acting in a way that shows they are desperate to please and be liked) *as they ever were.* He is therefore saying that chat show hosts are no different now from what they were like in the 1960s and 1970s.
B: His point is that more people are famous now than in the past, not that the guests are less famous than guests were in the 1960s and 1970s.
D: Celebrity is *ubiquitous* (famous people seem to be everywhere because so many people are famous); this does not mean that particular famous

people are always appearing on chat shows.

40 B: (see last paragraph)
The writer concludes *there must come a time* (it is bound to happen in the future) when celebrities *will stop doing these shows* (will stop appearing on these shows) because viewers will become angry at seeing them on these shows (they will *hate them* for *wasting* their – the viewers' – *time* talking about their *new films, books, records*).
A: The writer says that the performances on these shows are *disengaged* (done without interest or effort) and *low-calibre* (of low quality) and that no professional entertainer would do such poor performances if it was important to them personally (because their name was *above the heading* – it was a show or film that they were the main star of – and people had paid to see it; neither of these are the case with chat shows). This does not mean that chat shows will improve, it means that performers give better quality performances in other shows than they do in chat shows.
C: Certainly the writer has formed a low opinion of them but he doesn't say that viewers have done so yet. He says that *there must come a time* when this will happen – it will happen in the future.
D: The writer obviously feels that chat shows are awful but he doesn't actually say that they are worse than all other forms of entertainment.

PAPER 1:

SECTION A	25 marks
SECTION B	30 marks
TOTAL	55 marks

To be converted into a score out of 40 marks.

p17–19 PAPER 2

Each composition is given a mark out of 20. The total of the two compositions is then divided by two to give an overall score for the paper out of 20.

FURTHER PRACTICE AND GUIDANCE (p19)

Assessment of sample composition

1 Content

The composition addresses the task set at all times and concentrates both on the events of Einstein's life and why he was a significant figure. However, there is one major problem; the last part, in particular the final paragraph, does not really make sense. The nature of his dilemma is not clear (presumably the candidate means that it was whether to fight against the Nazis or co-operate with them but this is not what is written) and the final sentence does not make clear what he did and what the result of that was. In addition, the phrase *the opposition to energy* in the fourth paragraph does not make sense in the context and makes the whole sentence confusing. These are serious problems; if part of a composition does not communicate clearly, this will be penalized much more heavily than if it makes sense at all times and has a few linguistic errors.

2 Organization

The composition is very well organized, each paragraph covering a different stage in Einstein's life or a different aspect of him.

3 Linking

Most of the linking is relatively simple, using *and* and *but*. However, *so* in the second paragraph and *Therefore* at the beginning of the fifth paragraph are correctly used. Apart from the opening sentence, which is very fluent, most sentences are fairly short and simple. This is perhaps because this is a mostly chronological composition and it is hard to use more sophisticated linking to join a series of events. It should therefore not be viewed as a fault.

4 Use of vocabulary

There is some good use of vocabulary: *suspected* and *virtually* (almost) in the first paragraph; *stuttered* (had a speech problem), *saw no future in him* (thought he would not have a successful future) and *compelled* (forced) in the second paragraph; *thorny problems* (problems that are particularly hard to solve) and *reciprocal respect* (people respecting each other) in the fourth paragraph; *dilemma* (a difficult choice between two things) and *abandon* (give up) in the last paragraph.

Some of the vocabulary is not used appropriately: *characteristic* in the first paragraph should be *significant* or *important*; *engaging himself* in the second paragraph should be *involving himself*; at the end of the second paragraph *interests* seems more appropriate than *worries*.

5 Use of grammar

There are few grammatical errors and those are not really basic errors, although *At 1900* in the second paragraph should of course be *in 1900*. In the fourth paragraph, you *oppose something*, not 'to' something. *Nazi* is used incorrectly throughout; it should be plural to describe the people, not singular, and when used in the possessive it should be used in the phrase *of the Nazis* (it should therefore be *the menace of the Nazis, the violence of the Nazis, the brutality of the Nazis*). In the fifth paragraph, *jewish* should be *Jewish*. Apart from that, the use of structures is accurate and competent.

6 Style

The composition flows well and is reasonably natural in style.

This composition is generally competent, with few serious errors. However, the fact that its meaning is unclear in parts counts against it. It would be given a score of 10–11 marks out of 20.

p20–24 PAPER 3 SECTION A

PART 1

FURTHER PRACTICE AND GUIDANCE AND TEST(p20–21)

One mark per question (Total: 20)

1 **during**: The delivery man *called* (came to deliver something) while the interview for the article was taking place.

2 **that**: The delivery man saw the game on the table and is probably pointing at it when he speaks.

3 **introduced**: Somebody (probably the writer of the article) said to the delivery man, 'This is Leslie Scott and she invented the game you have just recognized'.

4 **face**: *Let's face it* = let's be honest about it, it should be accepted. The delivery man is saying that an honest view of the game is that it's *money for nothing* (it's a very easy way of making money).

5 **referred/related**: His *quip* (remark intended to be humorous) that it was *money for nothing* was connected with the simplicity of the game, not with any other aspect of the game (for example that it wasn't very good or that it wasn't well made).

6 **and**: This connects the way the bricks are arranged and what the players then do.

7 **on**: *On top* = at the top of the tower (pile) of bricks

8 **longer**: This forms part of the structure *the more one thing happens, the more something else is caused to happen*; in this case it means that as the bricks continue to be rearranged, the pile of bricks becomes more and more

unstable.

9 **whole**: *The whole lot* is a phrase that emphasizes that absolutely all of something is being described; in this case it describes the entire pile, every brick.

10 **while/when/whilst**: *While/when/whilst living* = while she was living, in this context

11 **as**: *As* here introduces the purpose of the bricks when they were bought, the reason why they were bought.

12 **named**: If something is *named after* something, it is deliberately given the same name as it. In this case, the game was given the same name as a nearby port, Takoradi.

13 **giving**: If you *give up* something, you stop doing it, you don't continue with it. In this context, the *-ing* form of the word is used to indicate that one thing happened immediately after another (she gave up her career and immediately started a business producing the game).

14 **into**: If someone *goes into business*, they start a business or company.

15 **changed**: If something is *changed to* something else, it becomes something else. In this case the name was *Takoradi Bricks* and it became *Jenga*.

16 **meaning**: *Meaning* here = with the meaning of. The inverted commas around *to build* emphasize that this is the definition of the word *Jenga*.

17 **agreed**: If you *agree to* something, you allow it to happen. In this case, the bank manager agreed to give her a loan for her business.

18 **single**: The phrase *not a single one* emphasizes that 'absolutely none at all' is meant. In this case, it emphasizes that she didn't even sell one copy of the game.

19 **took**: If you *take on* something, you accept it as a responsibility or as something you will deal with. In this case, the businessman decided to take responsibility for the game, which probably means producing and selling it.

20 **although/though**: These words are used with two things that contrast with each other, in the sense that what might be expected as a result of one thing is not in fact the case. It might be expected that Leslie would have stopped inventing games because she has made *a fortune* (a very great deal of money) from *Jenga* but in fact she still invents games.

PAPER 3 SECTION A

PART 2 FURTHER PRACTICE AND GUIDANCE (p23)

For explanations, see the explanations for the questions in the test below.

a 1, 4

b 2, 4, 5

c 1, 4

d 2

e 4

f 1

g 2

h 3

PAPER 3 SECTION A

PART 2 (TEST)

One mark per word or phrase in bold (Total: 12)

a **(you) any good to argue with her.** (1 mark)

If it *won't do any good to do* something, nothing will be achieved by doing it, the desired change won't happen; if it *won't do you any good to do* something, you won't get the result you want from doing it, it won't benefit you.

b **one occasion/a single occasion/the one occasion** (1) **have I had to** (1) have this car repaired. (2 marks)

On only one/a single/the one occasion = only once and emphasizes that something only happened once. If a sentence begins with this phrase, the verb has to be inverted so that the subject comes after the verb or, as here, the auxiliary.

c **the embarrassment of all the other guests/all the other guests' embarrassment, he told a disgusting joke.** (1 mark)

To the embarrassment of someone/to someone's embarrassment = with the result that someone was embarrassed. This structure can be used with other nouns describing feelings (*To my amazement/to the horror of everyone present, etc.*).

d **you out/you to any inconvenience** (1) **by phoning** (1) you so late. (2 marks)

If you *put someone out* or *put someone to some inconvenience*, you do something that is inconvenient for them and that causes them trouble. The structure *by -ing* is used here to describe the way in which the subject might be causing inconvenience.

e **the good** (1) **fortune to find** (1) another job shortly afterwards. (2 marks)

If you *have the good fortune to do something*, you do something or something happens to you which is lucky for you.

f **your insistence** (1) **that we came** (1) to this restaurant. (2 marks)

If you do something *at someone's insistence*, you do it because they insist that you do it, not because you want to do it. As the sentence begins with *It was*, the verb must be put into a *'that* clause'.

g **but pleased** (1) when I told her. (1 mark)

The phrase *anything but + adjective* = absolutely not, the opposite of

h **no resemblance to/relation to** (1) what really happened. (1 mark)

If something *bears no resemblance to something*, it is not at all similar to it, it is completely different from it.

PAPER 3 SECTION A

PART 3

One mark per question (Total: 6)

a **some reason (or other)**
If you say that something happens *for some reason (or other)*, you think that there must be a reason for it, but you don't know what that reason is.

b **of handing**
Short of doing something = apart from doing something extreme, without taking an extreme action. If you *hand in your resignation*, you inform your employer in writing that you are leaving your job.

c **of the ordinary**
If something is *out of the ordinary*, it is extraordinary, it doesn't normally happen or isn't normally the case. If *there is nothing out of the ordinary about something*, it is common or typical.

d **couldn't help/avoid**
If you *can't help/avoid doing* something, it is impossible for you not to do it because it is not something you can control.

e **make matters/things**
The phrase *to make matters/things worse*, introduces something that happens which makes a bad situation even worse.

f **once and for**
If you do something *once and for all*, you do it so that the result will be permanent and you won't have to do it again.

PAPER 3 SECTION A

PART 4

One mark per word or phrase in bold (Total: 12)

a **I'll have to acquaint myself** (1) **with the background** (1) to the problem before I can comment. (2 marks)

If you *acquaint yourself with* something, you find out about it so that you have some knowledge of it or are familiar with it.

b **Tom remained/was sound asleep** (1) throughout the thunderstorm. (1 mark)

If you are *sound asleep*, you are sleeping deeply.

c **I did my utmost to make** (1) their stay here enjoyable. (1 mark)

If you *do your utmost to do* something, you try as hard as you can to do it.

d **(If I were you,) I wouldn't make a habit/get into the habit** (1) **of spending** (1) more than you can afford. (2 marks)

When giving advice, *I wouldn't* can be used with the meaning *I think you shouldn't*. If you *make a habit of doing* something or *get into the habit of doing* something, you start doing it regularly or frequently.

e **The whole enterprise was fraught** (1) **with danger** (1). (2 marks)

If something is *fraught with* something, it is full of something unpleasant (*fraught with danger/tension/anxiety* = extremely dangerous/tense/anxious).

f **I have nothing but** (1) **admiration for Julie** (1). (2 marks)

If you *have nothing but* a certain feeling, you have that feeling completely. If you *have admiration for* someone, you admire them.

g **There's no denying (the fact) that** (1) he's excellent at his job. (1 mark)

There's no denying (the fact) that something is the case = nobody could deny it, it has to be admitted or accepted, it is obviously the case.

h **I told the manager in no uncertain terms** (1) that I would not tolerate such appalling service. (1 mark)

If you say something *in no uncertain terms*, you say it directly, forcefully and clearly so that the person you are addressing cannot fail to understand you. This expression is often used when the speaker is angry.

SECTION A:

QUESTION 1	20 marks
QUESTION 2	12 marks
QUESTION 3	6 marks
QUESTION 4	12 marks
TOTAL	50 marks

p25–30 PAPER 3 SECTION B

FURTHER PRACTICE AND GUIDANCE (p28)

Questions a–n

For explanations, see the explanations for the questions in the test below.

a travel writer and travel presenter

d that people couldn't see it/it was very small

e it means 'she's terrible' and it describes the writer

g d

h no

n **1** TV presenters in general
2 c
3 a

PAPER 3 SECTION B (TEST)

Answers similar to or covering the same points as those given here are acceptable provided they are clearly expressed.

a **the contrast between what she would notice/the way she would see things as a travel writer** (1) **and what she notices as a travel presenter** (1) (2 marks)

The writer begins with a fairly literary description and some fairly romantic images – a *barge* (canal boat) *nudges* (gently touches) the pavement, an *artichoke* (a kind of vegetable) salesman *deftly trims* (skilfully cuts small amounts from) his *wares* (an old-fashioned word meaning 'goods'); houses and tourists *shimmer* (shine as they are reflected) in the water. Then she says *Or they would if I was being a travel writer*, which means these are the things she would see and this is how she would describe them if she was working as a travel writer. However, as a travel presenter *all I can see* are very different things: the *muzzle of a camera* (the front of it as it points towards her), a *crate* (big wooden box) of tomatoes and a plastic bottle. These, she makes clear, are much less attractive objects and she is forced to look at them because they are all involved in her doing her job (she is obviously going to walk from the crate of tomatoes to the plastic bottle while speaking into the camera).

b **running away/escaping** (1 mark)

(colloquial) She is obviously very nervous just before she has to start speaking.

c **making mistakes when saying what she is supposed to say/getting them wrong** (1 mark)

Clearly she has a script that she must remember and say correctly without being able to look at it.

d **because her microphone is very small/invisible** (1) **and if the elderly people have poor eyesight and don't see the camera, they might think she is talking to herself, they won't realize she is making a film** (1) (2 marks)

Elderly shoppers *turn to stare* (look at her with curiosity or amazement). She is wearing a *radio mike* (a small microphone attached to the speaker and invisible to others) and if they are *short-sighted enough* (cannot see well enough) to *spot* (see) the camera, they will think she is talking to herself (this is considered to be a sign of madness) and not know that she is actually talking to a camera.

e **that she was no good at the job/a terrible presenter/useless** (1) **and that he wanted them to send someone to replace her who could do the job/say the lines properly** (1) (2 marks)

She thought the producer was going to phone Manchester (presumably where the TV company is based) and say *She's appalling* (terrible) and demand that they *get someone out here who can speak* (send a different presenter to Venice from Manchester who is capable of saying their lines correctly).

f **that everyone who works in the world of TV is informal with each other/calls each other by their first names** (1 mark)

If you *are on first-name terms with someone*, you have a friendly relationship with them and address them using their first name, not by using a formal way of addressing them, such as Mr..., Mrs..., Miss... etc.

g **Andrew and Nigel telling her that the sound or focus went wrong whenever she makes a mistake/the crew blaming technical problems, not her, whenever she makes a mistake** (1 mark)

She is *pitifully grateful* (grateful in a way that is rather pathetic or weak) because they are *reassuring* (they tell her not to worry), tell her that lots of things can go wrong and whenever I *mess up* (make a terrible mistake/do something very badly or inefficiently) they say there was a problem with the sound or the focus and don't say she got it wrong.

h that they're not really telling the truth, they're trying to make her relax (1 mark)

In David Niven's story, *the extras* (people in the background in a film who don't say anything) and *crew* (technicians involved in film-making) suddenly start to applaud when he has finished his first *take* (piece of recording intended for a film or record). When they do this, they are being *insincere* (they don't genuinely believe he has just done something excellent that deserves applause) – they do it *to make him relax*. The writer feels that something similar is happening here – she can *never entirely believe* Andrew and Nigel when they blame the sound and focus because she thinks that perhaps they are doing this to make her relax and they are not telling the truth because in fact she has made a mistake and there is no problem with the sound and focus.

i consider/think about for a period of time (1 mark)

She thinks about the differences between travel writing and travel presenting while she is waiting to continue with her part of the film-making.

j destinations (1 mark)

The writer says that as a travel writer you can *let a destination unfold around you* (find out about it as you go around the place). *Nothing happens* at some destinations but *at others* (at other destinations) events happen *perfectly*.

k show a lot of things that would otherwise have to be described in words (1 mark)

Writing for television, she says, requires *speed* (you have to do it quickly) and *economy* (you have to keep what you write brief) because the pictures make it unnecessary to describe certain things – they can be seen.

l she hadn't been a TV presenter before and she was too worried about saying her lines right to think clearly (1 mark)

Her *input* (contribution in the form of ideas and suggestions) was limited by *inexperience* (she hadn't done the job before) and because she was too worried about her lines (saying what she had to say) to be able to *think straight* (think clearly).

m that they show attractive places/scenes (1 mark)

The nickname given to *general views* suggests that these views are pretty. The word *pretty* cannot in fact be used as a noun; this is obviously a term used among people who make TV travel programmes only.

n She takes it as a compliment (1) **but she thinks that perhaps that is because she doesn't know enough to realize that it is not intended as a compliment** (1) (2 marks)

Being known as *the talent* might suggest that the others think that she is talented and she does find this *wildly flattering* (she thinks this is an expression of enormous praise, an enormous compliment to her). However, she adds that her reaction is *a sure sign of ignorance* (a definite indication of her lack of knowledge and experience), which implies that if she had more experience in television work she would know that the term was not used as a compliment. In fact, it would appear that it is a general term like all the others listed previously – APs, for example, would seem to apply to all Assistant Producers, so *the talent* is probably used for all presenters, whether they are good or not.

Questions a–n: Total 18 marks

PAPER 3 SECTION B

FURTHER PRACTICE AND GUIDANCE (p29)

WRITING A SUMMARY

1 **b** (lines 23–37) This is where she compares travel writing and making TV travel programmes.

2 The following points could be included:

travel writing: 1/3/4

making TV programmes: 2/4/5/6

The other points are all mentioned as being true but they are not presented as differences between writing and making programmes, so they are not relevant to the summary you have been asked to write.

PAPER 3 SECTION B

SUMMARY (TEST)

o *One mark each for the inclusion of the following points or points similar to them (in any order).*

1 **In travel writing you don't have to plan anything in advance, whereas when making a TV programme everything has to be planned first.**

A travel writer *can afford to let things happen* (they don't have to plan what they're going to do) and *let a destination unfold around you* (wait to see what develops in a place rather than going there with any particular intention). Making a programme involves *clockwork organization* (everything planned to be totally efficient with a strict timetable). You have to work out when to film buildings, get *complicated permissions* (presumably to film in certain places) and *pitfalls* (potential problems) have to be *anticipated* (foreseen).

2 **As a travel writer you can do things that are of no use to your article, whereas when making a programme you cannot waste any time.**

A travel writer can *conduct rambling interviews* (long, unstructured interviews) with people who are not useful to the article but are *good company* (enjoyable to be with) and go for *pointless walks just to get the feel of the place* (simply to find out about the atmosphere of the place). TV *can afford no such luxury* (cannot indulge in such pleasures). Interviewees, *however charming* (even if they are charming) *must be able to perform* (must do something in front of the camera that will be entertaining and can be used in the programme). It is essential that something happens in front of the camera because *There is no time to waste.*

3 **Travel writers are on their own whereas a lot of people are involved in making a programme.**

A travel writer *can move about unseen* but *there are quantities of people involved* in making a programme.

4 **Travel writing and writing for a programme require different styles of writing.**

A paragraph of writing *does not necessarily make a fine piece of speaking* because writing for TV involves *speed* and *economy*, which travel writing does not.

Total: 4 marks
Plus a maximum of 8 marks for general impression of summary skills, based on the following criteria:

- relevance
- general level of fluency
- accuracy of language
- absence of copying from passage
- length

SUMMARY TOTAL 12 marks

SECTION B:

QUESTIONS a – n 18 marks

SUMMARY 12 marks

TOTAL 30 marks

PAPER 3:

SECTION A 50 marks

SECTION B 30 marks

TOTAL 80 marks

To be converted into a score out of 40 marks.

PAPER 3 SECTION B

FURTHER PRACTICE AND GUIDANCE (p30)

SAMPLE SUMMARY

Inclusion of points:

1 This is included, in the middle of the first sentence and in the second sentence.

2 This is included at the beginning of the last sentence with regard to making programmes but not with regard to travel writing.

3 This is included at the beginning of the first sentence and in the second sentence.

4 This is included at the end of the summary.

Inclusion of points: Total 4 marks

General impression of summary skills:

1 Everything in the summary is relevant and nothing irrelevant has been included.

2 The summary flows well. It is very clear but it is not made up of sentences that are too simple and there is some good linking (for example, the use of *however* in the second sentence). However, the summary is to some extent a list of points rather than a comparison; travel writing and making programmes are not always linked in terms of the various aspects (planning, wasting time, etc.) which involve differences.

3 There is only one mistake (*chose* in the first sentence should of course be *choose* – a fairly basic error).

4 Nothing has simply been copied from the passage, all the ideas have been rephrased in a way that indicates full understanding of the passage (for example, in the first sentence, *wait for things to happen* rephrases the part of the passage about how you can let a destination unfold around you very well; the last phrase is a very good re-wording of the phrase a paragraph of writing does not necessarily make a fine piece of speaking).

5 At around 80 words, the summary is within the word limit.

Summary skills: Total 6 marks

SAMPLE SUMMARY TOTAL: *10 marks*

p31–34 PAPER 4

One mark per question (Total: 25)

To be converted into a score out of 20 marks.

PAPER 4 PART ONE

(see tapescript, p179)

FURTHER PRACTICE AND GUIDANCE (p33–34)

1 Tick **A**, **C**, **D**, **E**: (lines 19–25)

A: They said *You won't see me for dust* (I will disappear instantly), *I'll be on a desert island.* Hunter says that a lot of the winners *actually said those words beforehand* (before they won).

B: *Not one of them* is living abroad, but that does not mean that any of them did live abroad.

C: *People react to them differently* and this *makes them in the end be a little bit different, which they can't help* (they can't avoid becoming a bit different).

D: People *react to them differently.*

E: They *just want to carry on as normal.*

F: People *react to them differently* but Hunter does not say that they react with jealousy.

2 Tick **B**, **C**, **D**: (lines 26–40)

A: A lot of winners *say they will later* (give money to charity); they say they will *leave money* (give money to charity when they die).

B: Hunter begins by saying that *They all give money to their nearest and dearest* (their closest relatives) but then corrects this by saying *well, practically all, we know exceptions* (almost all of them, there are winners who don't).

C: Hunter says that in fact they generally don't give money to charity because they think that *charity begins at home* (this is a saying, which means that you should help your family and friends, not people you don't know).

D: They say they will leave money to charity in their *wills* (a will is a legal document in which you say what will happen to your money and possessions after your death).

E: They give money to their *nearest and dearest* but Hunter does not say that this is because their families ask them for money.

F: They give between 20% and a third of their money to their families but Hunter does not say that any families feel that this is not enough.

3 Tick **C**, **D**: (lines 41–58)

A: They managed to track him down (to find him after searching for him) but Hunter does not say that he tried to avoid them or that he wouldn't speak to them or cooperate with them.

B: They may have considered him unusual because he had had three wives and was only 33 years old but Hunter does not say they found him difficult to understand.

C: They called him the 'lottery rat' (if you call someone a 'rat', you mean that they are a nasty person) and *made him look like a horrible person.*

D: They called him a 'rat' and made him look like a horrible person because he had had three wives and was still only 33 and because he obviously had more than one girlfriend.

E: He and Paul Maddison were the biggest winners that Hunter followed but Hunter does not say that the press felt that he had won too much money.

F: They made him look horrible because of the number of wives and girlfriends he had but there is no suggestion that the press thought he lied to them.

4 Tick **A**, **D**: (lines 59–75)

A: He *wants to prove, which he hadn't been able to do before, that he can run a successful business* and winning 11 million *is a bit of a help* (Hunter means this as a bit of a joke; obviously such a large sum of money is a considerable help).

B: Although he has helped local people by giving 30 of them jobs and spending money advertising on the local radio station, it is not suggested that he set out to help local people; instead, this is a result of him expanding and investing in his business, which is what he really wanted to do.

C: There is no suggestion that he spent the money on his business so that other people wouldn't accuse him of wasting the money or becoming someone who could not control their spending.

D: Before he won, the business *wasn't doing very well* and it owed money. He wanted to prove that he was able to turn this failing business into a successful one.

E: He has been good for his home town, Hastings, but there is no mention of any feeling he has about the town.

F: Although he won an enormous amount of money, he was clearly serious about making the business a success, not because he needed the money any more but because he wanted to show that he could be a successful businessman.

5 Tick **B**, **C**, **F**: (lines 76–103)

A: Hunter confirms that the story is true. It has appeared in the *Daily Mirror* and it appeared in his book, but he does not suggest that people didn't believe it was true when they read it in his book and only believe it now that it is in the newspaper.

B: Hunter says that in some ways the newspaper has *played fair* (behaved in a decent and reasonable way), for example by using a photograph that does not reveal the identities of the couple.

C: He says that the story was *lifted* (in this context, this means copied without permission and without admitting that it was copied).

D: He is clearly unhappy that the story has been copied from the book and that the newspaper doesn't mention the book, but he doesn't suggest that this has been done in order to affect the sales of the book.

E: He confirms that the story is true and does not mention any details in it that are not true.

F: He says that *they* (the newspaper) *haven't given the book a mention.*

6 Tick **C**, **F**: (lines 104–134)

A: When Hunter tells the story about his meeting with the man, he does not suggest at any point that the man was keeping any information from him.

B: They seem to have had no problem keeping their win secret. Even when the man is talking about it to Hunter, he is not worried that his mother will hear because she has her televison on very loud.

C: He was *prejudiced against them* (he decided he wouldn't like them before he spoke to them) because the man *looked like a yob* (a rude, badly behaved young man) and the front garden was *a dump* (a place with rubbish in it or in very poor condition). In fact, however, he says that he was wrong about them, he had *bracketed them wrongly* (wrongly included them in a category of people that he didn't like).

D: It is typical for winners *to keep quiet* when they win (80% of them do so) but *the norm is* (the normal situation is) that they tell some of their family and then *swear them to secrecy* (make them promise not to tell anyone else) and that they don't tell *the street* (all their neighbours). However, this couple are *most amazing* and *most unusual* because they haven't even told the man's mother, despite the fact that they all live in the same house.

E: Hunter didn't ask why they hadn't told the man's mother.

F: He thought he *looked like a yob* and this made him *prejudiced* against him.

7 Tick **C**: (lines 135–155)

A: Hunter says that in the 18 months since they won, they've had time *to really think about it* and to *change their life and settle down.*

B: He says that *it's a shame* that their story has *come out* (been revealed) in the newspaper but he does not say or imply that he blames himself for that.

C: Hunter implies that by keeping their win secret for 18 months they have given themselves time to get used to it.

D: Hunter is asked whether keeping the win secret is *potentially damaging for the relationship* with the man's mother and he replies that *it remains to be seen* (this will only be known in the future; in other words, he doesn't know).

E: They have had time to get used to their win and *they haven't changed as people.* Hunter does not imply that they will change now.

F: Hunter say that when they told him their story *they were taking a risk that it would somehow come out.* Therefore thay accepted that it might come out but this does not mean that they actively wanted it to come out.

PAPER 4 PART ONE (TEST)

For explanations, refer to the explanations for the options in the Further Practice and Guidance pages above. The letters in brackets here refer to those options.

1	B	(see C and E)
	A	(see B)
	C	(see D and F)
	D	(see A)
2	A	(see C)
	B	(see A and D)
	C	(see E and F)
	D	(see B)
3	D	(see C and D)
	A	(see A and B)
	B	(see F)
	C	(see E)
4	B	(see A, D and F)
	A	(see B and E)
	C	(see C)
	D	(see B)
5	C	(see C and F)
	A	(see B and E)
	B	(see A)
	D	(see D)
6	B	(see C and F)
	A	(see D)
	C	(see A and E)
	D	(see B)
7	A	(see C and D)
	B	(see B, E and F)
	C	(see E and F)
	D	(see A and C)

PAPER 4 PART TWO

(see tapescript, p179–180)

8 **a box of salt**: (lines11–17)
The *carter* (a person who used a cart for transporting people or things) *made sure he had a box of salt in his cart.* Before he took *a stick of furniture* (a single piece of furniture) into the new house, he would *sprinkle it* (distribute the small particles of it) in every room.

9 **by/through the same door**: (lines 18–23) Callers were not allowed to *enter by one door and leave by another.*

10 **stepped on it**: (lines 23–29)
It was an *ill omen* (a sign of bad luck) if you dropped the front-door key when you arrived at your house but *misfortune was averted* (you could avoid bad luck) if you stepped on the key before picking it up.

11 **fire-gazing**: (lines 34–38)
If you *gaze at* something, you look at it for a long time without moving your eyes, because you are fascinated by it. A *spot of* something in this context means a period of doing something.

12 **news of a fortune**: (lines 38–46)
Any *square-shaped spark* (a spark is a small flame coming from a fire) *foretold the arrival of a letter* (predicted that a letter would arrive); if this *appeared with crackles* (explosive noises), it meant that the letter would *contain news of a fortune* (a fortune is a very large sum of money).

13 **jet of white steam**: (lines 47–54)
Something that is *hissing* makes a noise like 'sssss'; a *trawler* is a fishing boat; if a boat *gets up steam*, it increases the power of its engine in order to

move quickly; if you *head somewhere*, you go in that direction; a *jet* is a strong stream of something coming out of an opening.

14 opened an umbrella indoors: (lines 60–67)
Collapse = fall down.

15 dropped cutlery: (lines 70–73)
Dropped cutlery predicted who was about to visit. Cutlery = knives, forks and spoons.

16 sharp implement: (lines73–79)
A pair of scissors is used in this context as an example of *any sharp implement*, as the use of *or* indicates. An *implement* is a tool or piece of equipment.

17 turn over a mattress: (lines 88–92)
It was believed that *a mattress must never be turned over on a Sunday*, because that would mean *turning out* (removing) *your luck*. A *mattress* is the part of a bed that you sleep on; it may contain springs and it is usually covered with sheets or a duvet.

PAPER 4 PART THREE

(see tapescript, p 180)

18 R: (lines 1–43)
She says that she would tell people that her father was better than their fathers and that no-one tried to *counter* (argue against) that, so she *got away with it* (she wasn't challenged about it).

G says that *other people started commenting* about his father when he found fame on TV, but he doesn't say that he said anything to them about his father.

M refers to people asking his father for his autograph, realizing that this *meant something special to other people*, and being *looked on and treated in a different way* by other people because his father was famous, but he doesn't refer to saying anything himself to other people about his father.

19 M: (lines 44–68)
He says that *Whilst* (in this context, this means *although*) he might be *trying to pursue what might be termed* (what people might call) an ordinary career, *I'm not allowed because of my name*. This means that because he has a famous name, people won't let him have an ordinary career, which is what he would like to do. It seems from what he says that when interviewers are brave enough to ask him whether he is the son of his famous father and find out that he is, for some reason they then don't want to employ him.

R says that if you have an ordinary career, there's *a certain stigma attached to the fact that you're doing that job* (people look on it with disapproval). They wonder why you're working *in this dump* (this awful place) when your father is *like royalty* (considered to be a very special person). She doesn't say that she has been unable to get certain jobs, however.

G agrees that this situation is confusing but he doesn't say his father's fame has prevented him from getting any jobs.

20 G: (lines 69–92)
He says that *for us* (his family) *it was a lot harder than for the chap* (his father) *who's actually enjoying it and getting the benefits directly from it* (*it* = fame).

R says that it is hard to be *treated as an extraordinary person when you haven't done anything extraordinary* but she doesn't compare being a famous person with being the child of one.

M agrees with R but does not make any comparison.

21 M: (lines 93–113)
He says that people would ask him to say something *in his voice* (to sound like his father did when performing) and they would ask him to *do a comic turn* (perform a comedy act) like his father. He would point out to them that his father was a comedian, not him.

R found it difficult to act on stage because she thought people were comparing her with her father and this made her *paranoid* (worried that people were looking at her critically) but she doesn't say that she was asked to act like her father.

G agrees that he felt that he was being looked at (*there is that* = that is the case) but he doesn't refer to anyone speaking to him or asking him anything.

22 G: (lines 114–142)
They are asked whether they had to *tell all* (reveal everything about their fathers, including bad things). G says that he *took the easy way out* (avoided that by taking an easy option) by getting a co-writer and taking *the analytical approach* (they *set out to* – aimed to – *analyse* his father's career rather than his personality). Therefore they *didn't get any comeback* (didn't have a bad reaction) and people didn't say they were *slandering* (saying bad and untrue things about someone) his father.

R didn't feel that she had to protect her father's reputation because nothing can change it. She therefore didn't feel that she had to avoid criticizing him and in the book she and her sisters decided they were going to *say everything* (give all the details) and not *censor* (exclude because they didn't want people to know about it) anything about their lives with him.

M doesn't refer to any aims when writing his book.

23 M: (lines 143–184)
He says that some of the things he wrote in the book make him *cringe* (feel very embarrassed) because of the way he said them.

Neither G nor R refer to having any regrets about anything that is in their books.

24 G: (lines 143–184)
He says that his father's attitude was *never to take any of it seriously* and that you shouldn't believe people either when they praise you or when they criticize you. G thinks that this is *a very good way to live your life*.

M refers to how people react to his father today and what people say about him but he doesn't say anything about an attitude to life.

R does not mention having learnt anything from her father.

25 R: (lines 143–184)
She says that *sadly at the moment it looks like he will probably be the last great actor who plied his wares* (this literally means 'sold his goods', in this context it means 'performed') *mainly on the stage* (in the theatre, rather than in films).

M says that people still like his father's work and still talk about him admiringly but he doesn't say that there won't be anyone like his father again.

G does not refer to the future.

p35–38 PAPER 5

FURTHER PRACTICE AND GUIDANCE (p37–38)

DESCRIBING FEELINGS

ANGER

exasperated: very frustrated, impatient and annoyed
irate: very angry
incensed: very angry and wishing to express that anger
indignant: angry because you feel you have been badly and unfairly treated
sour: having an angry attitude because of bad experiences
animosity: a hostile and aggressive attitude towards someone
fume: to be or show that you are extremely angry

livid: extremely angry

FEAR

disquiet: the nervous or worried feeling that something bad has happened or might happen
fret: to worry or be very anxious
apprehensive: anxious and worried that something in the future will be unpleasant
intimidated: frightened, especially because you have been threatened or feel without confidence in a certain situation
trepidation: a feeling of fear or worry that something bad is going to happen or that a situation is going to be unpleasant
perturbed: caused to be anxious or worried because of something that has happened or been said
unnerved: caused to feel worried or nervous; caused to lose confidence

HAPPINESS

bliss: A moment or period of *bliss* is a moment or period of enormous happiness.
elation: a feeling of great happiness, especially because of something wonderful that has happened
relish: If you *relish something/doing something*, you get pleasure from it or enjoy it. If you do something *with relish*, you get pleasure from it or enjoy it.
jubilant: extremely happy and celebrating something marvellous that has happened
glee: great happiness, often because of someone else's misfortune
revel in: If you *revel in something/doing something*, you thoroughly enjoy it and get a great deal of pleasure from doing it.
chuffed: very pleased

UNHAPPINESS

dejected: sad and depressed; disappointed and without hope
cut up: unhappy and upset because of something bad that has happened
grieve: to feel extremely unhappy, especially because of the death of someone
despair: the feeling that there is no hope; extreme depression; to have this feeling
anguish: extreme unhappiness or distress; great emotional suffering because of something terrible that has happened
despondent: extremely unhappy; having lost hope
disconsolate: so unhappy that nothing can comfort you
demoralized: unhappy because of feeling discouraged or having lost confidence

RELATIONSHIPS

1 You try to think of things to say to each other because you have not met before and feel that you should speak to each other.

2 You agree with them totally about something.

3 Because you think they are acting foolishly or saying something stupid but you don't want to upset them so you pretend that they are being logical.

4 Because they might be useful to you – if you *keep in with someone*, you maintain a good relationship with them even though you no longer have much contact with them.

5 You tell them something personal, private and secret.

6 You speak to them angrily.

7 As if they are superior to you or to others; unfriendly and unwilling to join in with others in a friendly manner.

8 You get on well with them, often the first time you meet.

9 You are in a situation where you disagree very much with them about something and this disagreement continues.

10 Conversation about unimportant matters, that people who do not know each other well have.

11 You feel that you have a lot in common with them.

12 You get on very well together.

13 A group of people involved in something together get on very well with each other (this is a French word used in English).

14 Talking to or treating other people as if they are stupid or inferior and being rude to them.

15 You have a good relationship with them, which involves each person understanding and liking the other (this is a French word used in English).

TEST 2

p39–41 PAPER 1 SECTION A

FURTHER PRACTICE AND GUIDANCE (p41)

1 A craved
B aspired
C yearned
D hankered

2 A uninitiated
B blind
C ignorant
D unacquainted

3 A affinity
B sensitivity
C regard
D appreciation

4 A established
B proved
C verified
D vindicated

PAPER 1 SECTION A (TEST)

Note that all explanations in this part refer to the meaning or use of each option most closely related to the question, not necessarily to the only meaning or use of each option.

One mark per question (Total: 25)

1 D: If you **aspire to something/doing something**, you would like to have or do it very much if it was possible for you to achieve it.
A: If you *crave something*, you want it desperately.
B: If you *hanker after something*, you have a very strong desire for it.
C: If you *yearn for something*, you want it very much.
All the options are connected with 'wanting or desiring something very much' but only D can be followed by 'to+noun'.

2 C: If you are **blind to** something, you are unaware of it, perhaps by choice.
A: If you are *ignorant of* something, you don't know about it.
B: If you are *uninitiated in* something, you have no experience or knowledge of the way in which it operates.
D: If you are *unacquainted with* something, you don't know about it or have experience of it because you have never come across it.
All the options are connected with the idea of 'not knowing or being aware of something' but only C can be followed by 'to'.

3 B: If you have **no appreciation of** something, you don't understand or

recognize what it is like or what it involves.
A: If you *have/feel an affinity with someone*, you feel that you have a special, close relationship with them because you have things in common.
C: If you have *no regard for* someone, you do not respect them at all.
D: If you show *sensitivity towards* other people, you show that you are considering their feelings and wishes.
All the options are connected with the idea of 'understanding or sympathy' but only B can be followed by 'of'.

4 D: If you **prove yourself to be something**, you show that you are that thing.
A: If you *establish yourself as* something, you get into the situation or position of being something and remain there for some time.
B: If something *vindicates* you, it proves that you were wrongly blamed or accused or that you were right about something.
C: If you *verify* something, you check it and establish that it is true or correct.
All the options are connected with the idea of 'proving something' but only D can be followed by the structure 'yourself to be'.

5 C: **A provisional arrangement/plan** is one that is intended only to be temporary and may change later.
A: A *conditional offer* is one that depends on certain requirements being met.
B: An *indefinite period* is one that lasts for an unknown amount of time and possibly a very long time.
D: If something is *indeterminate*, it is very hard to be definite about what exactly it is (*a man of indeterminate age*).

6 C: A **solid** period of time is a period of time without an action or situation stopping or being interrupted at any time.
A: If something is *constant*, it happens all the time or very frequently (*constant interruptions/arguments/pain*).
B: If something is *incessant*, it happens all the time or very frequently and is annoying or unpleasant. (*His incessant complaints are really getting on my nerves/ incessant noise.*)
D: If something is *perpetual*, it is done or happens all the time or very frequently (*a job involving perpetual hard work/ live under perpetual pressure*).

7 A: **As yet** = until now, so far (when talking about something that hasn't happened but might happen)
B: *These days* = during the present period, in contrast with the past (*I used to do a lot of sport but these days I don't have time.*)
C: *So long* is an informal expression meaning 'goodbye').
D: *Just now* = at this precise moment or period, in contrast with other times (*I can't speak to you just now, I'm very busy.*)

8 A: If you **sigh with** boredom/ frustration, you express this feeling by breathing out loudly.
B: If you *gasp*, you make a sound that indicates you are having difficulty breathing (*gasp for air*); if you *gasp in/with amazement/excitement*, you express this feeling by breathing in suddenly and sharply. (*The audience gasped in amazement when he fell off the stage.*)
C: If you *pant*, you breathe in and out very quickly, perhaps because you have been running and are out of breath. (*She ran, panting, into the office and apologized for being late.*)
D: If you *blow on* something, you breathe out onto it (*blow on your hands to warm them up*).

9 B: If you **take the view that** something is the case, you have that opinion or belief.
A: Your *outlook on* something is your attitude towards it (*have an optimistic outlook on life*).
C: If you are *of the belief that* something is the case, that is what you believe. (*I'm of the belief that such things don't matter.*)
D: If you are *of the opinion that* something is the case, that is your opinion. (*She is of the opinion that she is cleverer than everyone else.*)

10 C: If you show **a flicker of emotion**, your face indicates just for a moment how you are feeling.
A: If you have *a gleam in your eye*, your eyes shine, perhaps because you are happy or excited. (*She was obviously enjoying herself because she had a gleam in her eye.*)
B: A *wink* is the act of closing one eye for a short moment and then opening it again, as a signal to someone or as a friendly act. (*He gave me a wink to show that he was joking.*)
D: A *flash of inspiration* is an occasion when a good idea suddenly somes into your mind. (*I had a flash of inspiration and came up with the perfect solution.*)

11 D: If something **rests on** something, it depends entirely on it.
A: If something *stems from* something, it is a result of it or is based on it. (*Her success stems from her willingness to take risks.*)
B: If you *count on something/doing something*, you rely on it and trust that it will be as you expect. (*A car you can count on./He was counting on getting that job.*)
C: If something *derives from* something, that is the reason for it or the source of it (*illnesses that derive from unhealthy lifestyles*).

12 C: **In all probability** = it is very likely that...
A: *The odds are* = it is likely that... (*The odds are that we'll be late.*)
B: *The chances are* = it is likely that... (*The chances are that she'll be angry.*)
D: If something is *in prospect*, it seems likely to happen. (*I had a terrible week in prospect.*)

13 D: If your voice is **hoarse**, you cannot speak clearly or loudly because you have been shouting a lot or because you are ill.
A: A *raucous voice* is one that is loud and has an unpleasant, rough sound (*raucous laughter*).
B: If a voice is *grating*, it has a harsh tone that you find unpleasant to listen to. (*His grating voice really irritates me.*)
C: A *shrill voice* is high, loud and unpleasant (*a shrill cry*).

14 D: If you **hurt someone's feelings**, you upset them and make them unhappy.
A: If you *harm* something, you do damage to it (*harm a relationship*).
B: If you *wound* somebody, you upset them and make them unhappy. (*I felt wounded by his insults.*)
C: If you *upset* someone, you do or say something that makes them unhappy or angry. (*It upset Alice when we all made fun of her.*)

15 A: If something **falls apart**, it ceases to be organized and satisfactory.
B: If a plan *falls through*, it is not carried out for some reason. (*Their holiday plans fell through because they didn't have the money.*)
C: If something *falls away*, it gradually disappears. (*Over the years, his popularity fell away.*)
D: If you *fall out with someone*, you have a disagreement with them and stop being friends, perhaps only for a period of time. (*Let's not fall out with each other about this.*)

16 A: **By far** = 'by a very large amount/extent', when used with comparatives or superlatives.
B: *Vastly* = 'to a very great extent', when used with adjectives (*a vastly superior offer*).
C: If something is *a long way from* something, it is not at all similar to it. (*His lifestyle now is a long way from how he grew up.*); *by a long way* = by far (*He is by a long way the best player in the country.*)
D: *Extensively* = 'to a very great extent', when used with a verb. (*The building has been extensively altered.*).

17 A: If you are **at the height of your fame/powers**, your fame/powers are at their greatest at the time mentioned.
B: The *high point of* something is the best moment or period in it. (*Winning

the Olympic gold medal was the high point of his career.)
C: If you are *at the top of your profession*, you are at the most senior level of it, or considered one of the best people in it (*a lawyer at the top of her profession*).
D: If you are *at the head of a queue*, you are at the front of it.

18 A: If something is **debatable**, others might disagree about it.
B: If someone is *argumentative*, they are aggressive and like arguing.
C: If people are *quarrelsome*, they quarrel with each other a lot (*a quarrelsome couple /family*).
D: If something is *a moot point*, it is a matter about which there is disagreement that has not been resolved. (*It's a moot point whose fault it was.*)

19 D: If you are **in a tearing hurry**, you are hurrying very much because you have no time at all to spare.
A: If you *dash* somewhere, you hurry there. (*We dashed out of the building when someone shouted 'Fire'!*)
B: If you *race* somewhere, you go there very quickly. (*Ambulances raced to the scene of the disaster.*)
C: If you *rush* somewhere, you hurry there; if you are *in a rush*, you are in a hurry. (*I can't stop now, I'm in a terrible rush.*)

20 C: If someone or something **changes out of all recognition**, they change so much that they look totally different from the way they used to look.
A: *Identification* = the act of identifying someone/something (*identification of a body*)
B: *In my recollection* = What I remember is ... (*In my recollection, nothing unusual happened.*)
D: If you *have familiarity with* something, you have knowledge and experience of it. (*Do you have any familiarity with this kind of computer?*)

21 B: If you **spell something out to/for** someone, you explain it to them very clearly.
A: If you *figure something out*, you find a solution or explanation for it, after thinking about it. (*I couldn't figure out how to repair it/figure out why it happened.*)
C: If you *clear something up (with someone)*, you resolve a matter after explanation or discussion. (*I want to clear up this misunderstanding with you.*); if you *clear something out*, you remove everything from it and tidy it (*clear out a cupboard/ wardrobe*).
D: If something *stands out from* something, it is obviously different from it (*a building that stands out from the others in the street*).

22 B: If you **part company (with someone)**, you separate from them after you have been somewhere together.
A: If you *split up with someone*, you separate from them or your relationship with them as part of a couple ends. (*Let's split up and meet back here later./ split up with a boyfriend/girlfriend.*)
C: If you are *separated from your husband/wife*, you are no longer living together but you are still married.
D: If you *break up with someone*, you separate from them and you are no longer a couple with them (*Sally broke up with Alan because she didn't love him any more.*); if something *breaks up*, its members separate and it ceases to exist as a unit. (*The band broke up shortly after their first hit record.*)

23 B: If it **pays/doesn't pay to do** something, it gives you an advantage or benefits you/it is a disadvantage to you or does you harm. (*It pays to tell the truth./ It doesn't pay to break the law.*)
A: If something *benefits someone*, it is good for them or gives them an advantage. (*The experience will benefit you in the long run.*)
C: If something *advantages you*, it gives you an advantage or is useful to you. (*Will that qualification advantage you very much?*)
D: If you *profit from* something, you gain from it. (*He doesn't want to profit from the misfortunes of others.*)

24 C: If something happens **against your will**, it happens despite the fact that you say you don't want it to happen.
A: If you *have no option but to do* something, you have to do it because you have no other choice. (*I had no option but to take the first job I was offered.*)
B: If you *have no desire to do* something, you really don't want to do it because it doesn't appeal to you at all. (*I have no desire to travel the world.*)
D: If you *have a preference for* something, you prefer it. (*Daniel has a preference for unusual clothes.*)

25 D: If something happens on **rare occasions**, it happens only rarely.
A: If something is *scarce*, it exists in only small quantities and is hard to find. (*Flats to rent cheaply are scarce in this area.*)
B: If something is *abnormal*, it is not normal and it is undesirable (*an abnormal medical condition*).
C: If something *seldom* happens, it happens infrequently. (*It seldom snows in this part of the country.*)

p42–49 PAPER 1 SECTION B

Two marks per question (Total: 30)

FIRST PASSAGE

26 D: (look at the first two paragraphs) The writer was concerned as to whether the deputy pianist *could follow my cues* (would be able to understand the points in the show when he had to start and stop playing) *without preparation* (without having had the opportunity to practise this with the writer).
A: The man obviously looked strange to the writer because he was wearing *overalls* or *a boiler suit* (a one-piece item of clothing that covers the whole body and is worn by workmen who may get dirty, such as a decorator, builder or mechanic) when he came on stage. He had paint on his clothes and presumably worked as a decorator but the writer does not imply that he doubted whether he really was the replacement pianist.
B: When the deputy pianist started playing, he *drowned out the conclusion of the deejay's announcement*, which means that he played so loud it was impossible to hear the rest of what the disc jockey said. However, the writer doesn't express a fear that he would play too loud during his act.
C: When the pianist took off his overalls and showed that he was wearing formal clothes underneath them, the audience clapped but this does not necessarily mean that they were laughing at him, nor does the writer express any worry as to whether they might laugh more at the pianist than at him.

27 C: (lines 19–28)
Number in this context means a song performed in a show.
The pianist played the opening song (and all the others) in the key of C, which was not the intended key. The writer was unable to sing in the key of C (*the key imposed* – the key he was forced to sing in). He tried to, but realized he was singing too high, so he changed to *a lower octave*. This was too low, so he sang higher (*changing upwards again*) and finally he spoke the words (did *a sort of declamatory recitative of my perky lyric* – recited his lively words as if he was making a speech) rather than singing them.
A: He knew that he wasn't a good singer; he describes himself as *a performer of limited range* and seems to accept the criticism of him as being *vocally impaired*. He says that it is *pretty well impossible* for even a good singer to *follow suit* – to do as the pianist was doing and perform a song in another key from the one intended without

practising this – and he doesn't consider himself a good singer. He doesn't suggest that he ever considered himself a good singer, so he wasn't surprised that he couldn't sing the song in the key of C.
B: The deputy pianist actually did something very difficult according to the writer – he managed to *sight-read unfamiliar tunes* (play songs he didn't know without practising them, only reading the notes on the paper and playing them instantly, and to play them in a different key from the one he was reading (*to transpose* them). The writer considers this an achievement (it's *not easy* to do it) and it would seem that the pianist played the songs well, even though he played them in a different key.
D: The problem was not that he played the wrong song but that he played the right song in the wrong key.

28 A: (lines 28–31)
One reason that he gives for not cutting the other songs is that his *gags were going well enough* (the audience were laughing at his jokes enough) *to lull me into a false sense of security* (to give him the false feeling that it was safe to keep the other songs in the act).
B: He may have panicked during the first song, trying all sorts of different ways of performing it that he would not have tried if he had given it *sober consideration* (thought about it calmly) but panic is not the reason why he continued with the other songs.
C: One reason why he kept the other songs was that his act *was tightly routined* (was very well planned with a strict timetable). Therefore, if he had cut the songs this routine would have been disturbed and he didn't want to do that, but he doesn't suggest that reducing the length of his act would have been unacceptable.
D: He decided on *taking each musical hurdle as it approached* (dealing with the problem of each song when it was time to perform each song and not worrying about that during the rest of his act) but he does not suggest that he thought any of the songs would be less of a problem for him than the first one.

29 A: (lines 32–36)
The audience had paid *good money* (a lot of money, with the expectation of value for money), but he had performed the songs either in a ridiculously high voice (*shrieked* them *like a strangling soprano*), a voice so low that it was impossible to hear him (*growling them inaudibly low*) or by *yelling* (shouting loud) like a *ham actor* (a very poor, amateur actor). They were therefore *bewildered* (they couldn't understand why he was performing the songs like that) and *hostile* (angry and unfriendly) because they had paid and were expecting him to perform the songs properly.
B: After the performance he decided to reduce the number of songs to three in future, but the audience's reaction was caused by the way he performed the songs, not the number of songs he performed.
C: The audience found his performance of the songs strange – there is no suggestion that they thought he wasn't trying.
D: The writer performed the songs in many different styles and in a way that was obviously different from the way he usually did them, but he does not say that he changed any words.

30 B: (lines 37–43 and the first paragraph)
The pianist gave as his reason for playing all the songs in C that it *Sounds better* in his opinion. The writer evidently finds this very strange, as his comment on having his house painted suggests. The writer sees this strange behaviour and comment from the pianist as proof of what he states in the first paragraph – that musicians in general are species from *the Twilight Zone* (a fictional world of creatures from outer space), who have *something different in their brains* which has replaced certain thought processes that normal people have (made them very peculiar). He says that they are *all marching to the beat of a different drummer* (they are all living in their own world, which is not the same world as everyone else lives in). The story of the pianist therefore illustrates what he says in the first paragraph.
A: The pianist's behaviour and explanation for it were obviously unpredictable, but the writer uses him as an example of all musicians, not just some.
C: The pianist was adaptable in a way – he played all the songs without any rehearsal and he changed the key of all of them instantly, as he read the notes – but he is not said to be different from other musicians, he is typical of all of them. Furthermore, the story shows how strange musicians are and the way he played the songs is an example of this, not of the adaptability of musicians.
D: There is no suggestion that the pianist was deliberately trying to cause the writer problems – according to the bass player, he always played everything in the key of C and the pianist seems to genuinely believe that it is a good idea to do that.

SECOND PASSAGE

31 B: (see first paragraph)
The gist of what the writer is saying in the first paragraph is that although things happen which people say are too terrible to talk about (*more terrible than words can express;* making us *too shocked to speak; indescribable; too dreadful to talk about*), they still talk about them (*we speak; we go on to try to describe it; we talk about it*).
A: The writer quotes from the front page of a newspaper but his main point is that he wishes people wouldn't talk about such horrible things. (*If only we really would accept that there are things more terrible than words can express.*) He is chiefly concerned with all talk about horrific things, not with the style of newspaper coverage.
C: The writer believes that there are things which are too terrible to find words for, but his main point is that this doesn't stop people from talking about them, not that they can't find the right words.
D: The story in the newspaper is about a murder trial, and the writer describes the crime as *horrific* and *terrible*, but the writer's main point is that people talk about such things, not that such things happen.

32 D: (see second paragraph)
The writer says that his *heart sank* (he suddenly became very unhappy) when he read about the murders, not because they were awful but *for a more selfish reason* – because he was *bored*. For this reason reports of the case *will be of little interest to me*. He realizes that people may not believe him so he emphasizes that he really means it by using italics for the word *really* in the sentence *I really don't want to read about it*.
A: This seems to be a particularly unpleasant case – the murders are *awful beyond comprehension* – but he doesn't aim in this paragraph to show how much worse they are than other murders and in fact he doesn't mention other murders.
B: His attitude to the reporting of such cases is that it bores him, but he does not say that this represents any change in attitude – it is highly likely that he has always felt like this.
C: He says that newspaper, magazine, television and radio news coverage of the trial will not interest in him and that *whole reams* (large quantities of paper) of all newspapers will be *a blank* (something he won't read) for him but this is because he finds such things boring; he does not comment on the quality of the reporting.

33 A: (lines 16–25)
People *are prone* (tend) to *declare their disgust* (say they are disgusted) when a certain newspaper gives *prominence* (importance) to certain stories but then they *eagerly buy it*. Both people who say the press ought to cover a certain story and those who say it shouldn't *devour the story* (read it eagerly) *avidly* (with great interest). In addition, he says that the *propensity* (tendency) to find things in newspapers *offensive, undignified or harmful* is similar to the tendency to be *drawn towards* (attracted to it) – in other words people are attracted to such stories almost as much as they are shocked by them.
B: The writer says that it is *doubtful* whether it's possible to learn anything by asking people if they are influenced by certain stories when they buy a newspaper. This is because they buy or read it regardless of what they say about whether it should cover certain stories or not, not because they can't explain what appeals to them about a newspaper.
C: He doesn't say that they keep changing their minds, he says that some people say a newspaper should feature certain stories and others say it shouldn't.
D: He believes that the research itself is pointless – he doesn't mention the way in which it is analysed or any conclusions that are drawn from it.

34 B: (lines 25–28)
He says that *the natural censors among us* (people who don't want others to be allowed to read or see certain things) are *driven* (motivated) by *an unacknowledged fear* (a fear they don't realize they have) of the bad side of their natures. In *the privacy* of a shop selling newspapers (where nobody else can see what they're doing), they are just like the *openly prurient* (people who make no secret of the fact that they are fascinated by shocking things) in the sense that they buy, read and *relish* (enjoy) such stories.
A: He says that they enjoy the stories they say they'd like to ban; he does not suggest that they should take into consideration other opinions on the matter.
C: He says that there are people who want to ban such stories but he does not say that he thinks there are a great many of them.
D: He says that such people *complain* but he does not say that their complaints have any effect on others.

35 C: (lines 29–38 and the passage as a whole)
He says that people like him are more *uncomprehending* (they don't understand why such things happen) than *shocked* by such stories and that such stories don't *arouse great curiosity* for them (don't make them keen to find out more). He accepts that such things are horrific – the crimes are *awful beyond comprehension* (second paragraph) and he refers to them as *nasty* (very unpleasant) *stories* (last paragraph), but he and people like him ignore these stories (they don't read the front page, on which these stories appear, they turn immediately to page two). Similarly, they feel no *horror* or *disgust* when they see people shooting each other in films. They *stare blankly* (with no emotion on their faces) and they are *uncomprehending* as to *what viewers see in this sort of thing* (what makes this sort of thing interesting to viewers). They are therefore not affected by and don't have any strong feelings about things that others find horrific and shocking.
A: He says that the reaction of people like him is very clear – they are bored by such stories. Moreover, he is quite clear that he considers such crimes to be terrible.
B: He talks throughout the passage about people's reactions to such stories but he does not say that this represents any change in society – indeed, he implies that this is not a new thing. Furthermore, he does not suggest that there has been any increase in such crimes.
D: He says that he and people like him have no particular views on violence, apart from that watching it or reading about it is boring. He is not saying that people like him have strong views that differ from other people's views on the subject.

THIRD PASSAGE

FURTHER PRACTICE AND GUIDANCE (p48–49)

For explanations, see the explanations to the questions in the test that follow.

Question 36

1 no **2** c **3** a

4 It was trim and tidy and it had green shutters.

Question 37

1 The city owns the house and it makes a lot of money from the house.

2 That there are 135,000 of them a year (he implies that this is a large number because it results in a big profit for the city).

3 because it is not looked after

4 He would be more sympathetic about the terrible state of the place.

Question 38

1 b **2** no **3** no **4** very little

Question 39

1 a (it had fallen into bad condition)

2 yes (lines 25–26)

3 no

4 c

Question 40

1 no **2** no **3** no
4 yes – his comments on the Restaurant and Dinette, the Mental Health Center and the licence plate.

THIRD PASSAGE (TEST)

36 C: (lines 1–10)
The house *purported to be* (it was claimed that it was) *a faithful reproduction of the original interiors*. However, the writer saw various things that made him believe this was not so – wires, water sprinklers (in case of fire) were *clumsily evident* (obvious when they should have been hidden because they would not have been in the original house); he says that he doubts very much whether vinyl (a man-made substance used to cover floors), and a plywood partition (a thin piece of wood used for dividing one room into two) would have been present in the original house.
A: He mentions that there was an admission charge and that the house was a disappointment, but he does not say that he was surprised or disappointed to discover that he had to pay to get in.
B: He says that there were recorded messages *at every window* but he is critical of what the messages were like – they seemed to assume that you were a *moron* (a very unintelligent person) – not the number of them.
D: The house was *trim and tidy* and it had *green shutters*. There is nothing to suggest that the writer found any of this strange. It was *set incongruously in the middle of the downtown* – it didn't fit in with the other buildings in the centre of the town, it looked totally out of place there; this means that he found its location strange but it doesn't mean that he found the house itself strange from the outside.

37 B: (lines 10–13)
The city = the city authorities. A lot of people (135,000 a year) visit the house, which is owned by the city, so for Hannibal it is *a little gold mine* (a source of profit or wealth). However, it is *shabby* (not looked after and in poor condition) and the writer considers this *awful*. He says it

wouldn't be so awful (unacceptable) if a literary society owned it but it is so awful because the city owns it. He therefore implies that the city of Hannibal shouldn't make so much money from it because they don't look after it.
A: A lot of people visit it and it is shabby, but the writer is not implying that its condition has been caused by the visitors.
C: The writer says the place is *shabby* and *awful* but the problem is not that it is open to the public, it is that it has been neglected. He seems to think it should still be open to the public but better looked after.
D: The writer says that if it was owned by a local literary society that was trying hard despite being *underfunded* (having too little money), it wouldn't be so terrible that the place is shabby – he would be more sympathetic about that, there would be a reasonable excuse. This doesn't mean that it would be better if a literary society ran it, only that its condition would be more acceptable in the circumstances.

38 C: (see second paragraph)
The museum contained cases of *Twain memorabilia* (items that belonged to or are connected with a famous person, in this case Twain). The writer gives these as the reason why the museum was better and does not appear to doubt that they were authentic.
A: When he saw the Mark Twain Drive-In Restaurant and Dinette, which were right next to the museum, the writer clearly disapproved of them because he says that when he saw them, he began to understand why the author *didn't just leave town but also changed his name* – in other words, they made him dislike the whole town. The sentence *It really lent the scene a touch of class* (it made the place look sophisticated) is ironic.
B: He obviously liked the exhibits but he doesn't say they were valuable. The phrase *precious little* means 'not very much at all'.
D: The writer says there was very little in the museum to connect the author with the house or town, which implies that he didn't learn much there about when Twain lived in the house or the town. He knew that Twain *got the hell out of the place* (left the place quickly because he didn't want to stay there) and was *disinclined* (didn't want) to go back, but he didn't learn that in the museum.

39 A: (see third paragraph)
The writer had always thought that river towns were *more interesting than other towns* because the river *served as a conduit* (acted as a channel linking one place with another) *to a larger world* (it seemed to connect the town with other, bigger places). In addition the river *washed up* (deposited) *a more interesting and sophisticated brand of detritus* (type of rubbish).
B: The business district was *dispiriting* (depressing) because there were a lot of empty buildings and *vacant lots* (areas of land intended for a particular purpose but not used), which indicates that the business district was not prosperous and had fallen into a bad state. He had always thought that river towns had *something about them* (a certain quality) that made them more interesting than other towns but he does not say that he had expected the business district to be prosperous.
C: He had always thought that they had a kind of *faded elegance* (that they had once been elegant but that elegance was now gradually disappearing) and that they had *a raffish air* (they seemed not to be very respectable but in an attractive way); this does not suggest that he had thought they were clean and tidy.
D: The writer says that Hannibal *had obviously had better days* (been a better or more prosperous town in the past) but he doubted whether those days were *all that great* (very good). He therefore mentions the town's past but he does not say that he had previously considered the history of such towns to be interesting or that their history was the only interesting thing about them.

40 D: (consider the passage as a whole)
The writer makes it clear that he disliked everything about the whole visit – apart from the museum, which wasn't too bad. He is very critical of the house – it is shabby and awful; the Restaurant and Dinette made him understand why someone might leave the town and he is sarcastic about them; he dislikes the fact that so many things have Mark Twain in their name; he imagines that the possibility of going *insane* (mad) would *grow increasingly likely with every day spent in Hannibal* (lines 30–32); his comment that the car licence plate for Missouri should read 'Show Me the Way to Any Other State' indicates that he dislikes Missouri very much (lines 35–37); and he leaves Missouri *without regret*. He is therefore harshly critical of the house, the town and the State throughout the passage.
A: He sees much that he dislikes – he feels the house is not as good as it should be (and perhaps he likes Mark Twain's books); the town depresses him – it is *sad and awful* (third paragraph) However, there is nothing in his tone to suggest that any of this worries him. He seems more annoyed than concerned and leaves without regret, the implication being that he won't think about the place again.
B: He dismisses almost everything he sees as awful – he does not seem to be interested in finding out why it is awful and doesn't seem curious to learn more about it.
C: Some of the things he says seem to be intended to amuse the reader (lines 20–21 *It really lent the scene a touch of class*; the comment about the Mental Health Center (third paragraph); the comment about the licence plate (last paragraph). However, all these examples are of remarks that are also highly critical and they do not make the passage light-hearted in tone.

PAPER 1:

SECTION A	25 marks
SECTION B	30 marks
TOTAL	55 marks

To be converted into a score out of 40 marks.

p50–52 PAPER 2

Each composition is given a mark out of 20. The total of the two compositions is then divided by two to give an overall score for the paper out of 20.

FURTHER PRACTICE AND GUIDANCE (p52)

Assessment of sample composition

1 **Content**
The composition certainly does address the issue given in the question throughout and the points made are all relevant. However, it is somewhat repetitious towards the end the fifth paragraph repeats a point made in the third paragraph and the final sentence repeats the first sentence.

2 **Organization**
The composition is very well-organized. It has a clear introduction, in which the matters that are going to be dealt with are raised, and a conclusion – it is perfectly acceptable to conclude that you don't have a firm opinion on the matter. The other paragraphs all deal with clear, separate points.

3 **Linking**
There is some good linking: *but still* (= but even so) in the first paragraph; *that is to say* (= which means) in the second paragraph; *Furthermore* at the start of the third paragraph; *On the other hand* (to introduce a contrasting point) in the fourth paragraph.

4 **Use of vocabulary**
There is some very good, more than simple vocabulary: *break free, conformity, your peers* (people of the same age as you) and *to find yourself* (to discover your real personality) in the first paragraph; *pressured, bearing upon* (having an influence on) and *follow in the footsteps of* (do exactly the same as) in the second paragraph; *anonymity* (not being known by other people) in the third paragraph; *arduous* (demanding) in the last paragraph. The only time that vocabulary is used inappropriately is in the fourth paragraph: you don't *have the possibility to do something*, you have the chance or opportunity to do it.

5 **Use of grammar**
Grammatically this composition is very good, with only very minor errors; in the second paragraph it should be *at a very early stage* not 'on'; *adolescent* in the fourth paragraph should be plural; the phrase *The adolescence situation* in the last paragraph is rather awkward and perhaps it should say something like *The situation regarding adolescence.* Apart from these, the structures used are more than simple and they are used accurately throughout, showing a good command of grammar.

6 **Style**
This composition is clear, natural and lively. The use of the question at the end of the first paragraph helps to grab the reader's attention. It flows well and shows a generally high level of English.

This is a generally very good composition in all respects. It would be given 14–15 marks out of 20. The fact that there is repetition prevents it from having a higher mark.

p53–57 PAPER 3 SECTION A

PART 1

One mark per question (Total: 20)

1 **and**: The *twists and turns* involved in something are the events and developments that take place, especially when there are many of these and they are complex or unexpected.

2 **had**: *Had something not happened* = if something had not happened. This structure is a variation of the third conditional.

3 **come**: If you *come to a decision*, you make a decision after some thought.

4 **effect/influence**: If something *has a profound effect/influence on something*, it affects/influences it very greatly.

5 **mean/imply**: This sentence means that the fact that the failures were soon forgotten doesn't make it also true that the people who had the ideas were wrong. In this context, if one thing *means* or *implies* another thing, the fact that the first thing is true makes the second thing also true.

6 **often**: The phrase *more often than not* means very often, in most cases.

7 **get**: If you *get something right*, you do it in the right way, with the result that it is successful.

8 **no**: If there is *no shortage of* something, there is a great deal of it or a great many of them.

9 **sure/certain**: If you *make sure/certain* that something happens, you do something so that it is certain that it happens.

10 **using/exerting**: If you *use/exert influence*, you deliberately influence something.

11 **similar**: This sentence means that the same kind of thing happened with the car tyre that happened with the alternatives to the petrol-driven engine – it quietly disappeared.

12 **need/require**: It *would never need/require replacing* = it would never need to be replaced, it would never be necessary to replace it

13 **for**: The substances mentioned were produced so that they could be used in making astronauts' boots.

14 **worn**: If an item of clothing *wears out*, it gets into a bad condition as a result of wearing it for a long time.

15 **had/has/held/holds**: If something *has/holds appeal for* someone, it is attractive to them. In the context, both past and present tenses can be used, as it seems likely that this situation is still the case.

16 **make**: If someone/something *makes it*, they become successful.

17 **against**: If you are *advised against doing* something, you are advised not to do it.

18 **without**: They *responded without enthusiasm* = they reacted in an unenthusiastic way. We know that they were not enthusiastic because of what we are told in the next sentence.

19 **catch**: If something *catches on*, it becomes popular or fashionable.

20 **would**: This part of the sentence means 'Most others thought that the product would fail.' The *would* here relates to the *wouldn't* before question 19. A dud is a complete failure, something that doesn't work at all.

PAPER 3 SECTION A

PART 2

One mark per word or phrase in bold (Total: 12)

a **good/excellent terms** (1) **with his ex-wife** (1). (2 marks)
If you are *on good terms with someone*, you have a good relationship with them, you are friendly with each other.

b **decision (that) I** (1) **made/took/reached/ came to easily** (1) OR **decision that** (1) **was easy for me (to make/take/reach/come to)** (1).
(2 marks)
As the sentence begins with *This is*, the second part of it must be in the form of a '*that* clause'. You can *make/reach* or *come to* a decision.

c **to popular opinion,** (1) **this is not a dangerous city** (1). (2 marks)
Contrary to something = totally different from, opposite to. *Contrary to popular opinion* = what many people believe is wrong because... *But* must therefore be removed from the original sentence.

d **what may,** (1) **I won't change my mind about this.** (1 mark)
Come what may = it doesn't matter what happens. This is used to emphasize that nothing at all will influence something or prevent it from being the case.

e **down** (1) **well with** (1) **the audience**.
(2 marks)
If something *goes down well with someone*, it is well received by them, they approve of it or like it.

f **in breaking the law** (1)**, he will get into trouble**. (1 mark)
If you *persist in doing* something, you continue to do something bad or annoying; if you *persist with* something, you continue to do it, despite the fact that it is difficult and you are not succeeding (*persist with a course*).

g **best of my knowledge** (1), there's no reason for James to be so unhappy.
(1 mark)
To the best of my knowledge = as far as I'm aware, what I know is...; this phrase implies that perhaps there is something you don't know.

h **off the idea**. (1 mark)
If you *go off something/doing something*, you were keen on it or to do it at one time but you stop being keen on it or

to do it because it stops being attractive or interesting for you.

PAPER 3 SECTION A

PART 3 FURTHER PRACTICE AND GUIDANCE (p55)

For explanations, see the explanations for the questions in the test below.

a 3

b 2

c 3

d 1

e 5

f 2

PAPER 3 SECTION A

PART 3 (TEST)

One mark per question (Total: 6)

a a state of
If something is *in a state of* something, that is the condition it is in.

b than makes up for
The sentence means that her determination more than compensates for her lack of natural ability; in other words, that the positive aspect is of more significance than the negative one. If you *make up for* something, you compensate for something bad by doing something good.

c suppose you could do
If you ask someone to do something and you begin *I don't suppose you*, you are saying that you don't expect them to do it but you are asking anyway. The form of the tag at the end means that *could* must be used in the first part so that the tag corresponds with the modal verb in the rest of the question. If you *do someone a favour*, you do something for them, that helps them, usually because they ask you to do so.

d the process/middle/act of getting
If you are *in the process/act/middle of doing* something, you are still doing it, you haven't finished it. If you *get something ready*, you prepare it or make it ready.

e take it as
If you *take something as read*, you assume that it is the case and that there is therefore no need to think or talk about it.

f the other way
If a situation is *the other way round*, it is the opposite of the way it was previously.

PAPER 3 SECTION A

PART 4 FURTHER PRACTICE AND GUIDANCE (p57)

For explanations, see the explanations for the questions in the test below.

a 2

b 3 and 4

c 1

d 1 and 4

e 2

f 2

g 1

h 1 and 2

PAPER 3 SECTION A

PART 4 (TEST)

One mark per word or phrase in bold (Total: 12)

a I wasn't in a position to lend (1) him any money because I didn't have enough myself. (1 mark)
If you are *not in a position to do* something, you can't do it because of the circumstances.

b It wouldn't be worth (1) **your while to take that course** (1). OR **Taking that course wouldn't be worth** (1) **your while** (1). (2 marks)
If it is *not worth your while to do* something or if something is *not worth your while*, there is no point in you doing it because you will not gain any benefit from it.

c Bad publicity had a detrimental (1) **effect on sales (figures)** (1). OR **was detrimental** (1) **to sales (figures)** (1). (2 marks)
If something *has a detrimental effect on* or *is detrimental to* something, it has a bad effect on it, it harms it.

d There is/can be (1) **little doubt that** (1) **the crime was committed by professional thieves/ professional thieves committed the crime.** (2 marks)
There is/can be little doubt that... = it is almost certain that...

e Either we tackle this problem now or it will get worse. (1 mark)
Either one thing happens or another thing will happen = if the first thing doesn't happen, the second, bad thing will happen.

f In the absence of a better alternative (1), I accepted the job. (1 mark)
In the absence of = because there wasn't, because something was not present.

g When he won the gold medal, **there was no mistaking his delight** (1). OR **There was no mistaking his delight** (1) when he won the gold medal. (1 mark)
If *there is no mistaking* something, it is very obvious and nobody could have the wrong idea about it.

h Her heart is set (1) **on becoming a doctor** (1). OR **She has set her heart** (1) **on becoming a doctor** (1). (2 marks)
If you *set your heart on something* or *your heart is set on something*, you want it very much and you are determined to do or have it.

SECTION A:

QUESTION 1	20 marks
QUESTION 2	12 marks
QUESTION 3	6 marks
QUESTION 4	12 marks
TOTAL	50 marks

p58–62 PAPER 3 SECTION B

FURTHER PRACTICE AND GUIDANCE (p61–62)

Questions a–n

For explanations, see the explanations for the questions in the test below.

b b

d **1** b
2 d

g **1** d
2 a

k a

l c

f b

m a

PAPER 3 SECTION B (TEST)

Answers similar to or covering the same points as those given here are acceptable provided they are clearly expressed.

a that it would have been an acceptable/ understandable thing for him to do if he had been reading something sad. (1 mark)
He says that he *wouldn't have minded crying* (he wouldn't have thought that there was anything wrong with crying) or *pausing to swallow down a discreet silent sob* (interrupting his reading for a moment to swallow hard

in order to hide a cry that might embarrass the audience) if what he was reading was sad. However, it wasn't.

b that he was finding it very difficult not to start crying/that he was very close to crying. (1 mark)
If you are *in serious trouble* , you have a big problem of some sort. In his case, the problem was preventing himself from crying.

c that it contained more details than necessary/too many details (1) **and that it didn't play a very important part in the story** (1). (2 marks)
The sentence described all the different things that the woman put into the bag with the muffin (see lines 5–7). He says that the sentence contained *more stirrers* (objects like spoons), *sugar packets and butter pats* (small pieces of butter) *than I needed* – he had put more objects into the sentence than was necessary. For this reason (*In that sense*), the sentence was *semi-decorative rather than functional* (its purpose was more to add interesting details than to make an important contribution to the story).

d suddenly make me feel upset/distressed/very sad. (1 mark)
This is an image. Literally, if someone *grabs at your lapels*, they suddenly take hold of the front part of the collar of your jacket or coat, usually as an act of aggression. *Grief* is enormous unhappiness/sorrow/distress, usually cause by the death of someone.

e because he had been proved right that the correct word (to describe what the muffin was wrapped in) was 'tissue', not 'paper'. (1 mark)
If you *exult*, you rejoice or celebrate because of something that has happened. The writer had had a disagreement with his editor (see line 15) – he said the correct word for what a muffin was wrapped in at a bakery was 'tissue', she insisted that it was 'paper'. When he visited the bakery, he saw that what was used there was indeed called 'tissue'.

f the phrase describing what the muffin was wrapped in. (1 mark)
The phrase had been 'tissue-wrapped muffin' in the book – the editor had agreed that the word was 'tissue' but the phrase was still different from his original phrase, which was 'tissue-protected muffin'. When he was *reading it* (the phrase) *aloud*, he could *turn it* (the phrase) *into* the one he had originally written.

g that the sentence had never attracted praise or been highly valued by him (1) **but it had remained in the story** (1). (2 marks)
This part of the paragraph had been *unrewarded* because he had never thought of it *proudly* (line 22), he had *forgotten* it. It was unimpaired *(still there, undamaged) – it had* hung on in there (managed to survive in the book).

h that he was in the middle of reading a story that was meant to be ironical/humorous/amusing, not sad. (1 mark)
If you are *in the midst of doing* something, you are in the process/middle/act of doing it. *Irony* is a way of being amusing by using a style or tone that suggests that what you are saying may appear serious but is in fact funny.

i his bitterness at having his own work rejected by publishers when he was trying to become a writer. (1 mark)
He felt *pure, mean-spirited* (bitter, having an ungenerous attitude) *contempt* (deep dislike) for writers who gave readings during his *rejection-letter days* (a rejection letter in this context is one that informs you that a piece of work you have sent has been rejected – we can infer from this that when he began trying to be a writer, publishers, magazines, etc. rejected his work).

j he thought the writers who gave them were showing off by reading stories that belonged on the printed page (1) **and that the writers were not very good at reading/didn't have the right personalities for giving interesting readings** (1). (2 marks)
He had thought that it was *self-congratulatory* (the writers gave readings because they were very pleased with themselves and felt it was a way of showing how well they had done by having their work published) *to repudiate the divine economy of the published page* (to reject/turn away from the beautiful conciseness of a book) and make people come together to listen to a *reticent* person (someone who is normally very quiet and does not like speaking or revealing their feelings) *reiterate* (repeat) something that had been published a long time before.

k they hadn't known that he had previously disapproved of readings. (1 mark)
If you do something *innocently*, you do it without realizing that something bad or unpleasant is involved. In this case, they had been *unaware of my prior disapproval* (they didn't know when they listened to him that he had previously had great contempt for people who did what he was doing then – giving readings).

l something too terrible to consider/think about/imagine (1 mark)
Unthinkable can also be used as an adjective (*Such high levels of violent crime were unthinkable years ago.*)

m the writer breaking down/crying OR **the listeners being puzzled about his mental state** (1 mark)
He says that he did *break down* (lose control and start crying), the fact that he had shown such intense feeling when reading something that was *supposedly comic* (meant to be funny) would make the audience *puzzled* (confused) about his *overall mental wellbeing* (whether he was in a generally good mental state or whether he had psychological problems normally). It was *this* (the fact the he cried/their reaction to him crying) that they would *take home with them* (remember as the most significant thing after the reading) and not anything he had read.

n whenever he tried to write something amusing in future, he would remember his shame at crying at the reading (1) **and so he would change it to something sad that would not be typical of him** (1). (2 marks)
If he tried to write something *light* (amusing/not serious or sad) after that, he would remember his *moment of shame* (when he cried that evening) and to *counteract it* (to make the memory of this less painful) he would have to write something *bleak and brooding* (depressing and serious) instead. To do so would be *wholly out of character* (totally untypical of him, completely contrary to his real personality). We can infer from this that to justify crying, he feared he would have to start considering himself a writer of sad and serious things, which is not what he really is. Thus the incident would *distort* his future *output* (change into an unnatural form what he wrote in future).

Questions a–n: Total 18 marks

PAPER 3 SECTION B

FURTHER PRACTICE AND GUIDANCE (p62)

WRITING A SUMMARY

1 The third, fourth, fifth and sixth paragraphs.
At the end of the second paragraph he says there were a *number of reasons* and he then lists these reasons. The final paragraph deals not with reasons why

he might cry but possible consequences of doing so.

2 The following points could be included:
3/5/6/8/9

The other points are mentioned, but not as reasons why he felt like crying, which is the subject of the summary.

PAPER 3 SECTION B

SUMMARY

o *One mark each for the inclusion of the following points or points similar to them (in any order).*

1 **He could read the phrase describing the muffin as he had originally written it, not as it was published.** At the end of the third paragraph he says *And that might have been enough to make me cry*. In this sentence *that* refers to *I could turn it into a 'tissue-protected muffin all over again'* (see also question (f) and the explanation for it).

2 **The sentence wasn't remarkable and he hadn't valued it but it was still there.** At the end of the fourth paragraph he says that *it* (the sentence) *had become the tearjerker moment* (the part of a story or film that makes people cry) that would make him *dissolve in grief* (break down and cry out of terrible sadness) *out of pity for its very unmemorableness* (because he felt sorry for the sentence simply because it was not memorable) (see also question (g) and the explanation for it).

3 **He regretted his previous contempt for authors who gave readings.** At the beginning of the fifth paragraph, he says that *Contrition* (regret for something bad that you have done) *made its contribution* (was another reason why he felt like crying). His regret was for his previous attitude to authors giving readings (see also questions (i) and (j) and the explanations for them).

4 **Although he had been nervous before the reading, he hadn't done anything embarrassing and he had been well received by the audience.** In the sixth paragraph he says that he had been extremely nervous but he hadn't done anything *too humiliating* (extremely embarrassing) and the audience had *tolerantly laughed once or twice*. At the end of the paragraph, he says that *all this* (being nervous, not doing anything too humiliating, the audience listening and laughing occasionally) *was too much* (it made him too emotional to prevent himself from crying).

Total: 4 marks
Plus a maximum of 8 marks for general impression of summary skills, based on the following criteria:

- relevance
- general level of fluency
- accuracy of language
- absence of copying from passage
- length

SUMMARY: TOTAL	12 marks
SECTION B:	
QUESTIONS a – n	18 marks
SUMMARY	12 marks
TOTAL	30 marks
PAPER 3:	
SECTION A	50 marks
SECTION B	30 marks
TOTAL	80 marks

To be converted into a score out of 40 marks.

p63–65 PAPER 4

One mark per question (Total: 25)

To be converted into a score out of 20 marks.

PAPER 4 PART ONE

(see tapescript, p181)

FURTHER PRACTICE AND GUIDANCE (p65)

For explanations, see the explanations for the questions in the test below.

1 C

2 A

3 A

4 B

5 C

6 A

7 A

8 B

9 C

10 B

PAPER 4 PART ONE (TEST)

1 **block of ice**: (lines5–9)
The sub-Arctic winter will turn the area into a vast frozen mass.

2 **their homeland**: (lines 18–26)
Someone's *homeland* is the country or region they were born in and come from.

3 **bleak and forbidding**: (lines 26–34)
If a place is described as *bleak*, it is bare and depressing. If a place is *forbidding*, it makes you not want to go there because it does not look nice or safe.

4 **hunting grounds**: (lines 41–45)
Hunting grounds are areas of land specially reserved for hunting animals.

5 **nomadic**: (lines 52–59)
A *nomadic existence/way of life* involves constantly travelling from place to place.

6 **canoes and paddles**: (lines 59–63)
A *canoe* is a small, narrow boat. A *paddle* is a pole with a flat end that is used for making a boat move through water.

7 **That man likes everything**: (lines 76–83)
Lejeune describes the Innu as *very generous* people, who don't feel strongly about possessing *the riches of the earth* so that they won't *grieve* (become very upset) if they lose them. The phrase *That man likes everything* is a big insult to the Innu, so it must be used to describe someone who is greedy or selfish.

8 **order of precedence**: (lines 88–92)
An *order of precedence* is the order in which people or things are placed or treated, from the most important to the least important. At an Innu meal, everyone is equal (each person is *as noble* – as important or respected *as the others*).

9 **ignorance and superstition**: (lines 110–114)
Lejeune *talks approvingly* sometimes of the Innu's *simplicity and naturalness*. This is in contrast to what he says *more often* about them, when he refers to their *ignorance* (lack of education or sophistication) and *superstition* (illogical belief that various things are signs of good or bad luck). These characteristics are normally associated with primitive people.

10 **holy occupation**: (lines 122–131)
They see hunting not only as *a means of survival* but as a *holy* (sacred; in accordance with religious belief) *occupation* (activity).

PAPER 4 PART TWO

(see tapescript, p181–182)

11 J: (lines 1–36)
She says that the decision to fund the centre concerns people's *creativity* and *enterprise* and that these matters are *right up my street* (something I am very interested in and enthusiastic about). She believes that people *should be* creative and enterprising and so she welcomes the decision to fund the centre and is glad that someone has *fostered* (helped and encouraged) the idea.
P says that the rock business is a *money-spinning* (extremely profitable) one and that huge amounts of money are invested in it and made from it. However, he is against the centre, which he describes as a *surrender* to something that has done a lot of damage and he does not say that it is a good idea to invest money in rock music, even if it is extremely profitable.

12 P: (lines 37–53)
He says that we have *wiped out* (completely destroyed) *real culture* and that rock music is *a substitute for culture*. He therefore believes that it cannot be considered the same as, for example, the music of Gershwin, which he believes is *real culture*.
J says that Gershwin's music isn't part of *British culture* because it was *imported* (Gershwin was from the US). However, she believes that rock music is part of *contemporary British culture* and therefore she does not believe that it should be considered to be in a separate category from culture.

13 P: (lines 53–65)
His exclamation *To compare Gershwin with rock* means that you cannot compare the two. He clearly dislikes rock music and likes Gershwin's music. One reason why he likes it is that it is *morally uplifting* (it makes you cheerful or optimistic) and he clearly thinks that good music should be like that.
J says that rock music is *humanity on the move* (people making progress) and that it makes a lot of money for the country but she does not refer to it making people happier.

14 P: (lines 66–100)
P says that *this stuff* (rock music) *has been revered* (people have had a great deal of respect and admiration for it) and that *it doesn't deserve* this. He adds that anyone who criticizes it is said to be *highbrow* (too serious and intellectual about cultural matters) or *snobbish* (believing that your taste is superior to that of other people) or *culturally deprived* (suffering from a lack of culture), and he clearly disagrees with this general view.
J says that the music business is *actually* based on small *venues* (places where concerts take place) and *small businesses*. She therefore implies that people wrongly believe it is based on big record companies. However, this is a belief about the structure of the business, not about the music itself.

15 B: (lines 101–128)
P says that rock music has had a social effect; it has encouraged *adolescent self-pity* (teenagers feeling sorry for themselves), *self-indulgence* (selfishly doing whatever you gain pleasure from) and has led to *the breakdown of parental authority*. He believes that people should realize that it has had these damaging effects.
J believes that it is important for young people to communicate *how they feel* and that *self-expression* is *a fundamental human right*. She clearly believes that pop music is a way in which young people communicate how they feel and a form of self-expression for them. If it didn't exist, she says, the result would be a more *ingrained society* (one with fixed, narrow attitudes) and that this would result in *a bigger problem*. She therefore believes that rock music is important in young people's lives because it allows them to express their feelings.

16 B: (lines 129–147)
P describes how, when the Rolling Stones first appeared, people *had to be trained in how to respond to it*. They didn't know how to react to the music and performance at first.
J says that the same is true of Beethoven, that people *had to learn how to deal with* his symphonies when they were first performed.

17 J (lines 148–167)
She says that people don't want to or can't *enter this educational spiral* (go into an educational process of increasing intensity) to get *the one violin place this year* (the only vacancy at college for studying the violin), so they have *gone round that* (found a way of avoiding that by taking a different route). They've said that if there is a *barrier* (something that stops them doing what they want to do, such as exams they can't *get* – pass), they will do what they want in another way, by which she means they will get involved in rock music.
P's point is that rock music is *conformism* (behaving according to the rules of what is acceptable behaviour), not self-expression. He does not refer to musical training, formal or otherwise.

PAPER 4 PART THREE

(see tapescript, p181–182)

18 D: (lines 1–19)
She describes people who *face an audience unaided by a supporting cast* as *brave souls* (people with courage).
A: Her *last foray* (attempt to achieve something) in the world of theatre was a one-woman show (she performed solo) and she *hated every single minute of it* but she doesn't say whether she was successful or not.
B: She says that Susie has *asked herself for many years why anyone would want to face a roomful of strangers entirely alone* but she does not say that she herself has wondered that.
C: She didn't enjoy performing the one-woman show but she doesn't say that she now regrets having done it.

19 D: (lines 20–46)
Half-way through the play, he feels *knackered* (this is a slang word meaning 'very tired'), he's *gasping for breath* (finding it hard to breathe because the play is physically demanding) and he says to himself that he *can't continue*.
A: He says that *the audience can't see* that he is very tired, but he doesn't say that he finds it hard not to show that he is tired.
B: He says that unpredictable things can happen, such as the audience laughing when he is not expecting it, but he does not say that he changes his performance or that it is hard for him to do so.
C: He gives *audience participation* as an example of the *added extras* in his show but he doesn't say that he has trouble getting them to participate.

20 A: (lines 47–65)
He says that it is his *only means of making a living at the moment*, which implies that that is why he does it.
B: He thinks that adults like to be told stories because it reminds them of their mothers reading them stories but he does not say that he does the show in order to bring back story-telling.
C: He says that he has *never seen* his style of performance before, so he does think it may be unique, but that is not why he does the show.
D: Susie says that he plays *all these characters* (a lot of them) and that this *must be exciting* but Guy doesn't comment on this.

21 D: (lines 66–84)
When he looks at his audience and sees, for example, that they are middle-aged and middle-class, he decides to use *material towards their interests* (things to include in his performance that will appeal to them). This illustrates his statement that the

best thing he can do in a performance is *the next thing that comes into my head with that audience on that night*, which suggests that he does not have a fixed plan for what his performance will include when he starts one.
A: He says that people *want to laugh* and that he gives them *an excuse to laugh*. Therefore he is sure they will laugh.
B: He mentions one type of audience but does not express any preference concerning audiences.
C: He tries to think of material that will appeal to a particular audience but he doesn't mention having close contact with them.

22 C: (lines 85–100)
He says that if you have to explain to someone how you want the performance to be, you *end up compromising and losing the objective* (the aim of the performance).
A: He says that having to explain what you want to people causes a problem, but he doesn't refer to having disagreements with anyone.
B: He says that you end up losing *the vibe* (the mood or atmosphere), *the buzz* (the excitement), *the feeling* if you explain to others, but he doesn't say that anyone he worked with was less keen than him.
D: It was the need to explain to others what he wanted that made him decide to work alone, not a feeling that he had been given too much responsibility.

23 B: (lines 101–118)
He says that he has done so many *gigs* (live performances) in which he has got *an encore* (the audience demanding that he continue performing after he has finished because they have enjoyed his performance so much) that he doesn't get great pleasure from that any more; instead he gets upset if it doesn't happen.
A: When he says *I'm getting less and less of that*, 'that' refers to *the enthusiasm, the buzz*, coming off stage with the *hairs on the back of the neck standing up* (extremely excited). He has started to feel like that less.
C: What has become *more commonplace* (less unusual) are *great nights* when he sees his audiences enjoying themselves. He is not saying that it has become so common for performers in general to get encores that it doesn't necessarily mean the performance was good.
D: He says that he doesn't get the same pleasure from it as he used to, not that he doesn't know how to react.

24 B: (lines 52–61)
She says that she *always believed I was perfect* when she worked with other actors and that if anything went wrong she believed that it must have been someone else's fault, (*it's obviously not me*).
A: She went through *a traumatic period* (a time of great unhappiness) when she felt that she couldn't *face being someone* who could make a mistake in front of an audience and she would have *an awful feeling* on stage when she had *lost the audience* but this was all after she started performing solo.
C: She blamed other people when things went wrong; she doesn't say that she expected things to go wrong.
D: She thought she was perfect and never thought she was responsible when things went wrong but she does not actually say that she was brilliant.

25 C:(lines 143–160)
She says that Glenn Gould is an example of someone *who could go into his own state of ecstasy* (extreme pleasure) while he was playing and reach a *level of meditation* (deep thought, involving the exclusion of everything else from the mind).
A: He *groaned and moaned* (made sounds as if he was suffering greatly) but in fact he was in *total ecstasies* (experiencing extreme pleasure), so he was enjoying himself, not finding it difficult to perform on his own. She found it difficult to perform solo, but she doesn't say that he did.
B: He was a musician and she would like to be one rather than being an actor, but she does not compare him with actors.
D: He enjoyed performing and he could communicate his *level of meditation* to an audience, which suggests that they enjoyed his performances, but he is not an example of how enjoyable audiences feel solo performances are in general.

p66–68 PAPER 5

FURTHER PRACTICE AND GUIDANCE (p68)

DESCRIBING MOVEMENT AND POSITION

WALKING

stagger: to walk very unsteadily, in a way that suggests you are going to fall (*Suddenly he staggered and then he collapsed.*)
wander: to walk from place to place in a relaxed, unhurried manner (*wander around the shops*)
meander: to walk slowly, without any apparent purpose and not in a straight line (*meander along the street*)
trudge: to walk slowly in a tired or unenthusiastic way (*trudge reluctantly into work*)
stroll: to walk in a relaxed manner, in a way that suggests a cheerful mood (*stroll in the park on a sunny morning*)
stride: to walk with long steps, perhaps quickly and energetically (*stride along in a determined fashion*)
saunter: to walk very slowly, as if you are in no hurry to reach your destination (*saunter along the road with nothing in mind*)
march: to walk quickly, as if you are keen to reach your destination (*He marched to the manager's office to complain.*)
amble: to walk slowly and in a relaxed manner (*amble along looking at the scenery*)
dawdle: to walk very slowly; to walk so slowly that this annoys the person with you (*Don't dawdle! Hurry up!*)
pace: to walk within a particular place (e.g. a room) in a nervous or impatient manner (*pace up and down the room anxiously waiting for the phone to ring*).

SITTING/LYING

slump: to sit down very heavily (*He slumped into a chair, exhausted*); to sit, leaning forward on a surface with your head down (*When she slumped onto the table, we knew she was ill.*)
slouch: to sit in a lazy manner, with the body not upright (*Don't slouch! Pay attention!*)
recline: to sit or lie in a relaxed manner so that your body is flat or almost flat (*recline on the sofa and watch TV*)
lounge: to sit or lie in a lazy manner (*lounging on the floor*)
perch: to sit on the edge of something or on something that you might fall off (*perch on the edge of a chair/perch on a wall*)

MOVING QUICKLY

tear: to move very quickly or run (*cars tearing along the road; I tore into the hospital.*)
race: to run or move very quickly (*race to the shops just before they close*)
scurry: to run or move quickly, often with short steps (*insects scurrying along*)
dash: to run or move quickly because you are in a hurry (*I dashed along the platform as the train was about to leave.*)
trot: to run slowly and in a relaxed manner (*horses trotting round the field*)
sprint: to run as fast as possible (*sprint at the end of a race*)
dart: to run or move suddenly and quickly (*He darted out of the room when the phone rang.*)
bolt: to run or move quickly and suddenly in order to escape (*The thieves bolted when they heard a police car coming.*)
scamper: to run or move quickly in an excited or frightened way (*The children scampered into the room for their party.*)

MOVING ACROSS

float: to move across air or water without falling or sinking (*leaves floating through the air; a stick floating down the river*)
drift: to move slowly through the air or along the surface of water (*a cloud of smoke drifting through the air; The boat drifted across the lake.*)
slide: to move across a smooth surface (*slide on ice*)
glide: to move slowly and smoothly along a surface or through the air (*glide across the dance floor; birds gliding across the sky*)
waft: (of a sound or smell) to move through the air (*The sound of music/The smell of cooking wafted through the air.*)

TALKING ABOUT PASSAGES

1 **b**

2 **what skysurfers do**
The passage tells the reader what skysurfing involves.

3 **the danger/excitement of it**
The reader is told that you must *have a head for heights* (not be afraid of being high up in the air) to do this sport, that sky surfers *throw themselves* out of planes and balloons, that they travel at high speeds in the air and that some of them do *somersaults and spins* (they turn over and around in the air) before opening their parachutes.

4 **a**

5 **Too right it is**

6 **That it is worth taking a small risk to have a huge amount of enjoyment.**
The phrase *Too right it is* refers to the question in the previous sentence and means 'Yes, it is absolutely true that *taking a small risk for a big buzz* (a huge feeling of excitement and pleasure) is *worth the trouble* '.

7 **c**

8 **There are two changes, from pleasure to surprise, from surprise/fear to relief**

9 **discovering that it was not a crocodile, it was a dolphin**
They were *surprised* and *not sure how to fend off* (defend themselves against the attack of) *what had to be* (what they assumed to be) *a huge crocodile*. In fact, the creature that they saw (the dolphin) had a *cheeky pink nose and squinty little eyes* (its nose looked like that of a playful creature and its eyes were small and looked as if it was having trouble seeing in the light) and they realized that it was *having a bit of fun at our expense* (playing with them and enjoying the fact that it was frightening them).

TEST THREE

p69–71 PAPER 1 SECTION A

FURTHER PRACTICE AND GUIDANCE (p71)

1	A	deposed
	B	expelled
	C	discarded
	D	evicted
2	A	symbol
	B	signal
	C	gesture
	D	hint
3	A	distorted
	B	smudged
	C	blurred
	D	warped
4	A	hummed
	B	muttered
	C	whined
	D	hissed
5	A	alleviated
	B	abated
	C	dwindled
	D	slackened

PAPER 1 SECTION A (TEST)

Note that all the explanations in this part refer to the meaning or use of each option most closely related to the question, not necessarily to the only meaning or use of each option.

One mark per question (Total: 25)

1 **A**: If you are **evicted** *from* a place where you are living, you are forced to leave by the owner.
B: If a political leader or king/queen is *deposed*, they are removed from the leadership or throne by opponents.
C: If you are *expelled from* a country, you are forced to leave it by the authorities.
D: If someone/something is *discarded*, someone gets rid of them because they are no longer wanted or considered useful.
All the options are connected with the idea of 'being forced to leave' or 'getting rid of'; only A refers to leaving a home.

2 **B**: A **gesture** is an action that is intended to indicate a feeling that you have and that you want the other person to be aware of.
A: A *hint* is something that you say or do to indicate that you want the other person to do something, but without stating it directly; if you *drop a hint*, you make this kind of indirect suggestion.
C: A *signal* is an action that tells someone to do/not to do something.
D: A *symbol* is something that represents an idea.
All the options are connected with the idea of 'things which indicate something'; only B refers to an action that indicates a feeling and is not necessarily done in order to get something in return.

3 **A**: If a photograph is **blurred** it is not clear or sharp because it is out of focus.
B: If a sound is *distorted* it doesn't sound as it should and is difficult to hear properly because of some problem.
C: If something is *warped* it is out of shape because of the effects of heat or damp.
D: If something liquid (e.g. writing, paint or make-up) is *smudged* it has spread accidentally because something has touched it.
All the options are connected with the idea of 'being out of shape or not being clear'; only A refers to a photograph being out of focus and therefore not clear.

4 **D**: If you **hum** a tune/song, you sing the melody (but not the words) by making a sound with your mouth closed.
A: If someone whines, they complain by making an irritating sound.
B: If people *boo and hiss*, they show their disapproval by making a loud sound of 'boo' and a sound like the letter 's'.
C: If you *mutter*, you speak very quietly and it is hard to hear what you say.
All the options are connected with the idea of 'making sounds with the mouth'; only D refers to music.

5 **A**: If a storm/noise **abates**, it reduces in strength.
B: If something *dwindles*, it gradually reduces to a small amount/number.
C: If speed *slackens*, it becomes less intense.
D: If a problem/bad feeling is *alleviated*, it is made less unpleasant.
All the options are connected with the idea of 'reducing'; only A refers to wind or a storm.

6 **D**: If it is **out of character** for someone to do something, they do something which is surprising because it is not typical of their normal behaviour and what others would expect them to do.
A: A person's *temperament* is how they tend to react, behave or feel in certain circumstances. (*Her temperament isn't suited to being in charge of other people.*)
B: Your *personality* is the way you are in general, the total of your personal characteristics (*have an unattractive personality*).

C: If it is *in your nature to do* something, you do it because that is what you are like as a person, what your natural character is. (*It's in Ruth's nature to worry a lot.*)

7 B: If you **occupy yourself with** something, you concentrate on it and you are busy doing it.
A: If you *devote yourself to* something, you give most of your time and efforts to it. (*She devoted herself to her family.*)
C: If you *immerse yourself in* something, you are totally involved in or concentrating on it. (*He tends to immerse himself in trivial matters.*)
D: If you *dedicate yourself to* something, you put all your energies into it. (*He wasn't willing to dedicate himself to sport.*)

8 C: **Sole** = only, and is used for emphasizing that there are no others.
A: *Pure* = nothing apart from, and is used for emphasizing the great extent of something (*She felt pure joy.*)
B: *Sheer* = a great deal of, nothing apart from, and is used for emphasizing the great extent of something (*sheer nonsense/hard work/misery/pleasure*).
D: *Mere* = nothing more than, nothing greater or more important than (*He's not the boss, he's a mere assistant.*)

9 D: If you **take issue with** someone on/over/about something, you say that you disagree with them about it and why you disagree.
A: If you *challenge someone to do something*, you tell them to do it and that you believe they will not be able to do it. (*I challenged him to prove that what he was saying was true.*)
B: If you *take offence at* something, you are offended or upset by it. (*She took offence at his rude remarks.*)
C: If you *take exception to* something, you are offended by it and think it is not justified. (*I took exception to the way the manager spoke to me.*)

10 C: If you are **in the wrong**, you have done something wrong or you are to blame for something.
A: If you are *at fault for* something, you are responsible for a mistake or something bad. (*Who was at fault for the disaster?*)
B: If you are *in error*, you have made a mistake. (*I was in error – I added up the bill incorrectly.*)
D: If you *make a slip*, you make a small mistake. (*I made a slip when I was cooking the meal.*)

11 C: If you **settle up** (with someone), you pay them what you owe them.
A: If you *settle for* something, you accept it, although it is not as good as you wanted. (*I couldn't afford the car I wanted so I had to settle for a cheaper model.*)
B: If you *settle on* something, you choose it after considering various choices (*settle on a place to go to on holiday*).
D: If you *settle in*, you become used to a new home/job, etc. and start to feel comfortable in it. (*Have you settled in at work yet?*)

12 A: If something **fits** something, it accords, agrees or is consistent with it.
B: If something *conforms to/with* something, it accords, agrees or is consistent with the way it usually is. (*These statistics don't conform with the usual pattern.*)
C: If something *tallies with* something, it is consistent with it, it does not differ from it. (*What he said today doesn't tally with what he told me yesterday.*)
D: If something *corresponds to/with* something, it isn't different from it, it is consistent with it. (*The contract didn't correspond with what had previously been agreed.*)

13 B: If you **don't take kindly** to something, your reaction is that you don't like or appreciate it personally.
A: If you are *pleasantly surprised* by something, it is a nice surprise for you.
C: If you react to something *cheerfully*, you do not get unhappy or angry about it. (*He accepted the bad news cheerfully.*)
D: If you react *agreeably* to something, you react pleasantly and in a friendly manner (*react agreeably to a request for help*).

14 D: **Failing** something = if something doesn't happen
A: If you *leave* something, you don't do it or pay attention to it, but may do so in the future. (*Let's leave that decision until later.*)
B: If you *exclude* someone/something, you do not include them in what you are referring to. (*I dislike everyone in this office, excluding you.*)
C: If you *omit* something, you do not include it, you leave it out (*omit certain details from an account*).

15 D: If you **run something/someone down**, you criticize them very strongly and say that they are terrible or worthless.
A: If you *hold down a job*, you keep the job, perhaps despite the fact that it is hard to do so. (*He's so inefficient that it's amazing he holds down a job.*)
B: If a building is *pulled down*, it is demolished or destroyed by workmen.
C: If you *talk down to* someone, you talk to them in a manner that indicates that you consider them inferior or stupid (*politicians talking down to the public*).

16 C: If you are **held in high regard** by someone, they have a great deal of respect for you.
A: If you *have a reputation for* something, you are known for it (*have a reputation for doing good work*).
B: If someone *has respect for* you, they feel that you are a good person who can be admired or should be treated well (*have respect for your parents*).
D: If someone/something is *of + adjective + renown*, it is famous in a certain way (*a city of great/international renown*).

17 A: **Presumably** = it can be assumed that...
B: *Supposedly* = it is said that something is the case, but it might not really be the case (*She is supposedly an expert on this subject.*)
C: *Assuming* = 'if', when it is considered that something is very likely to happen (*Assuming nothing goes wrong, I'll see you at 8.*)
D: *Granted* = accepting that something is the case (*Granted that he was in a bad mood, he behaved quite well.*)

18 B: If you **make it plain** that something is the case, you make it absolutely clear so that there can be no misunderstanding.
A: *Distinct* = clear and noticeable (*There was a distinct atmosphere of hostility in the room.*)
C: If you are *frank* when you speak, you are totally honest (*make a frank statement/ admission*).
D: If you are *straight with someone/about something*, you are honest and tell the truth. (*Be straight with me – tell me what you really think.*)

19 D: If a thought **enters your mind**, you have that thought.
A: If something *strikes you*, you suddenly realize it or think it. (*The reality of the situation struck her.*)
B: If *it dawns on you that...* , you suddenly realize something that perhaps you should have realized before. (*It dawned on me that I was making a big mistake.*)
C: If *it occurs to you that...*, you realize or think that something is the case. (*It occurs to me that I haven't phoned Joe for ages.*)

20 A: If something **has a/no bearing on** something, it has an/no effect or influence on it.
B: If something is *of no relevance to* something, it has no connection with it (*evidence that is of no relevance to the case*).
C: If something is *of no significance to something*, it has no importance or influence.
D: *The repercussions of something on something* are the serious consequences or results of it. (*He had to consider the repercussions of giving up his job on his family.*)

21 D: If something happens **on a regular basis**, it happens regularly.
A: If something bad is *persistent*, it happens continuously, without stopping, or is repeated very frequently (*persistent rain/pain/rumours*).
B: If something is *commonplace*, it is so common that it is not particularly interesting. (*Cottages like that one are commonplace in this area.*)
C: A *standard* action is one that is always carried out in the same way (*standard procedures*).

22 C: If you **take a liking to** something, your reaction is that you start to like it.
A: If you *have (an) affection for someone/something*, you have a pleasant feeling of liking them/it. (*I will always have affection for my home town.*)
B: If you *have (a) fondness for someone/something*, you have a special feeling of liking them/it. (*She has a fondness for her old school friends.*)
D: If something *holds an attraction for* you, you find it attractive or appealing. (*Golf holds no attraction for me.*)

23 B: **In the light of** = because of something that has happened or exists.
A: *In view of* = considering, because of, as a result of (*In view of the time, I think we'd better leave now.*)
C: *Taking (something) into consideration* = considering because it is something that needs to be considered when forming an opinion (*Taking the cost into consideration, it wasn't the best choice.*)
D: *On the grounds of* = because of, for this reason (*He got the job on the grounds of his previous experience.*)

24 B: If you **switch off**, you relax after a period of hard work, pressure, concentration, etc.
A: If you *give in*, you stop trying to do something because it is too hard. (*She was determined to succeed and nothing could make her give in.*)
C: If you *let out* a sound, you make that sound because you cannot stop yourself from doing so (*let out a cry*).
D: If you *wind up* something, you bring it to an end (*wind up a meeting*); if you *wind down*, you relax after working hard, being under pressure, etc. (*wind down after a hard day's work*).

25 A: If something **puts your mind at rest/ease**, it stops you worrying or being nervous.
B: If something is *a comfort to you*, it makes you feel less worried or unhappy. (*Their kindness during that awful time was a great comfort to me.*)
C: *Calm* = being or showing that you are untroubled or relaxed (*I envy his calm under pressure.*)
D: If something is *a relief to* you, it causes you to stop being worried. (*It was a relief to me to find that in fact nothing was wrong.*)

p72–77 PAPER 1 SECTION B

Two marks per question (Total: 30)

FIRST PASSAGE

FURTHER PRACTICE AND GUIDANCE (p74–75)

For explanations, see the explanations to the questions in the test that follow.

Question 26

1 we aren't told **2** yes **3** no **4** yes (see explanation of Question 26 below)

Question 27

1 c **2** b

Question 28

1 yes **2** c **3** c **4** yes

Question 29

(for evidence, see Question 29 below)

1 yes **2** no **3** no **4** yes

Question 30

1 c **2** less likely **3** no **4** no

FIRST PASSAGE (TEST)

26 A: (see first paragraph)
Zen had been expecting *some ostentatious pleasure pavilion* (a place created to impress others with its owner's wealth and to satisfy all the desires of its owner) but he was surprised that the trees, shrubs and plants had been *artfully* (skilfully) *arranged*, that the guardhouse had *some of the rustic* (typical of the pleasant, simple aspects of the countryside) *pleasures of the country cottage* and he was *inspired* (impressed by, reacting with enthusiasm to) *by the beauty of the spot*. He had therefore been expecting not to like the place but he did like it.
B: It was an *artificial island* but there is no suggestion that Zen did not already know this or that this fact surprised him.
C: There was a guardhouse (a military building for guards or prisoners), and Zen noticed that it had been *skilfully transformed into a residence* (a place to live in) that combined the *military severity* of the original building with the pleasures of a country cottage. Its appearance therefore surprised him but there is no suggestion that its actual presence surprised him.
D: He was *inspired less by the sense that there was anything to be discovered than by the beauty of the spot*. This means that its beauty interested him more than the feeling that he would find out anything there. He obviously looked at the trees, shrubs, plants and guardhouse and there is nothing to suggest that he had expected to see more things there.

27 B: (lines 13–30)
Zen *sniffed sceptically. as though this were a transparent fiction* (he breathed in through his nose in a way that indicated he didn't believe Calderan and that Calderan's story was obviously not true); his *sneer indicated the value he ascribed to alibis which depended on the corroboration of the suspect's relations* (the expression of contempt on his face showed that he placed no value on suspects' stories that they were somewhere else when a crime was committed if only their relatives supported this story). Therefore, Zen's actions were intended to make Calderan think that Zen was a perceptive man who could tell when people weren't telling the truth.
A: Zen *lit a cigarette with elaborate nonchalance* (in a way that deliberately indicated he was extremely relaxed); he therefore tried to create the impression of being very relaxed, he didn't try to appear full of energy.
C: He *barked* and *snapped*, which means that he questioned Calderan in a brief and angry way. He told him that he realized Calderan was afraid *the two accounts won't tally* (the story he told before and the version he would give now wouldn't be the same) because he had told a *pack of lies* (a series of lies) – Zen therefore was trying to make Calderan think he already knew the truth, not that he was likely to say or do things suddenly without having thought about them.
D: Zen has obviously decided to frighten Calderan but there is no suggestion that he wants him to think that his methods of questioning are any different from any other policeman. He doesn't compare himself with any of his colleagues.

28 B: (lines 29–34)
Zen was *browbeating* him (frightening him by threatening him and questioning him very aggressively) because he wanted to make him *sweat a little in return for his surly welcome* (feel nervous or scared as revenge for the fact he had been unfriendly and hostile to Zen when they first met).
A: Zen tells Calderan that he knows he is lying and asks him why he is doing so, but it is unlikely that Zen really believes this (if he did, he

wouldn't have been *appalled* – shocked and disgusted – at himself for the way he was questioning him) and it is not the reason why he carries on questioning him – he does that because he has taken a dislike to him.
C: Zen was obviously experienced in making suspects feel uncomfortable (he had *been a policeman too long not to try* to do so with Calderan) and he wanted to make Calderan uncomfortable but he didn't keep questioning him because he enjoyed frightening suspects in general, he did it because he was annoyed with him.
D: Calderan's first account had been that he went to his sister's that Tuesday (lines 26–28) and he says the same thing to Zen (lines 33–34).

29 D: (look at the references to Calderan in lines 13–39)
Calderan responds to the question 'What are you doing here?' as if Zen had no right to ask him the question; he maintains emphatically that he has not lied (*I told them the truth; I'm not protecting anyone*). At the end he *confronted Zen openly*, demanding to know why he had come and why he was *raking over all this again* (bringing up a subject that belonged in the past). All of this suggests that he feels he is being unfairly treated by Zen, is annoyed about this, makes this clear and defends himself.
A: He makes it clear that the story he told about where he had been that day is true and there is no suggestion in the passage either that it isn't true or that he is hiding something.
B: He seems to understand very clearly what is happening – he realizes that Zen is accusing him of lying and he is angry rather than confused about this. He does not hesitate when replying or have trouble understanding the implications of what Zen is saying.
C: Zen is trying to frighten him but he is angry not afraid. He has an expression of *mute hostility* (silent aggression) which does not change and he confronts Zen openly at the end. There is nothing to suggest he is frightened of Zen at any point.

30 B: (see last paragraph)
Since the case *had already been fully investigated* when *clues and memories were still fresh*, Zen concluded that he had no hope of solving the mystery now because it was three months later and therefore too late. His visit had therefore been pointless because it had made his investigation even more of *a mockery* (a foolish and pointless thing).
A: Since any clues were no longer *fresh*, Zen concluded that he had no hope of finding out anything new. He didn't feel that he had failed to notice something that would lead to him solving the mystery.
C: Zen realized he was unlikely to solve the mystery because memories were no longer fresh (people involved could not remember certain things); there is no suggestion that he thought he would have learnt something if he had asked Calderan different questions.
D: His conversation with Calderan had been unpleasant and ended with *further acrimonious exhanges* (more angry conversation between them) but he had left in a *relatively dignified manner* (calmly and without looking too foolish) and there is no suggestion that there would be any further consequences of this visit.

SECOND PASSAGE

31 A: (see first paragraph)
The writer says that there are *those of us* (some people, including the writer), who *deride ghost-writing* (dismiss as silly or mock the practice of famous people having their autobiographies written for them by authors).
B: Everything went well at the beginning for Rosemary Kingsland and then things started to go wrong, but the writer doesn't imply that this was an unusual experience for a ghost-writer.
C: PJ Proby had a *disreputable early career* (one which gave him a bad reputation) but the writer doesn't imply that his life story is uninteresting or that nobody will be interested in it.
D: The writer had felt that it was an easy job that involved *simultaneously switching on the flattery and the tape-recorder* (paying compliments to the person whose book it is and simply sitting there while they talk into the tape-recorder). But what happened with Rosemary Kingsland and PJ Proby *is a lesson* to her and others who had that view (it shows them that they were wrong).

32 C: (see second paragraph)
Proby *is prone to terrible mood swings* (his mood tends to keep changing all the time). Sometimes they *would start to talk and he would suddenly explode like a volcano* (without warning he would lose his temper and start shouting and screaming).
A: We are not told what made him lose his temper, but it is not stated that it was because she wanted him to talk about things he didn't want to talk about.
B: He did have financial expectations, the writer clearly felt were unrealistic (he wanted 1 million) but this did not *unduly bother* her (this did not particularly worry her) because she left it to the agent to deal with that matter (to *sort that one out*).
D: She *trusted* (expected and believed) that the *hefty* (enormous and heavy) book he was expecting could be cut from 400,00 words to 120,000 *without upsetting him*. There is therefore no suggestion that he has argued about reducing the length of the book.

33 D: (see third paragraph)
She decided to *stand her ground* (not give up, continue doing what she was doing) because by doing so she thought *At least.... I'd get the book* (At least I will have produced a book). This means that, despite all the problems, there will be a concrete result and this is what she wants and why she has persisted.
A: She knows that PJ thinks that he could write the book better, but there is nothing to suggest that she thinks that she is a good writer or that she is more qualified than anyone else to write his life story.
B: PJ thinks he *could have done it all better himself* but there is no suggestion that she wants to make him realize that she can write it better than he could.
C: She simply wants to finish the book; she does not comment on whether she thinks it will be good or not.

34 B: (see fourth paragraph)
Although she says he wasn't bad to have as a guest in her house, there were still *unexpected outbursts* (times when he suddenly lost his temper and started shouting) and when *things got too much for* her (when she couldn't tolerate the situation any longer), she took him back to London.
A: He was *required to talk about himself* for the book and the rest of the time he was *ruminating* (thinking deeply) and listening to music in his room but it is not suggested that he did this because he didn't want to talk about anything but himself.
C: PJ didn't like sitting at a dinner table with her family and there were outbursts when they had dinner, but she doesn't refer to what her family thought of PJ.
D: He did spend time on his own, but there is nothing to suggest that he disliked doing so.

35 A: (see last paragraph)
He calls himself *colourful*, which means interesting and unusual.
B: He says that he is *difficult* (difficult to deal with) but he doesn't say that he has personal problems. Kingsland has acted as *part-time mother-confessor, psychologist and interviewer* so it seems likely that he has discussed matters that trouble him and personal

problems with her but he doesn't describe himself as a troubled person.
C: He *admits* that he is not easy-going and that he is difficult, so he agrees with other people's descriptions of him.
D: He doesn't say he is totally unlike anyone else, just that he is *colourful*.

THIRD PASSAGE

36 A: (see first paragraph)
Orwell described stamp-collectors in a way that suggests he didn't like them (they are *a strange, silent, fish-like breed*, according to him) and their hobby *held little interest for* him, but a colleague's *most vivid* (clearest and strongest) image of Orwell at that time is of him watching a small boy buying stamps, which indicates some interest. The writer introduces this memory with the word *Interestingly*, which suggests that this image contrasts with what was described before (Orwell's low opinion of stamp-collectors and lack of interest in their hobby).
B: Orwell didn't like stamp-collectors but there is no mention of him being unfriendly to anyone; he watched the boy but we are not told that he said anything to him or any other child.
C: He noticed that stamp-collectors were all men and concluded that women couldn't see the attraction of it; as he had a low opinion of collecting he evidently agreed with women on this matter. However, there is no reference to him disliking women.
D: Orwell generalized about all stamp-collectors and about women. However, we are not told that such judgements were untypical of him because he was normally cautious or that these views are examples of a tendency to make judgements too rapidly, without enough evidence to justify them.

37 C: (lines 10–17)
By all accounts he did his job well = everyone who mentioned whether he was good at the job or not said that he did it well.
A: He was *more than a little annoyed by* some of the customers and described them as *a nuisance* (an annoying problem). There is no evidence in the passage that he actually lost his temper with them, though.
B: Although some customers annoyed him, there is no evidence that he had previously had a different attitude towards people in general.
D: It is true that *All types of customer frequented the place* (people of all kinds went into the shop regularly), from *baronets* (members of the aristocracy) to *bus-conductors* (they are meant as an example of the working class). We are not told, however, that the fact that people of all social classes went there surprised Orwell. What did astonish him was how many people ordered books but never came to collect them.

38 D: (lines 16–21)
Orwell concluded that ordering books *was satisfaction enough for them* (gave them as much satisfaction as they needed) because it gave them *the illusion that they were spending real money* (the false notion that they had enough money to spend on books). Presumably he decided that they *never intended to return* to collect and pay for them because they couldn't really afford them.
A: People ordering books and not collecting them *caused him unnecessary trouble* and were a *nuisance*; perhaps it was the same for other members of staff but there is no reference to the way in which these people ordered books, only to the fact that they did so.
B: He concluded that they ordered books because it made them feel that they had money they didn't really have but it is not suggested that they wanted the staff to believe this. We are not told that they wanted to impress the staff, only that they got personal satisfaction from ordering books.
C: There is no suggestion that these people felt that they should order a book or felt under any pressure to do so.

39 C: (lines 22–28)
If something is *sobering*, it makes you think seriously and lose your previous, more idealistic or optimistic notions. Working in the shop reminded him that *publishing was a business, not a philanthropic endeavour* (its aim was to make money not to give it away as an act of charity or kindness). He realized that books were *a commodity* (a product that is made to be sold) and that, just like other products such as sausages, they were produced in large numbers and *devoured rapidly* (used up very quickly).
A: He gained *real insights into* (deep knowledge of) readers' tastes and saw that books were produced to serve *the particular appetites of certain consumers* (to satisfy the preferences of certain people buying them) but it is not suggested that working there taught him that people were unpredictable.
B: He wanted to see books as being *precious and profound* (valuable and deeply serious) but realized they were like any common product. However, he makes no mention of marketing techniques.
D: He learnt that books were like sausages in the sense that they were products. This may have affected his attitude as a writer (we learn that he was a writer because of the reference to his essay at the beginning of the second paragraph) but there is no reference to him drawing any conclusions about how much money he might earn from writing.

40 C: (lines 28–34)
He described detective novels as a *frightful torrent of trash* (a terrible mass of rubbish) and to emphasize just how great the amount of this rubbish was he referred to how much total area the number of pages in them would cover (nearly three-quarters of an acre is clearly meant to represent a very large area of land).
A: Clearly they were popular because of the number of pages read every year but that is not why he mentions this large amount of paper.
B: The person who read four or five detective novels could remember everything about the books he read – it was *stored for ever in his memory*. There is no mention of Orwell's memory or any pride he might have had in it.
D: It is not the length of detective novels themselves that Orwell comments on but the total number of pages of all of them added together. That it is a large number is his point, not that the novels would be better if they were shorter; he thinks they are *trash* anyway. Moreover, there is no reference to how long detective novels tended to be.

PAPER 1:

SECTION A	25 marks
SECTION B	30 marks
TOTAL	55 marks

To be converted into a score out of 40 marks.

p78–80 PAPER 2

Each composition is given a mark out of 20. The total of the two compositions is then divided by two to give an overall score for the paper out of 20.

FURTHER PRACTICE AND GUIDANCE (p80)

Assesment of sample composition

1 **Content**
The composition answers the question very well, both describing a series of events and what the lasting impression was. There is nothing irrelevant and no repetition.

2 **Organization**
This is a very well-organized composition. The first paragraph gives the background to attending the event, the second, third and fourth paragraphs present the different stages of the event and the final paragraph describes the lasting impression.

3 **Linking**
Most of the linking is fairly simple but it is hard to use more sophisticated linking when describing a series of events so this is not a problem. The use of *but, nonetheless* in the fourth paragraph is very good.

4 **Use of vocabulary**
There is some very good use of vocabulary: *homesick* and *an imposed sort of 'exile'* (being forced to live abroad) in the first paragraph; *bearing* and *actual* in the second paragraph; *my attention was grabbed* and *'alien'* (foreigner, in this context) in the third paragraph. There are a few minor vocabulary mistakes: in the second paragraph *pilots* should be *drivers* (this candidate called them *drivers* earlier in the paragraph) and *catalogue* should be *programme* because it is at a sports event; in the fourth paragraph, the phrase is *in somebody's hands* (depending on somebody), not *on* and it should say *sitting in a good place* not *on*.

5 **Use of grammar**
There are very few grammatical errors: in the fourth paragraph, there should not be *a* before fifth and second place; in the last paragraph, it should say *the loudest I have/had ever heard*. Apart from that, the structures used are more than simple and they are all used accurately. A high level of grammatical knowledge is shown, for example in the use of the *-ing* clause in the first sentence of the second paragraph.

6 **Style**
The composition flows very well and communicates very well the candidate's experiences when attending this event.

This is a very good composition which fully addresses the task set. There are very few errors and there is much natural and fluent use of language. It would be given a mark of 15–17 out of 20.

p81–85 PAPER 3 SECTION A

PART 1 FURTHER PRACTICE AND GUIDANCE (p82)

For explanations, see the explanations for the questions in the test below.

1 B	11 B
2 C	12 C
3 A	13 B
4 A	14 D
5 D	15 D
6 D	16 A
7 C	17 B
8 C	18 C
9 B	19 D
10 A	20 B

PAPER 3 SECTION A

PART 1 (TEST)

One mark per question (Total: 20)

1 **Once/Having**: *Once assembled/Having assembled* = after/when they have assembled

2 **if/albeit**: *If/albeit* in this context = although it is true that...

3 **stands**: If letters *stand for* something, they are the first letters of each word.

4 **behind**: *The thinking behind* something is the ideas that have caused it to exist or happen in the form that it does.

5 **but**: In a sentence like this, where a negative is contrasted with a positive, *but* follows what is not the case and introduces what is the case.

6 **around/about**: How you *get around/about* is how you travel from place to place.

7 **makes**: *It* here refers to *cycling*, so the phrase means *Cycling makes their streets more pleasant*.

8 **gets/starts**: If something *gets/starts you thinking*, it causes you to consider something that you have not thought about before.

9 **expect(s)**: The structure after the gap (*object + infinitive*) makes other verbs of similar meaning impossible (*believe/think, etc.* would all have to be followed by a '*that* clause'). CHARM, like most words describing a group of people viewed as one unit, can be singular (a unit) or plural (a number of people).

10 **least**: *At least until October* = the numbers will continue to grow but may not continue to grow when October arrives (the growth in numbers may stop in October)

11 **put**: If something *puts you off*, it makes you not want to do something, it discourages you.

12 **which**: *In which* = in the vacuum that is created in front of the cyclists

13 **surely**: If you begin a question with *Surely*, you are saying that you assume that something is the case and that you would have difficulty believing that it is not the case. Another way of doing this is to begin the question with a negative auxiliary (*Don't you know about this?* = surely you know about this). Note that answers such as *nevertheless* are not possible because of the question mark.

14 **when**: *When faced* = when they are faced, on being faced

15 **point**: If you *make a point of doing* something, you make sure that you do it because you want it to have a particular effect.

16 **majority**: *The vast majority of* something is almost all of it or almost every one of them.

17 **foremost**: When you are talking about the relative importance of various things, the phrase *first and foremost* is used to talk about the most important one and to emphasize that it is more important than all others.

18 **way**: *Your way of doing* something is how you do it, how you achieve it, or how you cause it to happen.

19 **what**: The structure *What a* is used to emphasize the great extent of something, in this case how bad the roads are – they are *a hideous mess* (in a terrible state). This structure can be used in exclamations with this meaning. (*What a lovely present!/What peculiar people!*)

20 **rest**: *The rest of the time* is in contrast to the *couple of hours a month* mentioned at the beginning of the sentence. The roads are safe when CHARM are in them; at all other times they are *a hideous mess*.

PAPER 3 SECTION A

PART 2 FURTHER PRACTICE AND GUIDANCE (p84)

For explanations, see the explanations for the questions in the test below.

a 3

b 2

c 1

d 4

e 3

f 1

g 2

h 2

PAPER 3 SECTION A

PART 2 (TEST)

One mark per word or phrase in bold (Total: 12)

The numbers refer to the incorrect options in the Further Practice and Guidance questions.

a **be given** (1) **to ways** (1) of improving the transport system. (2 marks)
Firstly, the verb must be changed from a present active modal one (*We must think*) to a present passive modal one (*Thought must be...*). If you *think about* something, you *give thought to it*.
1 The verb has been inverted, with the modal before the subject, but it is still active and *about* should be *to*.
2 *Had for* should be *given to*.
4 *Taken on* should be *given to*.

b **no better pianist than him** (1) in the whole country OR **nobody/no-one who is a better pianist than him** (1) in the whole country. (1 mark)
The structures *there is no better x than y* and *there is nobody/no-one/ nothing/ nowhere who/that is a better x than y* can both be used instead of the superlative structure. These structures can be used with other comparatives. (*There is no more boring place than this./There is nowhere that is more boring than this.*)
1 This is correct except that *a* is missing before *pianist*.
3 The phrase *no such good* is impossible in any circumstances.
4 The phrase *nobody so good a* is also impossible in any circumstances.

c **you'd/you had listened/been listening to what I told you earlier** (1), **you wouldn't be asking these questions** (1). (2 marks)
This is a mixed conditional involving a past cause (*you didn't listen*) and a present continuous result (*You're asking these questions*).
The past cause must therefore be changed into the form of the third conditional (the past perfect tense is used and the verb changes from negative to positive). The present continuous result must be changed into the form of the second conditional (*would be doing* is used and the positive verb becomes negative).
2 The first part is in second conditional form (referring to the present); the second part is in third conditional form (referring to the past).
3 The first part is correct; the second part is in third conditional form (referring to the past).
4 The first part is incorrectly in second conditional form (in this case referring to present continuous time); the second part is also in in second conditional form, but it is not a continuous verb form as in the original sentence (this means it refers to habitual action rather than action at this moment, which is what the original sentence refers to).

d **as/though I was to pay** (1) such a high price, I had no choice. (1 mark)
This structure is *adjective + as/though + subject + verb*. It is another way of expressing a sentence which is a contrast, a sentence with the idea of 'but' in it (*Although I was tired... = Tired as/though I was ...* = I was tired but...). If you *don't want to do* something, you *are reluctant to do it*.
1 The verb has been inverted, with the subject after the verb and *as/though* are missing.
2 *That* should be *as/though*.
3 *I was* is in the wrong place; *as/though* is missing; *for paying* should be *to pay*.

e **wasn't much time/long/a long time** (1) **left/remaining/to go** (1) when the winning goal was scored. (2 marks)
Only a few minutes must be changed to a negative phrase with the same meaning (*not long/not much time/not a long time/not more than a few minutes*). *Remained* must be changed to *remaining*; the phrase *something remaining* is used to describe how much remains when the rest has gone or been used up. (*With an hour remaining before it would have been too late, the money arrived./There are only five people remaining from the original department.*) *Left* can be used with exactly the same meaning as *remaining*. *To go* can only be used with the meaning 'before the end'; it is appropriate here since it refers to the end of the match.
1 *Many minutes* = plural; the given verb (*wasn't*) is singular.
2 *Remained* should be *remaining*.
4 *A* is missing before *long*; the structure *to be long time* is not possible in any circumstances.

f **much the money** (1) **as the challenge** (1) that appealed to me about the job. OR **so much the money that appealed to me about the job** (1) **as the challenge** (1). (2 marks)
The structure *not so much one thing as another* is used to say that one thing is not as important as another.
2 *So as to* = in order to; this does not make sense in a comparative sentence, followed by *than*.
3 The definite article is missing before *money* and *challenge*.
4 *Much* is missing after *so*; adjectives (*financial* and *challenging* here) cannot be the subject of verbs.

g **me responsible for** (1) your financial problems. (1 mark)
If you *hold somebody responsible for something*, you blame them for it or believe that they are responsible for it.
1 *Hold out blame* is not a correct collocation.
3 *Responsible* cannot be used as a noun.
4 *Hold me to blame* is not a correct collocation; *as* is also incorrect.

h **of me/my being/getting promoted** (1) this year. (1 mark)
If *there is no question of something happening*, it definitely will not happen; if *there is no question of someone doing something*, they definitely won't do it.
1 If *there is no question that something will happen*, it definitely will happen; if *there is no question that someone will do something*, they definitely will do it.
3 An infinitive cannot be used after *no question*.
4 *For someone + infinitive* cannot be used after *no question*.

PAPER 3 SECTION A

PART 3

One mark per question (Total: 6)

a **down with (the)**
If you *come down with* an illness, you catch it and start to feel ill. Influenza is commonly known as either *flu* or *the flu*.

b **to say**
Needless to say = it is not necessary to say this because it is obvious, totally expected or predictable. *Yet again* indicates that Harry often arrives late; it is therefore not at all surprising that he did so again.

c **were we**
The structure here is *so + adjective + verb + subject* (the subject and verb are in reverse order) + *that*. It is used for emphasizing to how great an extent the adjective is the case (how stunned we were).

d **from start to**
From start to finish = throughout all of something, from the beginning to the end of something

e **no means**
By no means = *not at all* (when emphasizing that something is really not the case).

f **need of**
If you are *badly in need of* something, you need it very much and are suffering because of not having it.

PAPER 3 SECTION A

PART 4

One mark per word or phrase in bold (Total: 12)

a **Are you questioning my** (1) **honesty** (1)**?** (2 marks)
If you *question something*, you express or imply doubts about it or you don't believe or accept that it is the case. In this structure, *question* is followed by a noun, so *dishonest* must be changed to *honesty*.

b **He was shouting at the top of his voice.** (1 mark)
If you make a sound *at the top of your voice*, you make a very loud vocal sound.

c **In the forthcoming biography of him, he is/will be portrayed** (1) **as (being) an arrogant and selfish man/as (being) arrogant and selfish** (1).
(2 marks)
Firstly, the verb in the original sentence is in the future but *portrayed* is a past simple verb or a past participle. Therefore, a passive must be formed (if *portrayed* is used as an active past simple or as part of a present perfect or past perfect, the verb tense will differ from the meaning of the original sentence). Therefore a future or present passive must be formed. Secondly, for the sentence to make sense *The forthcoming biography* will have to become *In the forthcoming biography*. Thirdly, the structure after *portray* must be *portray someone as (being/doing) something*.

d **It has not escaped** (1) **me/my attention/my notice** (1) **that Rebeca is upset about something.** OR **The fact that Rebecca is upset about something has not escaped** (1) **me/my attention/my notice.** (2 marks)
If something *does not escape you/your attention/your notice*, you do not fail to notice it.

e **Her latest novel isn't on a par** (1) **with her previous one** (1). (2 marks)
If something *isn't on a par with* something else, it is not of the same standard or not as good as it.

f **This is my first attempt at cooking this dish.** (1 mark)
An attempt at something/doing something is an occasion when someone tries to do something. *Your first attempt* is the first time you try to do something.

g **I don't dislike Ronnie, it's just that he annoys me sometimes.** (1 mark)
This structure is as follows: a negative statement that something is not the case + *it's just that* followed by a statement modifying the first one by saying that the first one is not entirely true.

h **There are all manner of tourist attractions** (1) **in this part of the country.** (1 mark)
All manner of + plural/uncountable noun = a very large number of/many different kinds of. *Tourist attractions* are plural, so the verb must be changed from singular to plural.

SECTION A:

QUESTION 1	20 marks
QUESTION 2	12 marks
QUESTION 3	6 marks
QUESTION 4	12 marks
TOTAL	50 marks

p86–91 PAPER 3 SECTION B

FURTHER PRACTICE AND GUIDANCE (p89)

Questions a–n

For explanations, see the explanations for the questions in the test below.

a 1 You should feel sorry for science writers because they are unfortunate people.
2 most people don't understand it/most people find it difficult

b/c people who are not involved in the world of science/people who are not scientists

f 1 b
2 d

g science that people in general know about

i to examine it/to admire (the beauty of) it

l two

m b

j a

k c

PAPER 3 SECTION B (TEST)

Answers similar to or covering the same points as those given here are acceptable provided that they are clearly expressed.

a **Feynman says that you have to understand the language of mathematics to appreciate science but many people have trouble understanding it** (1) **so science writers have a hard job and one should feel sorry for them** (1).
(2 marks)
Pity the poor science writer = feel sympathy for the unfortunate science writer

b **you can't explain either of them to people who are not capable of appreciating/understanding them**
(1 mark)
Deaf ears = people who can't hear at all or who can't appreciate music; *convey* = communicate. *'The other culture'* is clearly used here to describe people who are not involved in science.

c **if you aren't a scientist, you can't understand/appreciate science**
(1 mark)
Lay = non-specialist; the word *layman* is used to describe someone who is not an expert on something technical; *the lay culture* is clearly used here with the same meaning as *the other culture* (see b).

d **that it is not possible to translate one language into another perfectly**
(1 mark)
However imperfectly = no matter how imperfectly this is done, although this is done to some extent imperfectly. This phrase refers to the act of translating one language, mathematics, into another, English.

e **that science writing involves imprecise/ insubstantial/abstract things** (1) **whereas science involves precise/substantial/concrete things**
(1) (2 marks)
Science writers have to *fall back on* (use because there is no alternative) *metaphor and poetry* (images to describe things in an imaginative and interesting way) like *puffs of gauze* (small quantities of light fabric). On the other hand, scientists work with numbers and equations *like rods of steel* (strong metal bars).

f **having to reach a compromise which involves presenting a big subject in**

an inadequate way (1 mark)
Science writers are *haunted by* (constantly troubled by) *the spectre of* (the terrible prospect of) a compromise involving having to *filter a lush panorama through a flawed lens* (this is a photographic description, meaning having to produce an image of a wide view of a scene – a *panorama* – with a lot of strong colours in it – *lush* – using a camera that has a *lens* – the glass part of a camera that you look through – that is not in perfect condition – is *flawed*).

g **because we have more contact with and knowledge of science in our personal lives and know how much effect it has had on us** (1 mark)
Absurd = ridiculous. The writer says that *we are more deeply and knowledgeably embedded in a scientific world than ever before* – people in general are more firmly fixed in or involved in (*embedded in*) the world of science than they ever have been and know more about it than they ever have done.

h **because it looks very complicated/we don't understand it at all** (1 mark)
If you *quiver*, you shake or tremble because you are afraid. An *equation* is a type of mathematical calculation. The writer is saying that we would be unable to deal with an equation but we do know how much science changes our lives.

i **he decided not just to explain the ideas/the finished product but to tell the story of how some scientists changed people's understanding of the world** (1 mark)
His main aim was not to explain what had been discovered, as if examining or admiring a finished *objet d'art* (work of art) – if you hold something up to the light, you hold it in a place where the light enables you to see it very clearly. His main aim was to tell the *dramatic story* of what these people did.

j **people with unorthodox views/methods in their profession/area of work** (1 mark)
Mavericks are people who don't follow the conventional methods or views. A *field* in this context is a profession or a part of a profession.

k **clear/straightforward** (1 mark)
If something is *cut and dried*, it is fixed, totally clear and there are no further complications or confusions involved.

l **they either avoid science completely in an attempt to be popular** (1) **or they consist only of technical explanations joined together** (1)
(2 marks)
They are either *gross popularizations* – obvious and poor attempts to be popular with the general public – or *stitched together collections of technical explication* – separate pieces of technical explanation joined together with no real connection between them.

m **they were full of entertaining/amusing stories but they left out the scientific work that in fact he was obsessed with** (1 mark)
They were *anecdotal* – they told amusing but unimportant stories for entertainmnent – but *omitted* – didn't include, left out – the scientific work that in fact he *breathed from morning to night* – was completely involved with, that occupied all his time and thoughts.

n **he didn't limit himself to Feynman's scientific work** (1), **he considered this in relation to wider matters** (1)
(2 marks)
Feynman's life *encompassed* (included/involved) much more than his *profound* (big and important) contributions to science. The writer found himself *drawn into* (found that in writing the book he was forced to get involved with) much wider issues than the *specific problems* Feynman dealt with. He then lists these much bigger issues.

Questions a–n: Total 18 marks

PAPER 3 SECTION B

FURTHER PRACTICE AND GUIDANCE (p90)

WRITING A SUMMARY

The sections of the text which are relevant and could be used for your summary are:

C/D/E/G/H/J/K

The other sections do not deal with misconceptions.

PAPER 3 SECTION B

SUMMARY (TEST)

o *One mark each for the inclusion of the following points or points similar to them (in any order). The sections referred to are those in the text on page 90.*

1 **People believe that science is separate from them and that if you're not a scientist you can't understand it but in fact people know more about science now than ever before.**
SECTION C (see also question (c) and the explanation for it) and SECTION G (see also question (g) and the explanation for it).

2 **Science isn't as straightforward as we learn it at school because scientists make mistakes and get confused.**
SECTION J (see also question (k) and the explanation for it).

3 **It is wrong to think that science writers have to make science popular by translating it.**
SECTION D and SECTION H

4 **It is not true that science writing has to adopt a particular style.**
SECTION E (see also question (e) and the explanation for it) and SECTION K (see also questions (l) and (m) and the explanations for them).

Total: 4 marks
Plus a maximum of 8 marks for general impression of summary skills, based on the following criteria:
- relevance
- general level of fluency
- accuracy of language
- absence of copying from passage
- length

SUMMARY TOTAL:	12 marks
SECTION B:	
QUESTIONS a–n	18 marks
SUMMARY	12 marks
TOTAL	30 marks
PAPER 3:	
SECTION A	50 marks
SECTION B	30 marks
TOTAL	80 marks

To be converted into a score out of 40 marks.

PAPER 3 SECTION B

FURTHER PRACTICE AND GUIDANCE (p91)

SAMPLE SUMMARY

Inclusion of points:

1 This is included in the third and fifth sentence.

2 This is not included.

3 This is included in the first part of the fourth sentence.

4 This is included in the last sentence and in the second part of the fourth sentence.

Inclusion of points: Total 3 marks

General impression of summary skills:

1 Everything in this summary is relevant.

2 The summary flows well and is well

organized, with some good linking (for example, the use of *Furthermore* and *In addition*).

3 There are a few errors: *put* in the second sentence should be 'puts' to maintain the present tense used throughout; in the fourth sentence it should be *a science writer*; also in the fourth sentence *it* after *which* is incorrect and should be removed; in the final sentence *instead* should begin a new sentence and the use of *would* is incorrect. None of these errors destroys the meaning of what is said in the summary.

4 There is some good rephrasing of what is in the passage. The third sentence shows a full understanding of what is meant by *layman*. The fifth and final sentences rephrase and summarize briefly the ideas expressed in lines 21–26 and 40–44 very well. The fourth sentence, however, is largely copied from the passage.

5 At about 130 words, the summary is too long. This is mostly due to the fact that the first two sentences form an introduction that does not make any of the required points. This introduction would be fine in a composition but the word limit for a summary does not make such an introduction possible. If it was removed, the summary would be of an acceptable length.

Summary skills: Total 5 marks

SAMPLE SUMMARY TOTAL: 8 marks

p92–94 PAPER 4

One mark per question (Total: 25)

To be converted into a score out of 20 marks.

PAPER 4 PART ONE

(see tapescript, p183)

FURTHER PRACTICE AND GUIDANCE (p94)

1 (lines 1–24)

A: N
K says that he asks people to spell certain rude words but this is not because he hasn't heard them before, it is so that people will realize what they have just said.

B: K
He asks people to spell certain words they have used as insults.

C: N
Neither of them says that some insults are worse than others.

D: N
K doesn't ask people to spell certain words because they don't make sense to him, he does it so that they will think about what they have said.

E: B
Neither of them appear to get upset about insults. They both ask people whether they have finished insulting them and they both laugh about this.

F: N
K does not ask for some words to be spelt for him because he intends to use them himself.

2 and 3 (lines 25–42)

A: N
J talks about not intending to give a ticket but she doesn't say that she changes her mind and then gives one.

B: B
K refers to drivers who say *you're never giving me a ticket*, which in this context means 'Surely you're not giving me a ticket'; these drivers think a ticket is being written. J supplies the answer to this (she asks *would you like one?*) so she is also talking about times when people wrongly assume she is writing a ticket.

C: N
K refers to people lying about how long their car has been illegally parked but he doesn't say that he gives such people a ticket.
J says that she tells people to get into their car or she will give them a ticket; she doesn't say that she gives a ticket.

D: J
She refers to writing in her pocket book but she says that she isn't *starting on a ticket*, which means that she must be writing something else.
K refers to a note in his book about how long a car has been in a certain place but he does not refer to writing this note.

E: B
J says that when you've started writing a ticket, *that's it* (you must finish it and give it). K confirms that this is still the case.

F: N
They both talk about people reacting badly to the idea that they are going to be given a ticket. Both of them say that they don't give a ticket and they weren't intending to anyway but neither of them says that they are kinder to some people than others.

4 and 5 (lines 43–70)

A: N
They both talk about the damage done by the behaviour of some wardens but neither of them says that this is because the job has got harder.

B: B
K says that some wardens *let us down* (cause people to have a low opinion of all the others); J says that with some wardens *the image* is completely wrong, which means that they cause all wardens to have a bad image with the public.

C: N
K talks about his compromise with the hairdresser and J also refers to this. Both of them then talk about wardens who are too aggressive with people but neither of them says that these wardens treat shopkeepers worse than anyone else. J refers to a warden going into a shop and being aggressive but this is an example of bad behaviour by wardens, not of how some wardens are severe with shops in particular.

D: J
J talks about wardens who *march round like dictators* when they are wearing their uniforms – she thinks that putting on the uniform changes them into people who want to use their power over people all the time. K talks about wardens with bad attitudes but he does not refer to a feeling of power.

E: N
K talks about the need to compromise with some people and J mentions K's compromise with the hairdresser but neither of them says that it's necessary to limit the extent to which you compromise.

F: J
She refers to wardens who walk into shops and say *Move it now* (*it* = a car).
K refers to the way some wardens talk to people but he does not actually mention orders.

6 and 7 (lines 71–102)

A: B
If you *pick on* someone, you constantly treat them badly. Both K and J refer to wardens who *persecute* certain people, which means the same.

B: N
K talks about a man who he would inform when he was in the street so that he could move his car if it was illegally parked. This does not mean that he allowed him to leave the car illegally parked.
J didn't like it that one man was given tickets every day, but she doesn't say that she let him park illegally.

C: K
He says that people who *always reoffend* (repeatedly break the law) *get on your nerves* (annoy you).
J agrees that there are people who always reoffend but does not say that this annoys her.

D: N
K gave the man tickets if he wasn't there to move his car when he let him know he was in the street. J didn't think the man should be given so

many tickets but it wasn't her who gave him the tickets.

E: B

J says that she told her colleague that it wasn't right to persecute a person like that. K says that some wardens *go a bit overboard* (behave in a way that is too extreme) – he is talking here about those who persecute people.

F: K

He warned him he was in the street so that he could quickly move his car without getting a ticket.

J thought the man was given too many tickets but she does not say she warned him he was going to get one.

8 and 9 (lines 104–143)

A: N

K doesn't like people shouting at him, it *does get on my nerves* (annoy me) but he doesn't say that it is a good idea to ignore them. J explains what she says to such people, so she obviously doesn't believe in ignoring them.

B: K

He is determined that people arguing with him do not go over his time limit – the amount of time he allows people to park illegally. He has this time limit *in my mind*.

J does not refer to allowing people to park illegally at all.

C: N

K implies that if people exceed his time limit for parking illegally because they are arguing with him, he gives them a ticket. J says that she warns people who argue that she may give them another ticket as well. Neither of them says they don't give people tickets because they argue (*let off* = allow someone to escape without punishment).

D: J

She says some people's attitude is that they are going to park in a place and the warden is not going to stop them.

K refers to people who shout at him but doesn't say that they go and park in a place paying no attention to a warden.

E: J

She says that she threatens to give them a second ticket (and therefore another fine) if they continue to argue.

K says that he will give them a ticket (not a second one) if they go over his time limit.

F: J

She says that if she threatens them with another ticket, they soon leave (they get into their cars, close the door loudly – *slam* it – and *they're off* – they go away).

K has a problem with people who argue with him but he does not refer to a way of stopping them.

PAPER 4 PART ONE (TEST)

See also the answers to the questions on the Further Practice and Guidance pages and the explanations above.

1 K

He sometimes asks people who are insulting him *how to spell a certain rude word* and then *they realize what they've said to you*. Clearly he realizes what has been said to him but pretends not to be familiar with certain words so that people will be forced to realize that they have said something bad to him.

J only says that, like K, she asks people who are insulting her whether thay have finished or not.

2 N

J talks about writing in her pocket book but not writing a ticket and not even considering doing so (*you haven't even thought about it*). When people complain that she is writing a ticket, she asks if they would like one and then tells them to get into their car (and go, presumably). She says that if they do so, *I won't do any writing* (won't write a ticket). She therefore wasn't planning to give a ticket and doesn't give one.

K refers to complaints that he is writing a ticket and to the fact that people lie about how long they have been parked illegally (they say they've only been there for 30 seconds, whereas he has a note in his book that their car was there twenty minutes ago). He does not, however, refer to writing a ticket after deciding not to.

3 N

J says that *once you've started your ticket that is it*, which means that when you have started to write a ticket, you must complete it and give it (*that is it* = that's the end of the situation, there is nothing that can be done to change the situation). K agrees and says that it's *still the same* (that rule is still in operation).

4 K

He agrees with J that he has *a good compromise with the hairdresser*. He accepts that the hairdresser has got a business so he tries to *keep it on a good footing* (keep their dealings with each other on good terms), particularly when the hairdresser has got customers. The implication is that he doesn't automatically give tickets if customers' cars are illegally parked because he is sympathetic towards the hairdresser.

J notices that K has a good compromise with the hairdresser but she then goes on to talk about the attitudes of some wardens but she doesn't say shopkeepers deserve special consideration, only that some wardens are too unpleasant.

5 N

K says that it *bugs* him (annoys or worries him) that some wardens *let us down* – they behave in a way that gives the pleasant wardens who are willing to compromise with some people a bad reputation. He dislikes the way they talk to people and their attitude. He does not say that their behaviour is understandable.

J refers to wardens that act like *dictators* when they *don* (put on) the uniform and says that their image is *completely wrong* and that they have *the wrong attitude*. She does not say that she can understand why they have this image and attitude.

6 J

She refers to a warden who persecuted (punished constantly and unfairly) someone by giving him a ticket every day and says that she told that warden that *I didn't think it was right to persecute like that*.

K refers to wardens who persecute people but does not say that he spoke to a colleague about this.

7: K

He talks about a man who he was *forever catching* (he was always finding his car illegally parked). He found this embarrassing so he found out where the man worked and would *buzz him* (press the button at the entrance to the building, like a doorbell) to let him know he was in the street so that he could move his car before he gave him a ticket. If he wasn't there, he still gave him a ticket.

J talks about what she said to a colleague, not about giving someone special treatment.

8 J

She talks about people with *grim determination* on their faces (looking very serious and determined). They see her and know that they should not park illegally but their attitude is that they are going to park illegally anyway and she is not going to stop them.

K talks about people who try to *browbeat* him (to frighten him by being aggressive so that he doesn't give them a ticket) but he doesn't talk about people ignoring him.

9 J

She tells people that they have been arguing with her for 10 minutes and if they continue arguing with her for another 10 minutes she will give them an additional ticket.

K talks about people *screaming and shouting* at him. He allows people to be illegally parked for a certain amount of time, even people who argue. He won't allow them to exceed this amount of time because they are arguing. However, he does not say that he warns them that he will give them a ticket if they argue for so long that they exceed this time limit.

PAPER 4 PART TWO

(see tapescript, p183–184)

10 sharp-witted: (lines 8–13)
Pictures suggest that she was a *formidable* (serious and somewhat frightening) *matriarch* (figure of female authority) but in fact she was *sharp-witted* (she was quick-thinking and dynamic).

11 lack of purpose: (lines 23–28)
What *spurred her to write* (gave her the motivation or inspiration to write) was *lack of purpose* (the feeling that she had no aim in life).

12 Household Management: (lines 30–35)
This means 'how to organize the running of a house'.

13 useful hints: (lines 35–41)
Countless = a very large number of. A *hint* in this context means a piece of advice.

14 Englishwoman's Domestic Magazine: (lines 44–51)
Domestic = relating to the home

15 family discontent: (lines 59–63)
She was driven by (her aim was and she put a lot of effort into) her desire to avoid *family discontent* (disagreements or dissatisfaction in families).

16 meticulous explanation: (lines 63–66)
Many say that her success was *owed to* (due to) her *meticulous explanation* (explanations that were very careful and included every detail, even the smallest details).

17 cautionary notes: (lines 75–83)
A *cautionary note* is one that warns people to be careful to avoid doing something. Her notes of this kind included warning people about *the evil of gossip* (that gossip was a very bad thing).

18 social graces: (lines 84–90)
We are told that *as a result of the Industrial Revolution* (the period in the 19th century when machines were invented), the *nouveau riche* (a French phrase also used in English to mean people who suddenly become wealthy as a result of changes in society or their own efforts, rather than because they inherited wealth from their family) were *thrust into moneyed lifestyles* (suddenly found that they had lifestyles involving wealth) but thought they were *lacking in the required social graces* (didn't have the knowledge of the social behaviour that was considered appropriate or polite for people with a lot of money).

19 nutrition: (lines 90–95)
She felt that her books could help *rich and poor alike* (both rich and poor people) and proclaimed (announced with great emphasis) that the poor would have fewer problems if they had some *rudimentary* (basic) knowledge of *nutrition* (the right food to eat in order to be healthy).

PAPER 4 PART THREE

(see tapescript, p184)

20 C: (lines 1–39)
He says that first-borns tend to be *more conventional, more conscientious* (taking care in everything they do), *more serious* and *more responsible* (sensible and not doing foolish things) *because parents value that in their offspring* (children) – in other words, they have those characteristics because those are the characteristics their parents want them to have.
A: He says that they have a special *niche* (role or position) in families *as a surrogate parent* (someone who acts as a substitute for a parent) *in caring for younger siblings* (brothers and sisters). However, he does not say that they dislike having this role.
B: He contrasts first borns, who are conventional, serious, etc. with younger children, who are *more sociable, more daring* (willing to take risks) *and adventurous, more unconventional and liberal* and who *tend to rebel* (to oppose authority). He does not, however, say that first-born children disapprove of these characteristics, only that they are different from their own.
D: Although younger siblings may enjoy life more, according to the characteristics he says they have, he does not suggest that first-born children would like to be like them.

21 B: (lines 40–67)
Sophie believes that whether you rebel or not depends not necessarily on whether you are a first-born or a younger child but on how *outrageous* (behaving in a way that is shocking and not socially acceptable) *or how rebellious your own parents are*. She says that her mother was outrageous when she was growing up *and seemed to be such* (and appeared outrageous to Sophie). This was why she *rebelled against her*. She reacted to her mother's outrageous behaviour by doing something the opposite of outrageous – joining the local church.
A: The presenter points out that Sophie is the second-born in her family; according to Frank's theory this means she is a rebel.
However, Sophie says that although the theory is *fascinating*, she is not sure *how far you can go along with it* (how much it is possible to agree with it). She believes that whether you rebel or not depends on other factors.
C: She doesn't say that her mother encouraged her to rebel at all, even though her mother was herself rebellious. Certainly, her mother does not seem to have been pleased when Sophie rebelled against her – they were an *atheist* (not believing in any religion) family, and Sophie going to church every Sunday was *a thorn in my mother's side* (a constant source of annoyance to her).
D: Sophie seems to think that if your parents are outrageous and rebellious, you *rebel against them but not necessarily against society itself*. This is not the same as saying that every child rebels when they are growing up, it refers only to the children of parents of a certain type.

22 D: (lines 68–81)
Her older sister, the first-born in the family, was, according to Sophie, *more conservative* than her, but she believes that this characteristic *is more due to the cautiousness of the parents* with a first child because *they don't actually know what to do* and so they are anxious not to do something wrong. With subsequent children, the parents *get more and more careless* because they *know that they survive* (experience with the first child has shown them that they don't need to be cautious because the first one has survived). She is therefore saying that first-born children are conservative because their parents are very worried and cautious when dealing with them.
A: She says that parents are cautious with first-borns because they don't know what to do and so presumably they are worried that they might make a terrible mistake, but she does not say that anything bad actually happened to her sister.
B: She says that when other children are born, the parents are less careful with them, but she does not say that in her family this made her older sister feel that she had to take care of or worry about her.
C: She makes a general point about parents and their children; what she says does not apply only or particularly to her own family.

23 A: (lines 82–88)
Sophie's nickname (*the policeman*) was given to her because she was the member of the family who tried to *get everyone on to the straight and narrow again* (to make the others behave in an acceptable, conventional manner). So, although she was *more outrageous* than her older sister, she believes that this fact shows that she did not conform to Frank's theory completely. She was sometimes conventional, serious and responsible – which Frank believes to be the characteristics of the first-born – but she was not the first-born. She didn't always exhibit the characteristics of younger children (rebellious, liberal, etc.) of Frank's theory.
B: It may appear that her family and childhood were strange – we know that her mother was outrageous – but she mentions the nickname to illustrate the more serious side to her character when she was a child, not to comment on her upbringing.
C: The nickname illustrates a contrast in her personality – on the one hand she was more outrageous than her older sister, but on the other hand she was also conventional. She does not say whether she felt this made her different from other children or in any way unusual.
D: She tried to get her family to behave well and for this they nicknamed her *the policeman*; there is no suggestion that they misunderstood her or got the wrong impression of her.

24 C: (lines 89–111)
She says that *many people do extraordinary things when they're way past the age of childhood* (when they're a lot older than children) and that what happens in life can suddenly change you into *a rebel later in life*. Therefore, even if Frank's theory about the characteristics of first-born and later children are true of people when they are children, they may not be true of the same people when they are a lot older.
A: She understands perfectly well what it involves, but she doesn't agree that it is true in every way (she only fits it *up to a point*) or that your personality is dictated by which child you were – she thinks that people's personalities are a result of *the individual circumstances of their family life and their lives*.
B: She says that this *hallmarking* (labelling) *of where you lie in the family* (whether you are the first, second, etc. child) *can't stick rigidly with you all your life* (the characteristics Frank believes you have if you are the first or a subsequent child don't remain without any changes all your life). As an example of this, she mentions people who change later in life, but she does not actually say that she knows anyone who has done this.
D: She says that *individual circumstances* are *more of a factor* (than whether they are first- born or not) concerning how people behave and what people are like. She does not say that in some circumstances Frank's model is true and in others it is not; she says that people's characters depend less on when they were born than on other things and that therefore Frank's model does not explain people's characteristics fully in any circumstances.

25 A: (lines 112–143)
He says that in *highly unconventional families*, the first-born copies the parents and is also unconventional, but that the later born are *confronted with* (faced with) a problem – *there's no more space to be unconventional* (the role of being unconventional has already been taken by the first-born) and so they *go in the opposite direction and become more conservative* (they choose to be completely different from their parents and the first-born).
B: They become very different from the first-born but there is no suggestion that they have a bad relationship with the first-born.
C: He does not say that they are harder to analyse than any other children. He generalizes about them, as he has generalized about all children and he does not say that the situation is more complex with regard to them. He uses them as an example of children with *additional influences* that he has taken into account in his research.
D: They become more conservative than their parents but he does not say that they disapprove of their parents.

p95–97 PAPER 5

FURTHER PRACTICE AND GUIDANCE (p97)

DESCRIBING PERSONAL CHARACTERISTICS

APPROVAL

amiable/cordial: friendly and pleasant
genial: kind and friendly
compassionate: kind and showing sympathy for the misfortunes of others
jovial: cheerful, pleasant and friendly
courteous: polite
dignified: acting in a way that is not embarrassing or shocking; calm and worthy of respect
tough: able to deal with problems and misfortunes in life and carry on
self-possessed: confident, not nervous, especially when faced with a challenge
discreet: making sure you don't embarrass someone, especially by not repeating secrets they told you or by not acting in a way that draws attention to you
self-reliant: able to survive or manage something without help from anyone else.
level-headed: sensible and realistic; unlikely to do foolish things
self-assured: confident
decent: morally good; honest
obliging: cooperative and helpful
principled: acting according to strong ideas of what is morally right
loyal: remaining a friend or supporter regardless of anything that happens
magnanimous: generous and tolerant, especially when such an attitude might not be expected
gutsy: very brave (*colloquial*)
affable: friendly and pleasant; easy to get on with

DISAPPROVAL

callous: cruel; having no feelings for others
spineless: having no courage at all; cowardly
grumpy: bad-tempered; tending to be in an angry mood
pompous: speaking or acting in a way that suggests you think you are very important
obnoxious: extremely unpleasant in any way
headstrong: acting in a way that you wish to, despite warnings of others
impetuous: tending to act without thinking first
pretentious: trying to impress people that you are sophisticated, particularly with regard to intellectual or cultural matters
overbearing: tending to dominate people and situations in a way that is not liked
complacent: self-satisfied; believing that you are fine and have no need to make any efforts or improve
cold: unfriendly and lacking in emotion
malicious: speaking or acting out of hatred and with a desire to make others suffer
surly: unfriendly, impolite and bad-tempered
soft: too kind to people, in a way that is considered weak
ruthless: acting in order to achieve what you want, regardless of the fact that this makes others suffer
moody: tending to change your mood frequently, making others uncomfortable

morose: quiet and miserable, in a way that makes it hard for people to be with you
underhand: doing things that affect others badly in secret so that they don't know
conceited: having too high an opinion of yourself; thinking that you are a very good person, when others do not share this view
offhand: rude by being too casual and not paying enough attention to the person you are speaking to
vile: extremely unpleasant and nasty
squeamish: tending to get frightened, upset or shocked much too easily
vindictive: nasty and trying to get revenge on people you feel have done something wrong to you
snobbish: considering yourself socially superior to others
hard: cruel and lacking in feelings
bigoted: having fixed, narrow and unpleasant views which you will not change
fickle: tending to change what and who you like and dislike frequently
obsequious: behaving in a way that others find annoying because you are much too anxious to please
tactless: upsetting or shocking people because of behaving or speaking in an insensitive way
self-righteous: talking or acting in the belief that you are morally right, in a way which others dislike

TEST FOUR

p 98–101 PAPER 1 SECTION A

FURTHER PRACTICE AND GUIDANCE (p 100–101)

1 **A** all in all
B as a rule
C at the most
D Over and above

2 **A** impression
B face
C evidence
D look

3 **A** As far as
B in terms of
C as for
D in that

4 **A** aside
B out
C apart
D off

5 **A** died
B let
C faded
D wore

6 **A** hold out
B stand by
C bear up
D keep at

PAPER 1 SECTION A (TEST)

Note that all the explanations in this part refer to the meaning or use of each option most closely related to the question, not necessarily to the only meaning or use of each option.

One mark per question (Total: 25)

1 **B**: **All in all** = after considering the good points and the bad points
A: *As a rule* = generally, what normally happens
C: *Over and above* = in addition to
D: *At the most* = at maximum, the maximum is...

2 **D**: **By the look of it** = it appears that...
A: *On the face of it* = that is how it appears but it may not really be like that
B: If you *give the impression of being* something, you appear to be that way.
C: *On the evidence of* something = judging from that, although it may not be everything that a judgement should be formed from

3 **B**: **In that** is used to qualify a statement by saying in what way it is true.
A: *As far as I'm aware/I know* = what I think is the case, although it may not be
C: *As for someone/something* = with regard to, concerning them, because they are different in some way
D: *In terms of* = with regard to, concerning a particular aspect, not the whole

4 **C**: If something **sets you apart from** others, it makes you noticeably different from them.
A: If you *set something aside*, you keep it for possible future use.
B: If something *sets someone off*, it causes them to start behaving in a certain emotional way.
D: If you *set out* information or ideas, you write them clearly and in an organized way.

5 **B**: If a feeling **wears off**, it stops being strong and gradually disappears.
A: If something *fades away*, it gradually disappears.
C: If a sound *dies down*, it stops being loud and gradually disappears.
D: If something *lets up*, it becomes less intense.

6 **B**: If you **hold out hope**, you continue to hope that something will happen.
A: If you *keep at* something, you continue to try to do it, even though you are failing.
C: If you *hang on*, you manage to continue to survive.
D: If you *stand by* something that you say, you continue to insist that it is true, despite other people's doubts.

7 **D**: A number of things **in a row** = a number of things one after the other, without any interruption
A: If you arrange things *in a line*, you arrange them so that they are straight, with each one behind another (*put toys in a line*).
B: A *sequence of events*, is a number of events that happen one after the other (*an unexpected sequence of events*).
C: A *series* is a number of things that are arranged or done so that one follows the other in a logical order (*ask a series of questions*).

8 **A**: If you **elaborate on** something, you give more information about it.
B: If you *amplify* something, you give more details about it. (*He refused to amplify his short statement.*)
C: If you *account for* something, you give reasons for it, or explain it. (*Nobody could account for the missing money.*)
D: If you *clarify* something, you make it clear because it is confusing (*clarify your intentions*).

9 **A**: If you **dispute/deny something hotly**, you dispute/deny it very strongly.
B: If you feel something *intensely*, you

feel it very greatly (*intensely dislike someone*).
C: If you *treat/criticize/punish someone harshly*, you treat/criticize/punish them severely and without sympathy.
D: If you feel something *acutely*, you feel it with great sensitivity (*be acutely embarrassed/aware*).

10 D: If you have a **keen interest** in something, you are very interested in it.
A: If you have a *fierce commitment to/passion for* something, you are very committed to/passionate about it indeed (*a fierce commitment to his political beliefs*).
B: A *sharp contrast* is a very great one.
C: A *grave condition* is a very bad and very serious one. (*He is in a grave condition and doctors fear for his life.*)

11 A: If your voice **quivers with emotion**, it becomes weak and trembles because you are feeling great emotion.
B: If you *flinch*, you react to something painful or frightening with a sudden involuntary movement (*flinch when given an injection*).
C: If you *cringe*, you move back or lower your body, indicating that you are very embarrassed or afraid. (*I cringed when I saw those old photos of me.*)
D: If you *wince*, you show on your face that you are feeling pain or embarrassment (*wince with pain*).

12 B: If you are **out of your depth**, you are in a situation where you lack the necessary knowledge or experience required to do something.
A: If you are *at a level*, that is the level you have reached. (*She's not at the highest level she can achieve in her career.*)
C: Your *limit* is the extent to which you can progress and no further. (*I've reached my limit as a musician.*)
D: If something is *in your range*, it is something you can manage (*look for a car in your price range*).

13 A: If you **don't hesitate to do something**, you do it without waiting to think about it or feeling that you shouldn't do it.
B: If you *dither*, you spend too long thinking about doing something because you cannot make up your mind. (*Come on, don't dither, make a decision.*)
C: If you *pause*, you wait for a short time before continuing (*pause to consider what to say next*).
D: If you *linger somewhere/over something*, you spend more time than necessary there/doing it because you are enjoying yourself (*linger in a restaurant over coffee*).

14 C: A **round of applause** is when people clap their hands to show appreciation or approval.
A: A *bout of* an illness is a period of suffering from an illness that is not very serious (*a bout of flu*).
B: A *stint* is a period of performing a certain duty (*do a stint as a trainee*).
D: A *spate* is a period in which a number of bad incidents happen (*a spate of thefts*).

15 D: If there is **an element of** something **in** something, it contains some of that thing.
A: A *factor* is something that contributes to the way something is or to an outcome. (*There were various factors in my final decision.*)
B: An *ingredient of* something is part of it that helps to form or produce it (*the ingredients of success in business*).
C: A *component of* something is one of the parts of it from which it is made (*machine components*).

16 B: **In the space of** = during a period of, especially when this is considered to be a short period
A: *In the interval* = during a pause, while something was not happening (*He left the room for ten minutes and in the interval we talked about him.*)
C: A *spell* of something is a period in which it is happening (*a spell of fine weather*).
D: *For the duration of* = during the whole period in which something is happening (*For the duration of his employment, he was a good worker.*)

17 C: If there is **ill feeling between** people, they dislike each other.
A: *Cross* = annoyed (*I'll get cross if you don't stop that.*)
B: *Adverse* = not favourable (*adverse weather conditions/an adverse reaction*)
D: *Vile* = horrible, disgusting (*a vile smell/colour*)

18 D: If you are **engrossed in** something, you are concentrating totally on it so that you do not notice anything else.
A: If you are *obsessed with* something, you think about it all the time (*He's obsessed with his own appearance.*)
B: If you are *preoccupied with* something, you are busy thinking about or doing it and therefore cannot do or think about something else. (*She didn't enjoy the film because she was preoccupied with her problems at work.*)
C: If you are *riveted by* something, it holds your attention completely and you are fascinated by it. (*I was riveted by his tales of travelling in exotic places.*)

19 A: If you **call a halt to** something, you bring it to an end or stop it from continuing.
B: A *stoppage* = a strike, an occasion when people stop working (*a stoppage at the factory*)
C: If something *comes to a close* or you bring something to a close, it ends or you end it. (*As the match came to a close,.../Let's bring this discussion to a close.*)
D: If something *comes to a standstill*, it cannot make any progress because something prevents it from doing so. (*Negotiations came to a standstill because neither side was prepared to compromise.*)

20 A: If something is **gloomy**, it is dark and depressing. It can also be used of people to mean sad and depressed.
B: If someone is *despondent*, they are extremely unhappy and have no hope. (*She was despondent when she lost her job.*)
C: If someone is *downcast*, they are depressed and disappointed. (*I was a bit downcast when my application was rejected.*)
D: If someone is *glum*, they are feeling miserable. (*He was very glum because his team had lost.*)

21 C: If you are **moved to tears**, something makes you cry because it affects you emotionally.
A: If you are *touched* by something, it affects you emotionally in a way that makes you feel good. (*I was touched by the kind things that she said about me.*)
B: If something *inspires you to do* something, it gives you the idea to do something and makes you want to do it. (*What inspired you to become a writer?*)
D: If something *arouses a feeling*, it causes that feeling. (*His attitude aroused my anger/suspicion.*)

22 B: If you **come to terms with** something, you accept that it is the case even though it is unpleasant.
A: *Acceptance* = the process of accepting that a bad situation is the case (*acceptance of failure*)
C: If you *come to an understanding with* someone, you reach an agreement with them that suits both of you. (*We came to an understanding not to mention the subject again.*)
D: If you *make allowances for* something, you take certain facts into account when reaching a decision. (*She never makes allowances for people who are less intelligent than her.*)

23 B: If someone **takes flight**, they run away.
A: If someone *retreats*, they go backwards because of a threat or danger (*a retreating army*).
C: If you *make your escape*, you run away or leave without being noticed. (*They made their escape under cover of darkness.*)
D: If you *make your/a getaway*, you escape or leave after committing a crime. (*The thieves made their getaway in a waiting car.*)

24 C: If you **reflect on** something, you think about it and the significance of it

after it has happened.
A: If you *contemplate doing* something, you consider the possibility of doing it. (*I wouldn't contemplate living anywhere else.*)
B: If you *review* something that has happened, you think about it afterwards (*review your past life*).
D: If you *weigh something up*, you think about it in order to decide on its value or to reach a conclusion about it (*weigh up the advantages and disadvantages of a course of action*).

25 A: If you **impress something on** someone, you make sure that they understand that it is the case and that it is important.
B: If you *instil something in* someone, you teach them it and the knowledge of it remains with them (*instil a sense of right and wrong in children*).
C: If you *highlight* something, you draw attention to it and say that it is important (*an article highlighting a new social problem*).
D: If something *underlines* something, it emphasizes it and shows that it is important. (*This mistake just underlines how careless you can be.*)

p102–106 PAPER 1 SECTION B

Two marks per question (Total: 30)

FIRST PASSAGE

26 C: (see first paragraph)
There was *something very human about the need to keep fire going by hand* – he liked the fact that people had to keep *shovelling* (using a spade to pick up coal and put it into the engine) *and watching* and they could never forget *their responsibility for the journey* (they were responsible for making sure the journey went well).
A: They were *already near the end of their golden age* (their greatest period). He was fascinated by them but this was not because they were becoming a thing of the past.
B: They *raced against themselves* in the sense that they used up the heat they generated so that heat had to be continuously generated to keep them going but he does not say that watching them go fast appealed to him.
D: He implies that the waste was safe (it didn't have to be *buried in lead-lined coffins*, which is what happens to dangerous waste such as radioactive waste). He says the waste was *exhaled* (breathed out) as carbon, sulphur and nitrogen or it turned into ash which scattered in the air and landed on people. Clearly one of the attractions for him was that you could see this waste but he does not say that he found the smell of it appealing.

27 B: (see second paragraph)
The writer says that people didn't know they were *using up and heating the earth too much* in those days, but even if they had known, it would have been right to *make an exception for steam engines* (treat them as a special case, in the sense of allowing them to damage the environment).
A: They were *the most beautiful machines produced in the industrial revolution* and so obviously they did change people's lives but he doesn't say anything about the idea of them changing people's lives in a bad way.
C: He says that the sound of them creates a feeling of beginning a journey more (*says more to us about getting under way*) than a *petrol-driven snarl* (the angry sound of a petrol engine) can, but he does not refer to them being more or less useful than cars.
D: They made an *explosive* sound (a loud sound, like an explosion) but he doesn't say that anyone has ever said they were too loud.

28 C: (see third paragraph)
We are told that various parts of the engines were *chipped and filed smooth by hammer and chisel* (made smooth by people using hand-held tools) after they came off the machines and that *Hands still made parts of these engines* (some parts were made by hand, not machine). The writer says that it is therefore *no surprise that drivers spoke of them as individuals.*
A: The writer mentions many of the characteristics of steam engines in this paragraph but he doesn't say that any of them resemble human characteristics.
B: According to the writer, it is true that you can see their function from their appearance – *most of its important parts are on display; there's no secrecy about a steam engine's force.* The writer goes into detail about all the parts you can see but he doesn't say this is why drivers spoke of them as individuals.
D: The writer says that even though drivers spoke of them as individuals they were all *essentially a boiler held in heavy frames on a set of wheels* (in other words they were all basically the same in construction).

29 A: (see fourth paragraph)
What *made it all so different from today's electric railways* was the *perilous* (dangerous) *balance of fire and water* involved with steam engines and *the need to be aware at every moment* of this. Clearly it was the engineman who had to be aware of this and react accordingly – he is the only person mentioned. It was therefore the engineman who could never allow the water *to fall below the top of the furnace or there would be an explosion.* The engine could be made to go faster by a good engineman but if the engineman was *incompetent,* there was the possibility of *disaster.* The way that the engine worked is the subject of this paragraph and the crucial role played by the engineman in this is emphasized.
B: The writer was amazed that *hordes of* (large numbers of) *people and commodities* could be carried at high speed in a machine that operated in the same way as a kettle but the way the engines worked is his main subject in this paragraph, not how much they could transport.
C: An incompetent engineman could cause an explosion or a disaster but there is no reference to the number of times such things occurred.
D: The writer begins by saying that the *simplicity of it fascinated* him. His subsequent description of the way the engines worked is meant to illustrate their simplicity, not to suggest that they were in fact complicated. He compares them to kettles, which he implies are also based on simple principles.

30 C: (see last paragraph and the passage as a whole)
The writer repeatedly describes them as beautiful. His feeling towards steam engines was *like love (first paragraph); they are* magical and *beautiful* (second paragraph); parts of them are *jewel-like* (third paragraph); there was *poetry* in them and they had *mystique* – charm and attraction (last paragraph).
A: He mentions developments in steam engines in the last paragraph, gives technical details of some of them and says they could be *endlessly refined, developed and decorated.* However, such developments are not a main point in the passage as a whole.
B: He says they were different from petrol-driven engines (second paragraph) and he compares them with the electric railways and kettles (fourth paragraph) but his main aim in the passage is to describe what fascinated him about steam engines, not to compare them with other machines.
D: It is reasonable to infer that he developed his love of steam engines as a boy but his main aim in the passage is to describe what he liked about steam engines then, not to tell the reader how much they make him recall now when he was a boy.

SECOND PASSAGE

FURTHER PRACTICE AND GUIDANCE (p105)

For explanations, see the explanations to the questions in the test that follow.

Question 31

1 doesn't say **2** c **3** no **4** d

Question 32

1 tongue-in-cheek **2** b
3 to indicate that he is not passionate about being a movie writer and that there were other things he might have preferred to do with his life
4 yes

Question 33

1 d **2** no
3 They don't show America's real history accurately.
4 yes (lines 12–15)

Question 34

1 no **2** no **3** no
4 yes (see explanation in test)

Question 35

1 no **2** spending so much time watching TV and films **3** Their parents don't spend enough time with them. **4** Children use them to reduce their parents' power over them.

SECOND PASSAGE (TEST)

31 B: (see first paragraph)
The writer says that celebrating the centenary (100th anniversary) of the movies is like attending someone's 100th birthday party. Although you acknowledge that surviving for so long is a remarkable achievement, you *cringe* (react with a very uncomfortable feeling) at the *absence of vitality* (the lack of health, vigour, energy) and at the *agony* (terrible pain) on the old face. He says that movies are like other things that are *past their prime* (old, having left behind the period when they were at their best and when their powers were at their greatest) or *grisly imitations* (horrible attempts to be like) the way they were when young. He is therefore saying that the celebration draws attention to the fact that movies are in much worse condition now than in their best period and that they are in a bad state.
A: He says that *you can't blame the movies* for celebrating their centenary (it's justifiable for them to do so) and he acknowledges by implication that he thinks the centenary is *a remarkable achievement*, just as living to be 100 years old is. He therefore isn't against the idea of a celebration.
C: He says that it is impossible not to notice (*there's no escaping*) that the celebration is embarrassing and *vulgar* (lacking in taste and sophistication), but this is not the same as saying that too much attention has been paid to it; it is a criticism of the kind of celebration that has taken place.
D: He compares the celebration with going to the birthday party of someone who is 100 years old but he doesn't say that he has actually attended such an event.

32 D: (see second paragraph)
He says that someone could spend *30 years thinking and writing about movies* without this meaning that *his mind is made up* (that he has reached a definite view). He therefore suggests that although he has spent all that time thinking and writing about movies, he hasn't come to a definite conclusion about them. He says that he is interested in thinking and writing and suggests that he only does this about movies because it is his *most available pretext* (it is the subject that gives him the most opportunity to do this), not because he has a particular view on them.
A: He says that the reader might suppose he is being *tongue-in-cheek* (pretending to be serious when in fact he is not being serious) but he denies this (*Really, I'm not*).
B: He implies that he still hasn't made up his mind about movies despite having thought and written about them for over 30 years – he does not say that he has changed his mind over that period or that he ever had a definite view that has now changed.
C: If you are *playing devil's advocate*, you deliberately express a controversial opinion or take an opposite view in order to stimulate a discussion or argument. He says that the reader will suppose he is doing that but when he states *Really I'm not*, he makes it clear that he isn't.

33 A: (see third paragraph)
He says that the *material in* (the content of) films has become *unreliable*. An example of this is westerns (films about cowboys and Indians in the US in the 19th century), which have changed from being *a resonant metaphor* (something used to represent something in a way that was effective and powerful) and become *a stupid distortion of the real history of America* (a stupid and inaccurate version of what really happened in America).
B: The same stories are repeated in movies – the writer says that there are a limited number of story forms in fiction (lines 12–15). Because there are now *so many movies and so many more versions of movies on TV*, it is true that *day after day the same stale mythic outlines are served up* (viewers are shown the same basic stories and these stories lack originality). However, this is not what the writer uses westerns as an example of.
C: The writer says that *excess of material* (the fact that there are too many movies) has become *wearying* (boring or tiring) and that people have become *cynical about their own legends* (they don't believe in them any more). However, although he is critical of the way in which westerns have changed, he doesn't say that they have become less popular.
D: He says that *Narrative tradition has been befouled* (the telling of traditional stories has been spoilt in a disgusting way) because films have changed those stories. However, he says that westerns used to be *a resonant metaphor*. He therefore implies that although westerns have changed for the worse, they used to be meaningful representations of the past.

34 D: (lines 21–26)
He says that films today require little effort from those watching them. Because *narrative suspense breaks down* (there is less need for viewers to wonder and get excited about what might happen next) the *complex involvement of a reader's sensibility in prolonged story* (the complex way in which a reader's mind and feelings get involved in a longer story than in a film) has become less likely (less likely to happen). Films *require less imaginative work* (you don't have to make the effort of using your imagination to watch them) because they don't need you to have *the powers of private insight and questioning* (the ability to gain your own understanding from them and to consider the issues they raise).
A: He refers to *the seductiveness of a spied-on fantasy* (the tempting appeal of a world unknown to you that you can observe as an outsider) that films have, but he does not suggest that films change your view of life or make people less hopeful about their lives.
B: He says that people prefer watching films to reading novels because it requires less effort but he doesn't suggest that films have any impact on what people want to achieve in their personal lives.
C: The writer says that films today require less effort than reading novels; he does not suggest that that they have any influence on the moral decisions that people make, nor that they affect them morally in any way.

35 A: (see lines 26–32)
Because children spend so much time with the TV on, this has a bad effect on their concentration, attention, introspection (thinking seriously and

silently) and linguistic response. They don't *relish* (enjoy) this life. They are *bitter* (angry for some time about something you consider unfair) and *vengeful* about it (they want revenge for it) because they know that watching so much film and TV has meant that they have had less attention from their parents than they want and they blame their parents for this. They feel *belittled and betrayed* (undervalued and cheated) by the amount of TV and films they watch because this has *cheated them of the company of their parents*.
B: He doesn't say that what they see in films or on TV makes them unhappy, he says that they would prefer to spend time with their parents.
C: They *employ* (use) *the catchphrases and attitudes of it to undermine* (weaken) their parents' influence/authority over them. It's not suggested that they are advised on what to watch by their parents.
D: They hold their parents responsible for the amount of TV and film they watch but he doesn't say they blame them for what they see on TV or in films.

THIRD PASSAGE

36 B: (see first paragraph)
They decided that *his training would reflect* (follow) *the casual* (informal), *spontaneous* (done without planning or careful consideration) *learning* he had already done. It would therefore not follow a rigid pattern.
A: They didn't keep changing their approach – they decided on one and followed it.
C: They didn't work out an approach specially for him, they left him to learn in an informal way.
D: He *has never been required to use symbols to get anything* – he uses symbols but he doesn't have to use them in order to get rewards.

37 C: (see second paragraph)
The words produced by the synthesizer have a *flat* and *monotonous* sound – they have no stress and they are all in the same tone. Kanzi can understand as many of them (two-thirds) as humans. He was not given any clues (*cues that might have tipped him to the meaning of the words*) such as *emotional content* or *unintentional stresses* which might have explained why he understood the words. The conclusion therefore is that he genuinely did understand them, even in the form produced by the synthesizer.
A: This may be true since the cues might have helped Kanzi understand the words but he understood as many words as humans did without them being stressed in any way, so this is not what the experiment suggests.
B: Kanzi understood many of the sounds produced by the synthesizer but it is not suggested that he understood them better than any other sound.
D: It is suggested that he probably can understand speech with emotional content as that might have helped him understand the words if it had been present; however, there was no emotional content in the experiment.

38 D: (see third paragraph)
Kanzi cannot understand the instruction to get the orange until the sentence structure makes clear to him what he is supposed to do. Even though this involves a relatively difficult grammatical structure, it is only when the sentence is in this form that he understands it.
A: There is no suggestion that Kanzi doesn't obey certain commands because he doesn't want to do certain things, only that he doesn't obey them if he can't understand them.
B: Kanzi can make some sense of the first instruction to get the orange – it is suggested that he knows he has to get an orange but suspects that there may be more than one and he doesn't know which one to get.
C: The first instruction isn't precise enough for Kanzi to know what to do, but it is not suggested that such things happen frequently in this kind of research.

39 A: (see last paragraph)
Kanzi gives several meanings to the word *juice* and critics suggest that this means he doesn't really understand it. The writer says this sounds like a *tricky argument* (a false point of view) because children do something similar. However, the critics say that children don't do the same as Kanzi – they use the same word for two things of the same kind, not two different kinds of things as Kanzi does (he uses *juice* to refer to the thing, the thing holding it, a place and an action).
B: The critics do compare Kanzi's abilities to understand with those of a child – they say he doesn't really have the same abilities and point out the evidence for this. They say that his abilities should be compared with those of a child because doing so proves that he can't really understand what the researchers say he can understand.
C: The critics say that because he attaches several meanings to each symbol, he doesn't really understand what the symbols represent; they don't say anything about what the symbols themselves are like or whether they were specially created so that the experiments would appear to prove his intelligence.
D: Children may use the same word for more than one object but it is not stated that they know where objects belong more than Kanzi does. Kanzi uses the same symbol for both an object and a place, but this does not mean that he confuses the places where objects belong more than children do.

40 A: (look at the passage as a whole)
The writer explains both what the researchers believe their experiments indicate about Kanzi – how much he can understand – (second and third paragraphs), and the views of those who are doubtful about this (last paragraph). The writer does not say whether he agrees or not with either view, he merely presents the facts.
B: The writer explains the evidence that the researchers believe indicates that Kanzi is intelligent but he doesn't say whether he is convinced of this or not.
C: The writer explains the doubts that some critics have expressed about the conclusions Kanzi's trainers have drawn from the experiments but he does not say whether he agrees with them or not.
D: The writer mentions certain possible similarities between chimpanzees and children in terms of their understanding in language – in the first paragraph he says that the trainers believe Kanzi uses symbols in the same way as children may learn to speak; in the third paragraph he says that Kanzi could understand certain types of question better than a two-year-old child, which is a difference not a similarity; in the last paragraph he explains the ways in which critics compare Kanzi's understanding with that of a child (again, these are differences, not similarities). Furthermore, the passage is about the experiments with Kanzi and what they may or may not prove about him; these experiments are not primarily aimed at comparing him with a child and so such a comparison could not be said to be the main purpose of the passage.

PAPER 1:

SECTION A	25 marks
SECTION B	30 marks
TOTAL	55 marks

To be converted into a score out of 40 marks.

p107–109 PAPER 2

Each composition is given a mark out of 20. The total of the two compositions is then divided by two to give an overall score for the paper out of 20.

FURTHER PRACTICE AND GUIDANCE (p109)

Assessment of sample composition

1 **Content**
The letter fully covers the task set, with nothing irrelevant or repetitious. The opening paragraph in particular shows an imaginative response to the question.

2 **Organization**
This is a very well-organized letter. The opening paragraph presents the background to the letter and its purpose, the second paragraph describes the writer's qualifications and experience, the third paragraph describes the writer's qualities and the final paragraph explains what the writer would like to happen in response to the letter.

3 **Linking**
There is some very good linking: *Since, As* and *along with* in the first paragraph; *apart from that* in the second paragraph; *Apart from* and *Moreover* in the third paragraph; *in terms of, if not, in case of* and *However* in the last paragraph.

4 **Use of vocabulary**
There is plenty of good, high level vocabulary: *a golden opportunity* in the first paragraph; *motivated, a positive approach to, working to deadlines* and *native tongue* in the third paragraph; *on file, of great value* and *utterly* (extremely) in the last paragraph. There is no inappropriate use of vocabulary.

5 **Use of grammar**
There are only a couple of errors: in the second paragraph, *my working experience* should be *my work experience* and *a manager assistant* should be *a manager's assistant* or *an assistant manager*; in the third paragraph, *equally as good* should be *equally as well* (this is a fairly serious error), and the phrase is *on my own initiative*, not *initiatives*; in the last paragraph *messures* is incorrectly spelt and should be *measure*, not singular (if something *measures up*, it is of the appropriately high standard). However, apart from these, the letter displays an excellent command of grammatical structure in some fairly long and complicated but totally accurate sentences (for example, the second sentence of the final paragraph).

6 **Style**
The letter is both fluent and natural and throughout maintains a friendly, semi-formal tone, which is entirely appropriate to the context.

This is a very well-constructed letter, which is not far short of being entirely fluent. It would be given 16–18 marks out of 20.

p110–114 PAPER 3 SECTION A

PART 1

One mark per question (Total: 20)

1 **in**: If something is *slow in happening/to happen*, it takes a long time to happen or does not happen as soon as it should.

2 **appointed**: If you are *appointed* as something, you are given a position with a certain title.

3 **for**: *For doing* is used to describe the use or purpose of something that is invented, created or produced.

4 **proved**: If something *proves to be* something, it is shown to be that thing after some time.

5 **among/amongst**: In this context, *among/amongst* = one of.

6 **recently/late**: The use of the word *even* and the content of the rest of this sentence show that the 1970s is regarded as being relatively recent; the writer is surprised that it took so long to search the fingerprint collection at a time when he would have expected the system to be more modern and to have become more efficient.

7 **if**: *If not* in this context = and possibly. *If not* is used to say that something even greater than the first thing stated may also be true.

8 **raising**: If you *raise the alarm*, you tell other people that there is an emergency so that they can react in the appropriate way. In this case, policemen told other people that a crime was taking place or had taken place.

9 **would**: *Would* is used to describe habitual or routine actions in the past that no longer happen.

10 **another**: *From one place to another* = from one police station to another police station/other police stations in this context.

11 **there**: Developing the telegraph system had begun before 1857 and the system was in existence in 1857.

12 **and**: This links the two technological developments mentioned.

13 **Even**: *Even so* = despite this, even though this is true. This sentence indicates that the government's worry (*concerned about* = worried about) was not necessary.

14 **far**: *Far from + adjective* = not at all, by no means and emphasizes that the adjective is not the case.

15 **without**: *Without getting* = and not to get. Even though they were in a *rough* (dangerous or criminal) area, they didn't get *a single* (not even one) assignment (task to carry out, in this context crime to deal with).

16 **duty**: *Night duty* = a period of work at night for people who work sometimes in the day and sometimes at night

17 **across**: If you *stretch something across* something, you extend it from one end or side of it to another. A *doorway* is the opening where a door is.

18 **been**: *There had been a break-in* = a break-in had taken place, someone had broken in (entered by force in order to commit a crime), there had been a burglary.

19 **other**: *Other than* = apart from/except for/but for/besides.

20 **with**: If you *fight something with* something, you use it in order to fight. *With which to fight crime* = to fight crime with, and completes the idea that the police did not have much that they could use for fighting crime.

PAPER 3 SECTION A

PART 2

One mark per word or phrase in bold (Total: 12)

a **to me** (1) **to sort this problem out (for you)** (1) (2 marks)
If you *leave it to someone to do something*, you give them or allow them to have the responsibility for doing it, so that they do it instead of you.

b **better off asking** (1) someone who really knows about the law. (1 mark)
If you say that someone *would be far better off doing something*, you are advising them that there is a much better course of action than the one they intend or than one that has been mentioned.

c **my suggestion** (1) **with laughter** (1). (2 marks)
If you *greet something with + noun*, that is your reaction to it. The verb *laughed* has to be changed to the noun *laughter*.

d **age/youth** (1) **in mind** (1), he has achieved a lot. (2 marks)

If you *bear something in mind*, you take it into account/consideration when making a judgement or decision or forming an opinion. *His* must be followed by a noun and *age* or *youth* are both appropriate nouns formed from *how young he is*.

e to her, her family (1) had reported her missing. (1 mark)
Unbeknown to someone = without that person knowing about it or being aware of it. *But* in the original sentence therefore must be removed.

f funny about (1) **me/my wanting** (1) to learn the saxophone? (2 marks)
The structure *What's so + adjective + about...?* = why is it so + adjective + that...? Since *about* is a preposition, the verb following must be in the *-ing* form; an object or possessive may come before the verb to refer to a person.

g her on her (good) taste in music. (1 mark)
If you *compliment someone on something*, you express praise or admiration for them with regard to something they do or have.

h to be popular with everyone he meets. (1 mark)
If you *contrive to do* something, you manage to do it, perhaps without having tried to do it.

PAPER 3 SECTION A

PART 3 FURTHER PRACTICE AND GUIDANCE (p112)

For explanations, see the explanations to the questions in the test below.

a 2

b 1

c 1

d 3

e 1

f 4

PAPER 3 SECTION A

PART 3 (TEST)

One mark per question (Total: 6)

a a chance of being
If someone *doesn't stand a chance of doing something*, they have no chance of doing it, there is no possibility that they will be able to do it. *Elected* is a past participle, in this case part of a passive.

b little time to
If you have something *to spare*, you have more of it than you need. If you have *very little* something, you have almost none of it. If you *rush somewhere*, you go there very quickly because you are in a hurry.

c much the
If something is *pretty much the same as* something else, it is almost the same as it or very similar to it.

d sooner or
Sooner or later = at a time in the future; whether it is a short time or a long time from now it will certainly happen. If you *persevere*, you keep trying to do something, even though it is very difficult and you are not succeeding.

e wonder they have
No wonder/It's no wonder = it is not at all surprising that...; if you *have a low opinion of someone/something*, you don't like them.

f effect from
With effect from = starting from (when used in formal language to talk about new rules and regulations, new systems or procedures and other official matters). If a rule, etc. *will apply*, it will come into force or operate.

PAPER 3 SECTION A

PART 4 FURTHER PRACTICE AND GUIDANCE (p114)

For explanations, see the explanations to the questions in the test below.

a 1

b 3

c 2

d 2

e 3

f 4

g 4

h 2

PAPER 3 SECTION A

PART 4 (TEST)

One mark per word or phrase in bold (Total: 12)

The numbers refer to the incorrect options in the Further Practice and Guidance questions.

a These pictures don't do (any/much) justice (1) **to the true beauty of the place** (1). (2 marks)
If something *doesn't do (any/much) justice to something*, it doesn't represent or describe it in a way that is accurate, fair or appropriate.
2 *Isn't of justice by* is not a correct phrase in any circumstances.
3 *Aren't a justice for* is not a correct phrase in any circumstances.
4 If *there isn't justice for someone/there is no justice for someone*, they are never treated fairly, especially by authorities.

b There is hardly anything (that) (1) **Hilary doesn't know** (1) about the history of this town. (2 marks)
Hardly anything = almost nothing. To rewrite the sentence using the phrase *hardly anything*, the structure *There is .... + 'that clause'* will have to be used. If Hilary *knows almost everything*, there is almost nothing she doesn't know, so the verb *knows* has to become negative.
1 The verb *has* is incorrect, as is the phrase *hardly nothing* – *hardly* must be followed by *any/anything*, etc. not by *no/nothing* etc.
2 *Hardly all* is incorrect; *hardly* is not a synonym of *almost*; *Hilary knows* is in the wrong position.
4 *Hardly every/everything*, etc. is not correct; *Hilary knows* is in the wrong position.

c Eventually, he reached the/a point (1) **when/where he couldn't** (1) stand the job any longer. OR **Eventually, it reached a/the point** (1) **when/where he couldn't** (1) stand the job any longer. (2 marks)
If you *reach a/the point when/where* something is the case, or *it reaches a/the point when/where* something is the case, the situation changes or develops until there is a particular result or something becomes the case.
1 *There was reached his point* is not possible in any circumstances.
3 *Reach to* is incorrect; *reach a time* is not a correct collocation to fit the meaning of the original sentence.
4 *The time reached* is not a possible collocation.

d His Italian has improved to such a degree that/to the degree that/to a degree where (1) he's virtually fluent now. (1 mark)

If something changes *to such a degree that* or *to the degree that* or *to a degree where* something is the case, it changes so much that the second thing becomes true.
1 It is not possible to talk about *a degree of a language*. A correct sentence could be constructed beginning *He has reached a standard of Italian* but the word *degree* could not be in it.
3 A *degree* cannot improve; it is *His Italian* that has improved.
4 Again, *a degree* of a language is not possible.

e **Travelling abroad on her own holds no fear for Anita.** (1 mark)
If something *holds no fear for someone*, they are not afraid of it or to do it. To rewrite the sentence, the subject has to become *Travelling abroad on her own*.
1 *Holds + adjective* and *holds + infinitive* are not possible in any circumstances.
2 *There holds no fear* is not possible in any circumstances.
4 *There holds nothing* is not possible in any circumstances.

f **She has lost hope of becoming** (1) a star. (1 mark)
If you *lose hope of doing something*, you no longer hope that you will be able to do it or that it will happen.
1 The noun *hope* is not followed by an infinitive. The passive structure is not appropriate here.
2 *Lost* (past simple) should be *has lost* because it refers to a present result (the original sentence refers to a present situation). *Hope for* is possible but must be followed by a noun; it cannot be followed by a verb, as is necessary here.
3 The passive is inappropriate; the infinitive is incorrect.

g **It's (only) a matter of time** (1) **before he gets** (1) himself into serious trouble. (2 marks)
If *it is (only) a matter of time before something happens*, it is certain to happen in the future but it is not certain when it will happen.
1 *No matter when* = it doesn't matter when; this does not fit the sense of the original sentence.
2 *As a matter of fact* does not fit the sense of the original sentence.
3 *The matter will be* is just possible as a phrase with the meaning *the problem will be*. However, this does not correspond to the original sentence.

h **Over the next few years, the business went from strength to strength.** OR **The business went from strength to strength over the next few years.** (1 mark)
If something/someone *goes from strength to strength*, they become more and more successful.
1 If something such as the wind *gets up strength*, it becomes strong, but this phrase cannot be used for a company.
3 *Strength* cannot *happen*.
4 *Increase strength to* is not a possible phrase in any circumstances.

SECTION A:

QUESTION 1	20 marks
QUESTION 2	12 marks
QUESTION 3	6 marks
QUESTION 4	12 marks
TOTAL	50 marks

p115–120 PAPER 3 SECTION B

FURTHER PRACTICE AND GUIDANCE (p118–119)

Questions a–n

For explanations, see the explanations for the questions in the test below.

b yes

c premise

d lack of rain/water

e the Kenyan people

f two – poor farmers and conservationists

h kill animals illegally

j share land

n d

g b

i 1 d
2 c

k d

l 1 c
2 a

m b

PAPER 3 SECTION B (TEST)

Answers similar to or covering the same points as those given here are acceptable provided that they are clearly expressed.

a **they think that fascinating things can be seen there because the problems between man and animals have been resolved** (1 mark)
The *spectacle* (a marvellous or impressive thing to look at or watch; presumably this refers to the wildlife) takes place in parks because the *perennial* (happening constantly) *conflict* (fight) between man and animal has been resolved, *mostly by removing the former* (by removing man from the parks).

b **they are critical of the new generation of ecologists and managers** (1) **and they prefer to believe in old-fashioned notions of the situation** (1) (2 marks)
The new generation of ecologists and managers are trying to *unravel* (resolve) the complexities that *lie behind* (that are involved in but are not seen) these images and ideas and they are *under fire* (they are being attacked) by campaigners who *prefer the older stereotypes* (older, fixed ideas about the nature or character of people or things, especially when these are not accurate).

c **a large number of elephants was put into the park because it was believed that they would establish their own balance** (1 mark)
The park was *overpopulated by elephants* (too many elephants were put in there) *on the premise that* (in the belief that, on the assumption that – a *premise* is a belief that ideas or actions are based on) the wildlife *would establish a balance of its own*.

d **the park became like a desert and when there was no water** (1) **the elephants couldn't move to a place where there was water** (1) (2 marks)
The park became *a near desert*. Even though it is large, it is *too small to sustain an elephant population 'naturally'* (to enable an elephant population to survive in their natural way). In times of *drought-stress* (when there is a big problem because it has not rained for a long time), the elephants couldn't go to somewhere where they *might survive* (where there was water) because they were kept in the park and there wasn't any water in the park.

e **most of Kenya's animals live outside the parks and the Kenyan people who have to live near them hate them** (1 mark)
Well over (considerably more than) 70% of Kenya's wildlife lives outside the parks and the animals' *neighbours* (the people) *loathe* (hate, intensely dislike) them because they kill people and destroy an enormous number of crops.

f **the fact that wildlife can be an advantage/ of benefit/useful to the local people and that it is acceptable to kill or let other people kill wildlife** (1 mark)
He must *persuade poor farmers that they can profit from the presence of wildlife* and explain to conservationists, who are opposed to the killing of wildlife that *peasants* (poor farmers) should be allowed to kill or sell permission to kill wildlife.

g **actions to show that you have good intentions towards someone** (1 mark)

A *gesture* is an action that is intended to indicate a certain attitude or feeling; *goodwill* = friendly feelings, a desire to cooperate or have a good relationship with someone.

h **because of the success of the anti-poaching measures, there are more animals in the park** (1) **and the fences are needed to keep them in/keep them away from the local people** (1) (2 marks)
Measures (actions) have been taken against *poaching* (the illegal killing of animals). This has been successful, so fewer animals are being killed. As a result, the number of animals in the park is increasing. The fences are needed to keep them in the park. These fences will become *less necessary* if local people start to feel better towards the animals because they see them as *profitable*. If this happens, they won't want the animals to be kept away from them and they won't want to poach them.

i **reduce the hostility of** (1 mark)
If you *defuse* a feeling or situation, you make it less strong or unpleasant; *animosity* is hostility, a strong feeling of dislike or aggression towards someone.

j **animals don't share land and don't have enough space (because cattle have been removed from the parks and there are too many elephants in the parks)** (1 mark)
Dr Western wants to see a return to *land-sharing* because the *diversity* (the variety, the wide range) of Africa's *savannah* (land with grass but not many trees) depends on the animals having enough space. When parks were created, cattle were *banished* (sent away) and the number of elephants increased because they *retreated* from (moved away from the threat of) poaching and went into the parks.

k **to indicate that the relationship between man and animals that Dr Western wants to create will be a happy/good one** (1 mark)
People (*cattlemen and park rangers* – people who deal with cattle and people who look after parks) and animals (*livestock* – farm animals – and wildlife) will *co-exist* (live together without problems) in a situation in which they are not *antagonistic* (aggressive towards each other).

l **people who don't agree will have to be persuaded** (1 mark)
Hearts and minds = people's feelings and opinions; if you *win someone over*, you convince them so that they agree with you.

m **opposition (from conservationists) to hunting and culling** (1 mark)
This refers to the attitude of conservationists. *Culling* is killing animals because there are too many of them.

n **to point out that Westerners who are opposed to the killing of animals in Africa are not really involved in the situation** (1), **they are admiring wildlife from a fortunate, comfortable position** (1) (2 marks)
Dr Western feels that he is *right to stress that the African people must benefit too* (by killing animals, see fourth paragraph) even if this means upsetting Westerners who are, in a sense, sitting down comfortably and admiring wildlife rather than having to deal with wildlife as a matter of everyday survival, as the Africans have to.

Questions a–n: Total 18 marks

PAPER 3 SECTION B

SUMMARY (TEST)

o *One mark each for the inclusion of the following points or points similar to them (in any order).*

1 **He wants the local people to profit from the wildlife by being allowed to kill animals.**

2 **He wants local people to be involved in decision-making and to know they have rights.**

3 **He wants wildlife to share land and have more space.**

4 **He wants man and animals to exist happily together so that fences can be removed and tourists can feel they are in a working countryside.**

Total: 4 marks
Plus a maximum of 8 marks for general impression of summary skills, based on the following criteria:
- relevance
- general level of fluency
- accuracy of language
- absence of copying from passage
- length

SUMMARY TOTAL: 12 marks

SECTION B:

QUESTIONS a–n	18 marks
SUMMARY	12 marks
TOTAL	30 marks

PAPER 3:

SECTION A	50 marks
SECTION B	30 marks
TOTAL	80 marks

To be converted into a score out of 40 marks.

PAPER 3 SECTION B

FURTHER PRACTICE AND GUIDANCE (p120)

SAMPLE SUMMARY

Inclusion of points:

1 This is not included.

2 This is not included. The third sentence might be referring to points 1 and 2 but it does not specifically do so.

3 This is included, in the second sentence, although it is not true that Dr Western wants to close the parks.

4 This is included, in the first sentence, the third sentence and the last sentence.

Inclusion of points: Total 2 marks

General impression of summary skills:

1 Nothing in the summary is irrelevant.

2 The summary flows well, with good linking of points (for example, *in order for that to...* in the second sentence, which refers back to the situation mentioned in the first sentence).

3 There are a few errors. In the first sentence, *eachother* should be two words and *harmonically* should be *harmoniously*. In the second sentence, *animals* should be *animals'*. In the last sentence *concequently* should be *consequently*. There is some very good use of structure and vocabulary, particularly in the last sentence (*working on an approach according to which, though animals will be free, tourists...* – this is a very complex sentence involving a 'though' clause in the middle and there are no errors in it).

4 There is no copying from the passage at all.

5 At about 90 words, the length is fine.

Summary skills: Total 6 marks

SAMPLE SUMMARY TOTAL: 8 marks

p121–125 PAPER 4

One mark per question (Total: 25)

To be converted into a score out of 20 marks.

PAPER 4 PART ONE

(see tapescript, p184–185)

FURTHER PRACTICE AND GUIDANCE (p123)

1 Tick **A, B, C** and **D**: (lines 1–32)
A: He conducts *close to 100 concerts a year* and plays in *20 or 25*. He says *I do an awful lot* (a very great deal of) *chamber music* but he does more conducting than playing.
B: He *did* (performed at) *a couple of chamber music concerts* when he was in London and he intends to do that *every time I go there now*, so he will be *playing the piano a little bit more*. He has decided to *start playing the piano more.*
C: He says that *so many* (a lot of) *pianists have become conductors* in the last ten years.
D: He is asked about the advantages of being versatile (having a number of different skills or talents you can use) and he replies that one advantage is that *you can't get bored.*

2 Tick **A, B** and **D**: (lines 33–51)
A: In his career, *there were sidetracks along the way* (times when he didn't follow a single path but moved away from it to do different things).
B: Even though he enjoyed being a commercial musician in films he *knew from day one* (from the very beginning of his time doing that) that he *wasn't going to do it for the rest of my life.*
C: Although he worked in films for 12 years, he does not say that he spent so long doing that because he was afraid to change what he did. In fact, he always knew that he would stop doing it one day.
D: The choices he made are *obvious considering what I do now* (if you look at what he does now, you know what decisions he must have made when he was very young).

3 Tick **B**: (lines 523–68)
A: He didn't want to write music that *would be played while actors talked*. This implies that he wanted to write music that people would listen to as music, not as an accompaniment to speech. It doesn't imply that he thought music should play a larger part in films.
B: He says he was trained as *a serious musician* but that as a teenager it was *irresistible* for him *to get away from that* (move to a different kind of music).
C: He says that *after a while I'd had enough* (he didn't want to continue doing it). That was a personal decision and it does not imply that it is hard for anyone to have a long-term career in film music.
D: He mentions *the discipline I had when I was a kid* and this refers to his training as a child, not to his work in film music as a teenager. This discipline was part of his training as a serious musician and he implies that it was one of the reasons why his *ambition was not to compose* film music.

4 Tick **A** and **D**: (lines 69–85)
A: The violinist *befriended* him (chose to become his friend) and *took me through* (explained to me) *the basic repertoire of chamber music*. He did this *out of the goodness of his heart* (because he was a kind person and expected nothing in return).
B: He says that he had his own group but he does not say that he had difficulty finding musicians to play with him.
C: He refers twice to playing chamber music but he does not mention composing it.
D: He says that *we* (he and his group) *played a lot of concerts.*

5 Tick **A** and **B**: (lines 85–109)
A: He says that *among the Hollywood composers and conductors, there were only a few of us* (he includes himself as one of them) *who were interested in that music so we always conducted them* (a few Hollywood composers and conductors, including him, conducted the orchestra).
B: They got *restless* (dissatisfied, impatient and keen to do something) *and bored with that kind of music* (film music) and so they formed the orchestra.
C: They wanted to play something other than film music and they played *whatever they felt like*; there is no suggestion that they formed the orchestra to learn anything new – it seems more likely that they played pieces they already knew.
D: It is true that they played in schools but this was because school auditoriums happened to be available. It is possible that children heard their performances but that was not the reason why they formed the orchestra.

6 Tick **A**: (lines 110–131)
A: He says that if someone who is only 16 years old decides to conduct the music of only one composer for the rest of his life, this is *doing him out of quite a lot of music* (depriving him of/preventing him from experiencing a lot of other music).
B: He says that it is not a good idea for *somebody who is gifted and talented* and is only 16 to limit their range of music too much, but he does not suggest that there are not many talented youngsters.
C: He gives an example of a 16-year-old who wants to conduct and he says that he tells conducting students that they should *keep an open mind* (not be too narrow or restricted in their attitude) but he does not suggest that young people who want to conduct are too single-minded; instead, he says that he tells them not to be.
D: He doesn't generalize about the characteristics of young people; he simply says that he tells them to be open-minded.

7 Tick **C**: (lines 131–149)
A: He says that musicians want to know what apprentice conductors want (how they want them to play) but there is no reference to musicians giving advice.
B: He says that apprentice conductors have to *transmit to living musicians what it is you're after* (what it is you want to get or achieve) but he doesn't mention any disagreement between musicians and apprentice conductors.
C: He says that apprentice conductors will have to wait a long time before they are asked to conduct *one of the great symphonies* so in the meantime they should do any conducting they can because by doing this, they are *learning to conduct.*
D: He doesn't say that it is hard to be good at conducting, only that it can take a long time for a conductor to be given the chance to conduct one of the great symphonies.

PAPER 4 PART ONE (TEST)

The letters in brackets refer to the options in the Further Practice and Guidance pages and the explanations above.

1 **C**
He says that because a lot of pianists have become conductors (see C), he has decided to get even (get revenge) by being a conductor who performs as a pianist. It is clear from his tone that he is joking, rather than being angry.
A: He says that he does more conducting than playing (see A) but he does not emphasize that being a conductor is more important to him than playing or that playing is insignificant in comparison to conducting.
B: He intends to do more playing (see B) but he doesn't say that this is because he thinks he should do it, only that he is going to do it.
D: He does say that being versatile stops you from getting bored (see D) but he does not say that he was bored

and that that is why he became versatile.

2 **B**
When asked about the choices he made when he was very young, he says that they're obvious considering what I do now – in other words, those choices resulted in the kind of career he now has (see D).
A: He spent 12 years as a commercial musician in films but he knew he wasn't going to do that permanently (see A and B). For this reason, he was glad to move away from that but he says that he enjoyed it and he does not suggest that he regrets it or views it as a mistake.
C: He doesn't mention having trouble making decisions. Remaining in films for 12 years does not seem to have been a problem, nor does giving up that work (see C).
D: Although these choices have brought him to his present position (see D) and he always knew that he wasn't going to work in films forever (see B), there were sidetracks (see A), which means that he did not stick to one particular plan for his career.

3 **B**
He was trained to be a serious musician but as a teenager it was irresistible (too appealing to be resisted) for him to move away from that (see B). He is therefore implying that film music isn't serious music.
A: He describes film music as music that is played while actors talk and it wasn't his ambition to write that kind of music (see A). He doesn't imply that film music deserves to have a higher reputation or to be listened to simply as music.
C: He had discipline when he was a kid but he doesn't imply that you need discipline to write film music or that having it helped him to do so (see D).
D: He stopped doing it because he didn't want to carry on doing it. He doesn't imply that most composers of film music only do it for a short time (see C).

4 **D**
The violinist Joseph Sigetti taught him about chamber music, which was very kind of him (see A). He describes this as extraordinary, which implies that he thinks he was fortunate to have met someone who would help him so much.
A: The violinist befriended him (see A), but he does not say that he set out to find someone who would teach him about chamber music.
B: He had a group (see B) and he played a lot of concerts (see D). Obviously at first he knew little about chamber music, as he was taught the basic repertoire but he doesn't mention any lack of opportunity to play it.
C: He talks only about playing it (see C and D).

5 **B**
They obviously found that playing film music was not demanding enough for them because they got restless and bored playing only film music and that was why they formed the orchestra (see B).
A: Children may have heard them playing but the orchestra was not formed with children in mind (see D).
C: They wanted to play music they enjoyed playing; there is no suggestion that they felt a need to improve as musicians (see C).
D: Hollywood composers and conductors did conduct the orchestra (see A) but it was not formed so that they could practise doing so.

6 **A**
When asked whether musicians should diversify (be involved in a wide range of activities), he says that he doesn't think it does any harm (has any bad effects). He then gives an example of a young person being too limited in their attitude and goes on to say that he tells them not to be like that (see A).
B: He says that he tells apprentice conductors not to specialize too much or be too limited (see A and C) but he doesn't say that most of them are too limited or that few of them diversify.
C: He says that gifted and talented youngsters shouldn't specialize too much (see A and B) but he doesn't say that diversifying is only a good idea for people who are particularly gifted or talented; he thinks it is a good idea for all youngsters.
D: He doesn't say that young musicians are more or less capable of diversifying than anyone else and he doesn't generalize about their characters or abilities (see D).

7 **C**
Apprentice conductors should not be too fancy in their outlook (they should not have ambitions that are too high and unrealistic). They shouldn't wait to be asked to conduct one of the great symphonies as this won't happen for a long time; they should be willing to do any conducting they can in order to gain experience (see C).
A: He doesn't refer to failure or say that apprentice conductors will find it hard to succeed (see D); he says that they should take any opportunity to conduct anywhere, for example to conduct a musical or at a circus.
B: He says that musicians want to know what is required of them by apprentice conductors but he doesn't say that musicians can be difficult to deal with (see B).
D: He doesn't refer to musicians telling apprentice conductors anything; he refers to them wanting to know something (see A).

PAPER 4 PART TWO

(see tapescript, p185–186)

FURTHER PRACTICE AND GUIDANCE (p124)

8 and 9 (lines 10–49)

A: T
When American baseball players *went out on strike a couple of years ago, cable television in the US carried* (broadcast) *some matches.*

B: T
When two professional baseball teams from America *played an exhibition game* in London, *the stands were half empty* (only half the number of spectators that could sit in the structures for spectators attended the game).

C: T
When the baseball players were on strike, showing cricket on cable TV was meant to *act as a kind of methodone for American fans suffering from withdrawal* (this refers to drug addiction; methodone is given to heroin addicts to help them overcome the effects of giving up heroin).

D: T
At the exhibition game in London, there were also *hot dogs* (food typically eaten at American sports events), *a frenetic organ* (an organ being played in an excited manner), *a giant prancing chicken* (someone dressed as a huge chicken and walking around in front of the crowd) and *all the razzamatazz of American sport* (all the loud activities that accompany an American sports event in order to entertain the crowd).

E: T
Cricket is played in Washington DC by *ex-patriots* (people living abroad) *to the bemusement* (confusion and surprise) *of passing spectators.*

F: F
Cricket has been shown on TV but there is no reference to the way in which it was staged.

G: T
In both places, the games are for *ex-patriots* (Americans living in Britain and British people living in the USA).

H: F
There is no reference to anything being left as a sign that a game of cricket has taken place.

10 and 11 (lines 50–70)

A: F

Some baseball phrases have entered British vocabulary, but it is not suggested that they are used incorrectly by British people.
B: T
Americans think that cricket is *more like a puzzle than a game.*
C: F
There is no mention of Americans thinking that changes should be made to cricket.
D: T
The British people who think about baseball at all think that it is *a peculiar mutation of cricket* (a strange version of cricket that has developed from it).
E: T
Americans *shake their heads* (react with disbelief or disapproval) at the thought of a game (cricket) that can last for a long time without any real result (*without either side winning*).
F: F
Americans think cricket is pointless but there is no suggestion that British people accept this view.
G: F
Americans think it strange that a game of cricket can end without a winner but there is no reference to how they react at the end of a game of baseball.
H: T
British people think that because a game of baseball *can be settled in an afternoon, it can't be all that serious* (because a game of baseball only lasts for a single afternoon, unlike cricket which lasts for days, it can't be a serious game).

12 and 13 (lines 71–87)
A: F
People have a certain image of both games. In England, cricket is associated with *the village common* (a piece of land in a village for public use), which could be considered the countryside. In America, baseball is associated with *the field behind a neighbourhood school* but this could be in a city.
B: T
The idea of the village common is *a rural idyll* (a scene considered perfect and giving a feeling of great happiness in the countryside) for English people.
C: T
For Americans, there is *nothing quite so evocative* (nothing causes such powerful feelings or associations) as a baseball pitch in a field behind a local school.
D: F
There is *a sweet romance about both games*; it is not stated that one has a more romantic image than the other.
E: T
They are both played *despite the clock* (without any concern about the length of time they last) rather than *against the clock* (having to be completed within a certain time limit).
F: F
Other games are said to have a *hectic pace* (to be played at a very fast pace), unlike cricket and baseball. There is no mention of games that last as long as cricket or baseball.
G: T
Both games are said to have a *lackadaisical* (rather lazy, without energy) *charm* and to *prize* (put a high value on) their *easy grace* (being relaxed and elegant).
H: T
Most other games are said to have a *hectic* (very fast) *pace.*

14 (lines 88–107)
A: F
At cricket matches, there is occasionally *a subdued moan* (a quiet low sound) from the crowd if there has been *particularly good play.*
B: T
At baseball games, the crowd *hoots and hollers* (makes loud, high-pitched sounds and shouts) and there is *a party atmosphere.*
C: F
Cricket fans read their newspapers and *rummage around* (search for things in) their picnic baskets during a game.
D: T
The crowd *hoots and hollers* during a game.

15 (lines 108–137)
A: T
For English people, cricket *stirs an imagined past* (makes them think about a previous age in the country, which he says in fact did not exist). They believe that if any sport is played in heaven, it is cricket.
B: T
For Americans, baseball *recalls an imagined innocence* (makes them think of a previous time when Americans were simple and optimistic, which he says in fact did not exist).
C: T
Cricket *seems to belong to the English* and is not popular with *the Welsh and the Scots.*
D: T
Americans think that *the world would be a better place* if more people played baseball.

PAPER 4 PART TWO (TEST)

See also the answers to the questions in the Further Practice and Guidance pages and the explanations above.

8 B: The baseball game in London had *all the razzamatazz of American sport.*

9 B: In Hyde Park in London, you can see *smudges* (marks caused by rubbing) *in the grass like big thumb prints*, which indicate where baseball has been played.

10 B: Some British people think that baseball is *a peculiar mutation of cricket.*

11 C: Americans *shake their heads* when they realize that a game of cricket can last for days but end without either side being the winner.

12 E: Both games have a romantic image in the countries where they are played. In America, the image is of a baseball pitch in a field behind a local school; in England it is of a cricket pitch on a village common.

13 E: Both games are said to be *lackadaisical* and to have *an easy grace*, unlike *most other games*, which are played *against the clock.*

14 C: It doesn't matter if cricket fans *come late* and *leave early*. They read their papers and look for things in their picnic baskets. They only react to what happens in the game occasionally. They regard a cricket match as *a day out*. All of these indicate that they do not see the game itself as particularly important.

15 B: Americans think that *if there were a little more baseball in it*, the world would be better.

PAPER 4 PART THREE

(see tapescript, p186)

FURTHER PRACTICE AND GUIDANCE (p125)

For explanations, see the explanations for the answers in the test below.

16 B

17 B

18 B

19 A

20 C

21 A

22 B

23 A

24 B

25 B

PAPER 4 PART THREE (TEST)

16 his/an/the attic: (lines 1–10)
An *attic* is the room at the top of a house below the roof, often where things are stored rather than where people live.

17 lay more cables: (lines 18–27)

They were confident that *if they needed more capacity* (if they needed to increase their ability to send signals), they *just* (simply) *had to lay more cables* (had to put more cables – covered wires – down).

18 dismantled: (lines 27–33)
If you *dismantle* something, you take it apart so that all the pieces are separate.

19 far-reaching: (lines 34–43)
If something is described as *far-reaching*, it has an enormous effect, particularly on the future of something.

20 over the horizon: (lines 44–54)
The *horizon* is the point at which land or sea and the sky meet when you are looking at them.

21 hoisted in a kite: (lines 54–59)
If something is *hoisted*, it is lifted into the air by use of something that can carry its weight; a *kite* is a toy that consists of a piece of fabric that is attached to a piece of string and that goes up into the air because of the power of the wind.

22 signed the microphone: (lines74–89)
The photograph shows her *handling the microphone* while she is singing but after that she signed the microphone to mark the occasion.

23 factory made receiver(s)/radio(s): (lines 90–107)
Listeners were *making their own receivers* and Marconi *couldn't allow this to happen for too long*, so his company started to manufacture their own receiver, the Marconiphone.

24 monopoly (of radio): (lines 107–112)
Other companies were not happy about his *monopoly* (domination of the market of, as the only person operating in that market).

25 wholesome: (lines 115–126)
What was broadcast was almost entirely wholesome (morally correct and acceptable; not controversial).

126–128 PAPER 5

FURTHER PRACTICE AND GUIDANCE (p128)

DESCRIBING FACIAL EXPRESSIONS

glum D: If you look *glum*, you look serious and unhappy.
grin P: If you *grin*, you smile broadly; *a grin* is a big smile.
glare D: If you *glare (at someone)*, you look at someone with an angry expression on your face; *a glare* is an angry look.
grim D: If you have a *grim* expression on your face, you look serious because you are angry or worried.
sulky D: If you have a *sulky* expression on your face, you look as if you are being silently angry about something that has happened to you or been said to you.
wince D: If you *wince*, your face has an expression of pain or great embarrassment.
gloomy D: If you have a *gloomy* expression on your face, you look depressed and as if you have lost hope.
scowl D: If you *scowl*, you have a very angry expression on your face, with your eyebrows closer together and your eyes narrower.
sullen D: If you look *sullen*, you are quiet and your face shows that you are displeased.
grimace D: If you *grimace*, your face becomes twisted because of pain or great displeasure; *a grimace* is a facial expression of pain or great displeasure.
smirk P: If you *smirk*, you have a small smile on your face, usually because you think that someone or something is ridiculous or foolish; *a smirk* is a slight smile that indicates this feeling.
frown D: If you *frown*, your face shows that you are angry, displeased or confused; your eyebrows get closer together and your forehead is tense; *a frown* is a facial expression of this kind.

DESCRIBING VOCAL SOUNDS

Note: All of these verbs can also be used as nouns with the same meaning, except for 'snap'.

jeer D: If you *jeer (at someone)*, you shout insults at someone.
snap D: If you *snap (at someone)*, you speak to or reply to them in an angry and brief way.
moan D: If you *moan (at someone)*, you complain, often at length, in a way which is considered annoying.
chuckle P: If you *chuckle*, you laugh quietly.
roar P/D: If you *roar with laughter*, you laugh very loudly; if you *roar* because you are angry, you shout very loudly and angrily.
sob D: If you *sob*, you cry loudly.
scream P/D: If you *scream*, you make a very loud, high-pitched noise; you might *scream* because you are excited, delighted, etc. or you might *scream* because you are angry, frightened, etc.
grumble D: If you *grumble*, you complain quietly, in a low voice.
groan D: If you *groan*, you make a long, low noise that indicates pain, disappointment, unhappiness, boredom or frustration.
snigger P: If you *snigger*, you laugh quietly and secretly, especially at the misfortune of someone else.
curse D: If you *curse*, you say very rude or insulting things because you are angry.
giggle P: If you *giggle*, you laugh with a high-pitched sound or you laugh in a situation in which you know it is inappropriate to laugh.
sigh P/D: If you *sigh with relief, pleasure*, etc., you breathe out strongly because you are relieved, pleased, etc; if you *sigh with boredom, impatience*, etc., you breathe out strongly because you are bored, impatient, etc.
sneer D: If you *sneer (at someone)*, you speak in a tone that indicates that you think someone or something is stupid or inferior.

TALKING ABOUT PASSAGES

1 b

2 **there are drawbacks; a mixed blessing; the pros; the cons**
Drawbacks are disadvantages; if something is *a mixed blessing*, it has both advantages and disadvantages; *the pros* of something are the advantages of it; *the cons* of something are the disadvantages of it.

3 **outdo**

4 a

5 **that playing computer games is bad for children**
The allegation is that playing computer games *rots* (gradually destroys) *a child's mind*.

6 **And a good thing too.**
This refers to the previous sentence, in which it is stated that computer games are *a number one demand*. The writer believes that this is good because computer games are *the nursery slopes of computer literacy* (this is an analogy with skiing; the nursery slopes are where beginners learn to ski and the writer is saying that computer games are the way in which children start to learn how to use computers).

7 c

8 **with the use of italics for *adding*.**
This emphasizes that, in the writer's view, many of the inventions *acclaimed* (welcomed with enthusiasm) *as lightening life's burdens* (as making life easier) in fact increase *our workload* (the amount of work we have to do).

9 **that he or she is not of the younger generation**
The writer refers to people who are *among my generation* and asks whether the way we live now *is really so much better*. This suggests that the writer has lived during a period in which the inventions he/she refers to did not exist.

LISTENING SCRIPTS

TEST 1 PART ONE

You will hear part of a radio programme about people who have won an enormous amount of money on the national lottery in Britain. For questions 1–7, choose the best answer, A, B, C or D.

Presenter: Hunter Davies has spent a year following the lives of big lottery winners, finding out how they've changed and whether their new-found wealth has brought them happiness. His book is called *Living on the Lottery*. Hunter, welcome. Tell us about the book.

Hunter: Hi Chris. Um, in my book I did 25 different people and they, like the vast majority of people, they said that before they won they said, if I win the lottery you won't see me for dust, I'll be on a desert island. A lot of them actually said those words beforehand and not one of them a year later of those 25 is either living abroad or has got a house abroad. When it happens to them they just want to carry on as normal. But what happens of course is that they try to carry on as normal but people react to them differently. And that makes them in the end a little bit different, which they can't help.

Presenter: Is there a common denominator in the first thing that people do?

Hunter: They all give away money to their nearest and dearest, well practically all, we know exceptions, and they give from 20% to a third to their mums, dads, brothers, sisters, children. They don't give away any money to charity – out of my 25 only one person has given money altruistically. A lot say they will later, in their wills. They often say, we'll leave money, but they don't, they think charity begins at home.

Presenter: Who's the biggest winner you followed, there's someone with 22 million...

Hunter: That was the two blokes from Hastings, Mark Gardiner and Paul Maddison, and they won, I think, it's 18 months ago now and I followed their lives. Mark was the so-called 'lottery rat' because in 24 hours the press, they managed to track him down, he was only 33, three wives, girlfriends and everything else and they made him look a really horrible person, which I think he's not. And a year later he's happily married and he's changed, single-handedly almost, the economy of Hastings by pumping money back into the town.

Presenter: What kind of things has he done?

Hunter: They had a firm called *Croft Glass* which wasn't doing very well, in fact they had debts and they owed the taxman, and he now runs it totally and he's hired another 30 people and he's put several million pounds into it and he's bought another factory and he spends £30,000 a month on the local commercial radio station advertising because he wants to prove, which he hadn't been able to do before, that he can run a successful business. Having 11 million of course behind you is a bit of a help.

Presenter: Good news for Hastings obviously. Hunter, I don't know if you've seen the front page of *The Daily Mirror* today...

Hunter: I have, yeh.

Presenter: Apparently *The Mirror* claims they've found, they've tracked down the winners of £2.8m, a couple, I think they're in their late 30s or 40s who haven't told their children or parents, they've been keeping the secret, or so *The Mirror* claims, for 17 months.

Hunter: It's not just *The Mirror* who are claiming it, that's from my book.

Presenter:... right, OK.

Hunter:... it's lifted from my book.

Presenter: I was going to say a good bit of journalism from *The Mirror* but they've lifted it from the book?

Hunter: And they haven't given the book a mention.

Presenter: It's true then?

Hunter: It is true, there are one or two things that at least *The Mirror* have played fair, there are one or two things like the photograph which doesn't show clearly who they are. This is the most amazing couple. Roughly 80% of people these days who win the lottery keep quiet, so there are actually 200-odd millionaires walking round Britain today whom nobody knows about. Now the norm is to tell some of your family and you give them some money and you swear them to secrecy but you don't tell the street. But this couple were most unusual in the sense they didn't tell his mother. I went, when I first went to see them in their house, and I was prejudiced against them because he looked like a yob and the front garden was a dump. I'd sort of bracketed them wrongly, they were the most loving couple. And I was saying, 'Well what are you going to do with the money and does your mother know?' because it was her house, and he said, 'No, we haven't told my mother'. And I said, 'You haven't told your mother and you've had this 2 point whatever it is million?' I said, 'Won't she see me coming, a stranger coming to the door and hear us talking?' He said, 'No, her television's on even louder than ours she won't hear a word.'

Presenter: But could that not be potentially damaging for the relationship, that they withheld this fact?

Hunter: Er... well it remains to be seen. They've had 18 months to really think about it and they told me about it, which was very kind of them because they were taking a risk that it would somehow come out, and it has, I know how it's come out and it's a shame really. And they've had time to change their life and settle down... they haven't... but the thing is they haven't changed as people. He did say to me, which he said to *The Mirror*, and I believe it entirely, that the biggest single exciting happiest moment of his life was meeting his wife, not winning the lottery and that won't change.

Presenter: OK, stay with me Hunter, I'm now going to talk to.... (*fade*)

TEST 1 PART TWO

You will hear a talk about old beliefs associated with houses in Britain. For questions 8–17, complete the sentences.

Most of us are superstitious, even if we don't really like to admit it. But few of us could compete with our ancestors, who clung to the comforts of a thousand superstitions, many of which now seem either faintly comic or utterly absurd.

Moving house has always been seen as a critical time. Superstitions about moving house varied according to where you lived. In Wales, the carter carrying your furniture always made sure he had a box of salt in his cart. Before a stick of furniture was taken indoors, he would sprinkle it in every room of the new house for good luck.

Knocking on people's doors could be a tricky business at any time. Callers were not allowed, for example, to enter by one door and leave by another, as to do so took the luck of the house with them. It was also an ill omen to drop the front-door key when you arrived at your house and were about to go in, but misfortune was averted if you quickly stepped on the key before picking it up.

You'd think that having got through the rituals associated with doors and getting into the house, you'd have been able to relax. Alas, not so. Once you were in the sitting-room it was almost obligatory to do a spot of fire-gazing. This was a mix of family fun and fortune-telling in the days before radio and television. A square-shaped spark shooting up from the wood or coals foretold the arrival of a letter – an important event in the days when a letter was a rarity. And if the square-shaped spark appeared with crackles, it was time to celebrate, because the letter would contain news of a fortune.

There were other beliefs about fires among certain people. For example, in some fishing communities, a jet of white steam hissing from a lump of black coal indicated to the fisherman's wife that her husband's trawler was getting up steam to head home. And in certain parts of the country, a flake of soot flapping and dancing about warned that a stranger would call soon.

It's hard to imagine the reason for many of these beliefs, but there are explanations for some of them. For example, it was believed that the roof would collapse if an umbrella was opened indoors. The supposed reasoning behind this was that the spirit of the house would be offended because its job as protector of those it sheltered was challenged.

The greatest hoard of superstitions and omens was always to be found in the kitchen. Dropped cutlery predicted who was about to visit: a knife for a man, a fork for a woman and a spoon for a child. Another belief, and one that some people still adhere to today, was that if ever a pair of scissors or any sharp implement was given as a gift, a small coin had to be handed over in exchange so as not to cut the friendship.

Venturing upstairs was certainly no escape. A good night's sleep depended on the bed being aligned with the floorboards and not pointed towards the door. There's a reason for that one. Corpses were carried out through the door feet first, so people didn't want to sleep with their feet pointing towards the door. It was also believed that a mattress must never be turned over on a Sunday, as that would be 'turning out your luck'. Other bedroom tips included making sure that your pillowcase ends pointed outwards to allow nightmares an easy escape.

So, although life might have been more colourful in the past, it must have been pretty tiresome when you could hardly do anything at home without breaking some taboo or other.

TEST 1 PART THREE

You will hear part of a radio programme, in which the children of famous fathers are interviewed. For questions 18–25, decide which of them makes the statements. Write G for George, R for Ruth or M for Mark.

PRESENTER: Here with us are George Vine, son of the great comedian, Ruth Smart, daughter of the great actor and Mark Tate, son of the great comic actor. Now, whether the familiarity of their surnames is a cross they've had to bear is something we may find out. First of all, was the fame of your father something you were always aware of as children? George?

GEORGE: I think for me 1961, that was a real start because he made it in television that year. Up until then I knew that my father was famous but it was on a limited scale, he was only famous to that particular audience he was appearing in front of. When television started and he became a national name, then other people started commenting and then obviously I was aware of it.

PRESENTER: Ruth?

RUTH: I wasn't really aware through my early childhood at all. I mean, there was that sort of fantasy that my Dad's better than your Dad which just no-one seemed to try and counter very often so I kind of got away with it for quite a long time.

PRESENTER: And Mark?

MARK: I was aware long before I knew what it meant. I saw him on television, I saw him in movies and we would walk the street and people would stop him for his autograph. And it wasn't till I was about 8 or 9, maybe 10 that I began to realize that this actually meant something special to somebody else, which was the important thing, you suddenly, you're looked on and treated in a different way even though you don't believe yourself to be so.

PRESENTER: Has your father's name affected your own careers? Mark?

MARK: When you go for an interview for a job and the guy says 'Name?', you say Mark Tate, and it takes a few more questions before they brave it up to ask you the question and then everything's different. Whilst I might be trying to pursue what might be termed an ordinary career, I'm not allowed because of my name.

PRESENTER: Ruth?

RUTH: And if you do an ordinary career, there's a certain stigma attached to the fact that you're doing that job. People used to say to me 'What are you doing in this dump, you're father's like royalty'. Now how do you sort of deal with that?

PRESENTER: It's very hard I should think. Isn't it George?

GEORGE: Well it's confusing, it's not so much hard it's just a bit confusing it takes a while to let things go through your mind.

PRESENTER: Be honest, have you found it awful to be the child of a famous father? Ruth?

RUTH: I mean if you're treated as an extraordinary person when you haven't done anything extraordinary, that's the difficulty, that's the really hard thing, isn't it Mark?

MARK: Yes that sums it up, doesn't it George?

GEORGE: Well I'd say that it's had a lot more pluses and a lot more pleasure than minuses.

PRESENTER: No inhibitions, George?

GEORGE: No, I would say that I was inhibited definitely because how can you live in the shadow of that persona when that person is living within the shadow himself? I mean my father was just as surprised by his own fame as his family was. But for us it was a lot harder than for the chap who's actually enjoying it and getting the benefits directly from it.

PRESENTER: I wonder if people compared you with your parents, whether you felt that that was happening. Ruth?

RUTH: I felt it and still to this day I don't know if they were or if I was totally paranoid. Every time I stepped on the stage I couldn't concentrate, I didn't know what I was doing, I was just thinking I'm being compared.

PRESENTER: What about the others, did any of you feel that you were being, well not necessarily when you were doing something but just in the street, being looked at? George?

GEORGE: Well there is that, isn't there Mark?

MARK:... there's also people who say 'Could you just do it in his voice, could you just do a comic turn?' and I say 'Actually I wasn't the comic, he was.' You do feel under scrutiny.

PRESENTER: Now you've all written books about your fathers? Did you have to tell all? George?

GEORGE: Well I took the easy way out with my book, I went for the analytical approach and I brought in a co-writer and it worked because we didn't get any... um... well the book was a bestseller, but we didn't get any comeback about this is slandering my father's wonderful name and all that sort of thing. But we didn't set out to do that, we set out to analyse his career.

PRESENTER: Ruth?

RUTH: I never felt the need to protect my father, his reputation as an actor cannot be changed, you only have to look at the movies, you know, whatever anybody else says. When I wrote the book with my sisters we felt that we were just going to say everything, we weren't going to censor it, that was our lives with him.

PRESENTER: And Mark?

MARK: I mean, looking back now I you know I cringe at some of the things I said because of the way I said it not necessarily what I said.

PRESENTER: Now, what sort of legacy, you've talked about the ins and outs and the downs and the ups of being the offspring of the famous, is there a legacy, a desirable legacy above all that your fathers have left you with? Mark.

MARK: His legacy today is to see children laughing at him. I find now that people say 'I really admired your father' and I'm moved. I can't just sort of dismiss them and say 'Leave me alone.' I'm there now to say thankyou on his behalf and even give them a bit of my time and discuss what they want to discuss, that's part of his legacy to me.

PRESENTER: George?

GEORGE: For me I suppose it's never to take any of it seriously because he certainly didn't. He never believed that he was as good as he was and never believed when he was told he was as bad as he was in the early days. I think that's a very good way to live your life.

PRESENTER: And Ruth?

RUTH: Yes I think my father left a legacy of inspiration to a younger generation of actors. I think quite sadly at the moment, it looks like he will probably be the last great actor who plied his wares mainly on the stage and his inspiration was in the theatre. His inspiration still goes on, people still come up to me and say he inspired them to act.

TEST 2 PART ONE

You will hear part of a radio programme about the Innu, a group of North American Indians. For questions 1–10, complete the sentences.

JAMES WILSON: Deep inside Labrador, hundreds of miles from the nearest house or road, two elderly Innu hunters are checking their fish nets. A few months from now the sub-Arctic winter will have turned the area into a vast 60ft-deep block of ice and reduced the landscape to a monochrome world. They are among the last native North Americans who have grown up in a world whose outlook was not formed by exposure to European culture. Their culture gives us perhaps the clearest glimpse possible today of what the world was like in much of North America before the Europeans arrived.

The Innu are the indigenous population of most of the Labrador/Quebec peninsula in North Eastern Canada. The main reason for their remarkable survival is that, unlike other indigenous North Americans, they have faced very little European competition for their homeland. Although it was probably visited as early as the 10th century AD by Vikings from Greenland, only a handful of colonists chose to settle there permanently. Chilled by the Arctic current flowing down from Hudson's Strait, it seems to European eyes a bleak and forbidding place. For eight months of the year the landscape lies under a deep white blanket, and the brief summers are infested with black flies and mosquitos. As a result, it's only very recently that outsiders have started to encroach on the Innu's heartland in the interior. In the 1960s, the government decided to settle them in permanent villages on the coast and start opening their hunting grounds to development. Some, however, have resisted settlement. They continue to spend most of the year with their families in the 'country' far away from schools, television and interference from the authorities.

Before settlement the Innu way of life was nomadic. For most of the year small bands of perhaps two or three families would travel through the interior in search of caribou and other game, walking on snowshoes and pushing their possessions on a sled. During the summer they would come together in larger groups at the coast to fish, make canoes and paddles and meet friends and relatives. It was a hard, heroic existence.

The first detailed account of Innu life comes from the writings of Father Paul Lejeune, a missionary who spent the winter of 1634 with three Innu families. His record is one of the earliest European descriptions of a North American native people and much of what he wrote would be immediately recognizable to someone who spent time in an Innu camp today.

VOICE OF LEJEUNE: They are very generous among themselves and even make a show of not being attached to the riches of the earth so that they may not grieve if they lose them. One of the greatest insults that can be offered to them is to say 'That man likes everything.' Those who are to be entertained, having been invited to a meal, they come, each with his dish and spoon and enter the cabin, each one taking his place as he comes. They seat themselves around the kettle which is over the fire. Their chairs are the ground covered with pine branches and no order of precedence is observed. All the members of the party are as noble as the others. I do not believe that there is a nation under heaven more given to bantering than them. Their life is passed in eating, laughing, and making fun of each other and of all the people they know.

JAMES WILSON: Lejeune is fascinating not only because he shows us how little the Innu have changed but also how little we have changed. Like other Europeans then and later he interprets their life as an image of our own past. Sometimes he talks approvingly of their simplicity and naturalness, seeing them as figures from a golden age from which we have lapsed. More often he sees them as still living in a state of ignorance and superstition from which Europeans, thanks to civilization, have moved on. This description, echoed by others in more modern times and based on European concepts of cultural development, bears almost no relation to the experience of the Innu. For them the idea that they are anachronisms, survivors from our collective past, would be incomprehensible. They see themselves as part of a sacred reality in which animals, human beings and the land are joyfully intertwined. This view of life is far more than a generalized respect for nature; it is rooted in a system of belief which sees hunting not simply as a means of survival but as a holy occupation.

TEST 2 PART TWO

You will hear a discussion on the radio about the decision to set up a college for rock music in the UK. For questions 11–17, decide which of the speakers expresses the views. Write J for Jane, P for Paul or B for both of them.

PRESENTER: Now a decision has been made to spend £10m on the UK's first centre dedicated to rock music. Is it a waste of money or a good idea? I have with me Jane Willis, a lecturer in popular culture, and newspaper columnist Paul Spicer. Jane first, a good idea or not?

JANE: This decision is about creativity and people's enterprise and this is, you know, right up my street. People should be creative, they should be enterprising and thank goodness someone somewhere in the country has fostered this idea. In fact, it's not a new idea, it's a development of many existing things that have been developed over the last ten years.

PRESENTER: OK Paul, would you agree with that, thank goodness someone's doing it?

PAUL: I think it's yet another surrender by our culture to an invasion that's done a tremendous amount of damage. No-one's prepared to say this because there's so much money invested in it. I mean the rock business when you see it at first hand is an enormous money-spinning outfit – vast quantities of money are invested in it and indeed vast quantities of money are being made. You suddenly realize why it has such a huge power in society but it's undermined real culture over the past 30 or 40 years.

PRESENTER: That's a very snobby attitude, isn't it?

PAUL: We have wiped out real culture, rock music as this place is going to celebrate it isn't culture, it's a substitute for culture, it's not like the music of, say, Gershwin, and I think we should begin to realize that.

JANE: I think that Paul's comment... I mean yes we've imported kinds of music.... the music of Gershwin isn't exactly British culture is it? But you know, there are great things going on that should be celebrated as contemporary British culture,... er... this is humanity on the move as far as I see it. And this is a big business. A billion pounds was earnt in the rock record industry and that's just the record industry part of the music industry last year. That's a big economic generator for this country.

PRESENTER: Paul?

PAUL: To compare Gershwin with rock Gershwin is musically literate and morally uplifting, they're not even remotely comparable. It's this inability to distinguish between the two which does so much damage.

PRESENTER: Now, Jane, the rock industry could fund this on its own, couldn't it? It doesn't need money from other sources.

JANE: Well the rock music industry could but unfortunately it's so refracted in its opinions, you know, inside the actual infrastructure of the record companies which is where the money is. The music business is actually founded on loads of small venues up and down the country, it's hundreds of small businesses all promoting and finding new talent, new ideas new directions and new scenes. There have been so many innovations over the last 30, 40 years across all forms of popular culture and I think this centre is going to celebrate that.

PRESENTER: Now Paul, you're taking a very highbrow tone about all of this.

PAUL: It's nothing to do with being highbrow, it's to do with saying this stuff has been revered in recent years in a way which it doesn't deserve and it's to do with saying it has a moral content that has an effect on the way people behave and it's a damaging one and yet we roll over and let it tickle our tummies. Whenever any attempt is made to criticize it you're immediately called highbrow or snobbish or in some other way culturally deprived.

PRESENTER: But isn't rock music just generally worth spending money on because it is part of our culture isn't it?

PAUL: Well it's part of something, whether you can call it culture is another matter. It's main effect is social. It's done an awful lot to promote for instance adolescent self-pity, self-indulgence and I think almost certainly the breakdown of parental authority.

JANE: Listen, the whole social environment we live in today is, you know, a product of the past and will evolve in the future and I think if we don't have dialogue, if we don't have communication, if we don't have young people communicating how they feel then we have a much more ingrained society and a bigger problem will evolve from that. The right, the fundamental right to self expression is in my opinion a fundamental human right and if you don't exercise that, if you bottle it up, then you will have a massive problem.

PAUL: And yet people originally, when it began, had to be trained in how to respond to it. When the Rolling Stones first appeared in South London, the promoter had to persuade people to stand on table tops because they didn't know that was what they were supposed to be doing and then they danced on table tops and the Stones got this reputation for being terribly avant garde. People had to be trained originally to respond to it but once that began it changed our society.

JANE: But the same thing can be said for a Beethoven symphony, the first time it was performed I think, people had to learn how to deal with that, didn't they?

PAUL: I'm trying to make the point about self expression.... um it's not self expression... it's the most monstrous conformism. Almost no teenager is allowed to escape this they all have to conform with this one type of music.

JANE: I think there's still a case for rock music and I think that people, if they're stopped and told, you must enter this educational spiral to achieve, you know, the one violin place this year, people have gone round that and that's why popular culture has evolved. They've said, no, if you put a barrier here, I can't get those exams, I want to do it another way, and that's the way I come round to rock being involved with popular culture.

PRESENTER: I can't see the two of you agreeing at all about that but thankyou very much to both of you, that's Jane Willis and Paul Spicer. And now it's coming up to........

TEST 2 PART THREE

You will hear a radio item about solo performers. For questions 18–25, choose the best answer, A, B, C or D.

PRESENTER: My very last foray into the world of theatre was in a one-woman show which I played to a 2000-seater auditorium and I hated every single minute of it. Maybe that's why I left the loneliness of the stage for the comfort and camaraderie of the studio. But there are many brave souls who still choose to face an audience unaided by a supporting cast. Susie Maguire, herself a graduate of the stand-up comedy circuit, has asked herself for many years why anyone would want to face a roomful of strangers entirely alone. Now she's decided to ask the same question of some other artists. She began by talking to actor Guy Masterson about his one-man play.

SUSIE: Bringing together the dozens of characters in your version of *Animal Farm* is one of the hardest of tasks for a solo artist, isn't it?

GUY: Yeh. There are moments half-way through the play when I think, 'What am I doing here?', because it's so physical, I get so knackered doing it, I'm gasping for breath, although the audience can't see that. I say, 'I can't continue'. Obviously you do and you finish it and by the end of course you feel you know why you're doing it.

SUSIE: But you relish a challenge, don't you?

GUY: It's totally up to you there's no-one to fall back on. And then of course you've got the added extras like audience participation, occasionally they laugh in the wrong places or whatever – not in the wrong places, in places you didn't expect. That throws a new energy into it. If you can control the audience reaction, you guide the audience down the story, then yes, it is the biggest thing you can do I suppose.

SUSIE: But you have a lot of fun doing that don't you, you're playing all these characters, it must be exciting, it's not one static, cerebral performance it's a completely integrated...

GUY: My style of performance, I've never seen it before, it was just born out of... er...imagination if you like, and I think every solo performer has their way of doing that. I think audiences, adults, love to be told stories, it's a long time since they were sat down with mother and told a story. I think this is essentially getting back to that.

SUSIE: Are you insane to be doing this?

GUY: Probably, but it's my only means of making a living at the moment.

SUSIE: Stu Who, well known on the comedy club circuit works without a script. Unlike Guy Masterson he goes out there and just 'feels' his audience.

STU: I am a comedy plumber. People want to laugh, all I'm doing is going in and clearing out their drains and I'm giving them an excuse to laugh a lot of the time. The best thing to do will be the next thing that comes into my head with that audience on that night. Cos if I look out and see a very middle-class, middle-aged audience my mind will immediately relate to them and go towards material that suits them – not so much that suits them, that I'm pandering to their taste, but material towards their interests.

SUSIE: Stu used to work with other performers but he says he now finds it easier to face an audience alone.

STU: It takes too much time explaining to someone else the way you want it if you can just go and do it yourself. And often you end up compromising and losing the objective, the actual artistic thing, where you're trying to get a feeling and you spend that much time trying to explain the vibe, the buzz, the feeling, that you end up losing it yourself because you've been so busy explaining it. Sometimes it's easier just to get on with it.

SUSIE: After you've done your hour and a half or whatever on stage and you come off, what's the reward for you?

STU: I've been through the enthusiasm, the buzz,... ah... come off and hairs standing up on the back of the neck, standing on stage and looking at an audience and they're really enjoying it on great nights and that. And I'm getting less and less of that because it's becoming more and more commonplace. It seems really really big-headed but you get to a point where you've done that many gigs where you get an encore, you don't actually get a buzz from the encore, you get upset if you don't get an encore.

SUSIE: Actress Clare Coulter does a one-woman show but she didn't plan to be a solo performer. The first time she tried it, it was a traumatic experience.

CLARE: As an actor with other actors on the stage I had always believed that I was perfect. Nothing I did was ever wrong and when something went wrong on stage and it was clearly felt in the audience that something had really gone wrong I would think to myself, 'What person could possibly have done what they've done, it's obviously not me'. And then when I was on stage alone that awful feeling of, you know, you've lost the audience and you just don't know what you've done but it was *me* and I had a really traumatic period where I thought I can't face being someone that could actually do that to an audience and could make that mistake and I wanted to quit.

SUSIE: But you enjoy it now?

CLARE: Actually, I've always wished that I could be a musician. I've always wanted to wear a black dress and go out on the stage and sit down in front of a grand piano and run my hands over those keys. Glenn Gould was always someone that I kind of envied, the way that he kind of hunched over the piano and groaned and moaned to himself and went into total ectasies. (*both laugh*) And there's an example of someone who could go into his own state of ecstasy as he worked and worked and worked. There is a level of meditation up there which you can give to an audience.

Presenter: Clare Coulter giving her views on solo performance to Susie Maguire. Well whether you're working on your own or with other performers...

TEST 3 PART ONE

You will hear part of a radio programme about traffic wardens, whose job is to stop people from parking illegally and give them a ticket if they do. For questions 1–9, decide which of the two speakers makes the statements. Write K for Keith, J for Julia or N for neither of them.

Announcer: Time for a new series of *The New Recruit*, in which someone new to a career talks to an old hand in the same profession. We go to meet the traffic wardens. Keith Lodgee, who joined the force just a year ago, is about to start his beat, accompanied by recently retired Julia Scott.

Keith: Julia, did you always get, you know, all the insults?

Julia: Yes.

Keith: The way they treat you, you take all the swearing and all the insults...

Julia:... and then you say, have you finished?

Keith: Yes and they hate that, don't they? And you look them in the eyes and you say, have you finished sir and you ask him how to spell a certain rude word (*both laugh*).... and they realize what they've said to you, you know.

Julia: Oh yes. And you've got your pocket book out and, you know, you write in your pocket book and you're not starting on a ticket, you haven't even thought about it...

Keith: No, and they say, 'Oh you're never giving me a ticket' (*laughs*)...

Julia:... and you have to say, no would you like one? Get in that car.

Keith: 'I've only been here 30 seconds'. Oh really sir, I've got you down in my book about 20 minutes ago...

Julia: That's right. If you get in your car now I won't do any writing...

Keith:... that's right...

Julia:... cos you've got to once you've started your ticket that is it...

Keith:... it's still the same, yeah. (*pause*)

Julia: So you've obviously got a good compromise with the hairdresser back there.

Keith: Yeah I try to, I mean she's got a business and I've got a job to do and if you keep it on a good footing, especially when she's got customers... and it's the same with most of the businesses, we try to have that compromise. But it bugs me that there are a few, I suppose like in any job, there are a few that let us down, you know, with their attitude, the way they talk to people.

Julia: That's right, oh you get one or two of the traffic wardens who, they don a uniform and they walk out and they think, right this is it, and they march round like dictators...

Keith:... yeah...

Julia:... which does the job no good at all...

Keith:... no...

Julia:... the image is completely wrong, you know they walk into shops and say 'Move it now' which is the wrong attitude. You've got to have a bit of liaison with people...

Keith:... yeah you do get some that, um sort of persecute, you know, you get the people that always reoffend they always do it...

Julia:... yes they do...

Keith:... they get on your nerves, and some traffic wardens tend to go a bit overboard.

Julia: We had one like that and he was absolutely shocking, and I mean not just one day, every day did that poor man get a ticket. He finally finished up in court...

Keith:... really?

Julia:... and he had to pay them. This warden just gave him tickets. I said to him I didn't think it was right to persecute like that you know...

Keith: Yeah I did have one I was forever catching, it got a bit ridiculous. I caught him about two times a week and I only work part time as you know (*laughs*). It was a bit embarrassing and in the end I found out where he worked and he worked in an office and I said every time I was on the street I would buzz him. He still got tickets off me if he wasn't in his office then it was tough luck, he still got a ticket, but if he was in his office I said 'I'm here' and then he'd jump, he'd move it quick (*laughs*).

Keith: Have you got any prejudices against certain drivers? I know I have.

Julia: Oh yes. You can tell the attitude with some of them the way they sit at the steering wheel. You know, their faces, grim determination, 'I'm going to park there and you're not going to stop me'.

Keith: I have a problem with businessmen bless them (*laughs*)...

Julia: Do you?

Keith: I hate it when they... er... try and browbeat me...

Julia:... yeah, look down on you...

Keith:... I do find that a problem. I have to grit my teeth and just be firm, cos even if they're shouting at me, because I've got a certain time limit in my mind – I don't know if you have – but I always give them a certain amount of time you know for parking illegally, just in my own mind to be fair. And even if they're screaming and shouting at me and calling me this and that, I still think he's not going over my time limit sort of thing. I try to be fair but oooh it does get on my nerves...

Julia:... yes it does...

Keith: Well how do you deal with it? You've had more experience than me.

Julia: Well I used to say to them, look you've been stood here now arguing with me for what 10 minutes?...

Keith:...mmm...

Julia:... another 10 minutes and you're going to get another ticket. And then they bounce into the car, the door slams and they're off.

TEST 3 PART TWO

You will hear a talk about Mrs Beeton, an English woman who wrote some extremely popular cookery books in the 19th century. For questions 10–19, complete the sentences.

If she were alive today, Mrs Beeton would serve as a typical example of the modern career woman. Growing up as she did in Victorian England, she broke the mould at a time when a woman's place was firmly in the home.

Far from being the formidable middle-aged matriarch depicted in pictures accompanying her great works, Isabella Beeton was sharp-witted and had a taste for social life and fashionable dresses. And she never did reach middle age, dying at 28 from a fever following the birth of her fourth child in June 1865.

Born in 1836, Isabella Mary Mayson was the oldest child of 14. Growing up in such a large family, she swiftly recognized the value of an orderly home and a well-run kitchen, which she called 'the great laboratory of the household'. She was married at 20 to Samuel Beeton, a publisher who played a crucial part in her success. Soon after marrying, 'lack of purpose' spurred her to write. She was determined to pursue a career based on her culinary expertise and her published works, including the definitive kitchen bible, *The Book of Household Management*, were not only best-selling classics in the Victorian era but avidly followed for years afterwards. Head cooks, housekeepers and kitchen maids faithfully followed the advice imparted from the 4,000 recipes and countless useful hints this indomitable lady began to compile from the age of 23.

How did she do it? Isabella confessed freely that she was not the originator of all her recipes. Many were culled from other cooks throughout the land, some of whom allegedly remained unpaid after sending their ideas to *The Englishwoman's Domestic Magazine*, a monthly journal published by her husband. But however they were sourced, the actual compiling of the series of works is thought to have precipitated Isabella's early death, attributed by *The Concise Universal Biography* to her being 'a martyr to overwork in the cause of culinary art'.

Why did she do it? Isabella Beeton was driven simply by the desire to avoid 'family discontent', caused by what she saw as 'a housewife's badly-cooked dinners'. Her success, many say, was owed to her meticulous explanation at a time when cooking had become a lost art. No stone was left unturned in her quest for perfection. She provided detailed recipes, itemizing cost and labour, the number of people they would serve and when it would be timely to serve them. Chapters were devoted to household servants, all of whom should have 'their duties clearly assigned to them'. Cautionary notes were written on the evil of gossip and the importance of 'good temper'. 'A wife should never let an account of her husband's failings pass her lips,' she wrote. There were homilies on childhood illness, first aid and even the laws concerning tenancy, taxation and tradesmen.

Her thinking and ideas came to be the saving grace of many nouveau riche of Victorian England. Thrust into moneyed lifestyles as a result of the Industrial Revolution, they found themselves lacking in the required social graces. But Mrs Beeton believed that her books could help rich and poor alike, proclaiming that with a little rudimentary knowledge of nutrition, the poor would survive with fewer problems.

Today, a revival in 'old-fashioned food' has rekindled interest in Mrs Beeton's works.

TEST 3 PART THREE

You will hear part of a radio programme about birth order. For questions 20–25, choose the best answer, A, B, C or D.

PRESENTER: Frank Sulloway of the Massachussetts Institute of Technology has spent 20 years researching the relationship between the position we hold in the family and the sort of people we are. He's examined thousands of historical figures and events before reaching the conclusion that people are designed to respond to birth order in predictable and universal ways. Frank, can you outline for us the characteristics of first-borns and subsequent children that you came across?

FRANK: Yes, first-borns have a special niche in the family, they tend to occupy a role as a surrogate parent... er... in caring for younger siblings. They tend to conform to parental authority so they're more conventional, more conscientious, more serious and in general more responsible, because parents value that in their offspring. Their younger siblings come along and that... um... serious niche has been taken and so the younger sibling is looking for an unoccupied niche that will distinguish them from the elder sibling and they tend to rebel against what the elder sibling's doing, so they're more open to experience, they're more sociable, they're more daring and adventurous, they're more unconventional and liberal in general in their attitudes. And in Western history, they've been the great rebels.

PRESENTER: Frank, stay with us because we're going to talk some more about this theory of yours because with me is Sophie Parkin, who's the daughter of the fashion editor, novelist and artist Molly. You're the second-born in your family, are you a rebel? Does what Frank's saying hold true for you?

SOPHIE: I think this theory is absolutely fascinating but I'm not sure how far you can go along with it because at the same time, it's this thing of how... um... outrageous or how rebellious your own parents are. I mean, you rebel against *them* but not necessarily against society itself. And so... um... well say for instance with my... er... own parenting which was quite outrageous, my mother was quite outrageous and seemed to be such and I rebelled against her. For instance, when I was 11, I came from a strictly atheist family and so I went and joined my local church and indeed joined up into the choir and this was a thorn in my mother's side every single Sunday.

PRESENTER: But in general you agree with Frank's theory?

SOPHIE: I think Frank's correct about my older sister, who was perhaps more conservative in her way but maybe the conservatism of the first-born is more due to the cautiousness of the parents who, because they're the first-born, they don't know actually what to do, and as soon as the second child comes along or the third or the fourth, you get more and more careless (*laughs*) because you just think, well I know that they survive. And I suppose in many ways I've been much more outrageous than my sister, but at the same time I also got the nickname in my family of 'the policeman' because I was always the one who wastrying to get everybody on to the straight and narrow again.

PRESENTER: So in a way you *don't* feel you fit in with Frank's model?

SOPHIE: I think I do up to a point but I mean, I tend to believe that each person is an individual and that the individual circumstances of their family life and their lives must be more of a factor as to how a person reacts or acts or behaves in any given circumstance. And after all, we all change, as you know, it is possible that, you know, you come as one thing into this life and you leave as quite another. And... um... many people do extraordinary things when they're way past the age of childhood, you know, right into their 60s. So this hallmarking of where you lie in the family can't stick rigidly with you all your life because other life circumstances change you into suddenly becoming a rebel later on in life.

PRESENTER: What do you think Frank?

FRANK: Well, I couldn't agree more. We all know that no single variable explains human behaviour completely or... er... even predominantly. And so in fact I've looked at many of these additional influences. For example, when later borns come from highly unconventional families, the first-born tends to imitate their parents' social values so the first-born would be just as unconventional. And the later born is suddenly confronted with a problem – there's no more space to be unconventional, so they will often in fact go in the opposite direction and become more conservative....

PRESENTER:... that's a bit like Sophie isn't it?...

FRANK:... exactly, because they're looking for a unique niche and that overrides the normal tendency to be unconventional. You have to understand that siblings are influenced in general by things like birth order but they're also influenced by what your sibling ahead of you in the sequence did and what your parents value and how all of that works itself out in the family.

PRESENTER: Thanks very much Sophie and Frank. And do let us know what you think about that because I'm sure..... (*fade*)

TEST 4 PART ONE

You will hear an interview with a well-known person in the classical music world. For questions 1–7, choose the best answer A, B, C or D.

ANNOUNCER: Now Tommy Pearson chats with his celebrity guest, André Previn, at Tanglewood, a music academy in the USA.

INTERVIEWER: Mr Previn, you're here at Tanglewood as a conductor, mostly, which is what we will know you best as in the UK, but I suppose you're best described as a musician, are you not?

PREVIN: I like to think so, yes (*chuckles*)....

INTERVIEWER:.... because you're so versatile. What are the advantages do you think of being a versatile musician?

PREVIN: Well it's.... one thing is selfish and that is that you can't get bored because you know I conduct.... er.... I would think about close to 100 concerts a year but I also play in about 20 or 25 so I do an awful lot of chamber music. It's interesting because just last month in London I did a couple of chamber music concerts and I will do that every time I go there now, so I will be playing the piano a little bit more. I don't know, maybe it's a reaction I found that in the last ten years that so many pianists have become conductors that

I thought I'd get even and start playing the piano more (*both laugh*).

INTERVIEWER: When you were very young, you composed music for films. I would assume you had choices to make then, which choices did you make?

PREVIN: Well, I suppose they're obvious considering what I do now, you know. I mean I had some sidetracks on the way – I worked as a commercial musician in films for about 12 years, not to the exclusion of doing other things but I have to admit that there I was in Hollywood doing films and I also am happy to tell you that I enjoyed it but I knew from day one on that I wasn't going to do it for the rest of my life. So after 10 or 12 years I was glad to move away from that.

INTERVIEWER: It must have been an amazing experience to be so young and suddenly composing for films. How did you avoid being sucked in then, you say from day one you wanted to go on... ?

PREVIN: Oh I think because I was always as a child I was trained to be a serious musician and while it was irresistible for me as a teenager to get away from that for a while, I really, I suppose the discipline I had when I was a kid, I always knew that my ambition was not to compose music that would be played while actors talked. So after a while I'd had enough.

INTERVIEWER: So what sort of things did you do to forward yourself then in that direction?

PREVIN: During that time?

INTERVIEWER: Uh hum.

PREVIN: Well, I.... for one thing, I played an inordinate amount of chamber music. I had my own group in Los Angeles and we played a lot of concerts and I went through a lot of different 35 chamber music. And there was a great violinist called Joseph Sigetti who befriended me and kind of took me through the basic repertoire of chamber music, simply out of the goodness of his heart which was extraordinary. And the other thing is that there was, you know the musicians who played in the studio orchestra at the film studios, they were really musicians of the highest possible order and they had all come from the great symphony orchestras to lead a more sedentary and an easier life. But after a while they did get restless and bored with that kind of music so they formed a rehearsal orchestra which met in...oh... any kind of school auditorium that was available once a week, with whoever was available that night and they would play Brahms symphonies, Beethoven symphonies, whatever they felt like. And among the Hollywood composers and conductors, there were only a few of us who were interested in that music so we always conducted them and... er... so I did manage to learn and study and keep my hand in during those days.

INTERVIEWER: When you're young it's very easy to have goals you want to achieve and maybe to specialize quite early. Do you think that's a healthy thing or do you think a musician should have perhaps the same attitude that you had.... ?

PREVIN: You mean to diversify?

INTERVIEWER: Mmm.

PREVIN: I never think it does any harm, I mean I think that if somebody who is gifted and talented who is 16 years old and says, 'For the rest of my life I'm just going to conduct one composer', I think it's doing him out of quite a lot of music. No, I think that you have to keep an open mind and I do like to tell conducting students, that when you are an apprentice conductor it's very hard because it's the one musical pursuit that you can't practise at home. You have to have an orchestra in front of you and I do firmly believe that any situation in which there are musicians sitting in front of you who ask of you 'What is it you want here?' is a terrific experience and a great learning experience. So very often I say to conducting students that if you're going to wait to be asked to do one of the great symphonies, it's a rather long wait. But in the meantime if there is anything, I don't care, a musical, or the circus, it doesn't matter, if you can transmit to living musicians what it is you're after, you're learning to conduct. So it's much better not to be too fancy in your outlook.

ANNOUNCER: Tommy Pearson was talking to André Previn. And tomorrow Tommy's guest will be...

TEST 4 PART TWO

You will hear a radio talk given by someone from the United States who spent some time living in Britain. He talks about the sports of the two countries – baseball and cricket. For questions 8–15, decide which of the sports he is referring to. Write B for Baseball, C for Cricket or E for each of them.

ANNOUNCER: And next this morning 'Letter From Over Here.' Raymond Seitz served as US Ambassador to Britain for several years, a unique vantage point from which to consider the many differences between our two countries. They're clearly revealed in our two national sports, baseball and cricket.

RAYMOND SEITZ: If you look hard enough you can see some cricket in America and a little baseball in Britain. But in both places the games are for ex-patriots, a kind of subversive over the shoulder souvenir of home. On a summer afternoon in Washington DC, in the parklands that run beside the Ptomac near the Memorial Bridge the cricket playing community of ex-patriots sometimes practises the sport to the bemusement of passing spectators. And when American baseball players went out on strike a couple of years ago, cable television in the US carried some cricket matches to see whether the English game could act as a kind of methodone for American fans suffering from withdrawal. But the experiment failed to stimulate much interest. For baseball in Britain you can go to Hyde Park – there smudges in the grass like big thumb prints show where the American colony in London has gathered over the years to play a little weekend baseball. And a couple of years ago, two professional teams from America came to London; they played an exhibition game, an occasion supercharged by hot dogs, a frenetic organ, a giant prancing chicken and all the razzamatazz of American sport but the stands were half empty, a second game was cancelled. So with the exception of loyal ex-patriots, neither national sport has made the transatlanic crossing with much success.

Those British who think of baseball at all look at the game as a peculiar mutation of cricket, as if a laboratory experiment had gone horribly wrong. Some baseball phrases such as 'touch base' and 'play hardball' have crept into the British vocabulary and baseball caps are now ubiquitous in Britain. But otherwise baseball has made few inroads here. After all, if a game that looks a little like cricket can be settled in an afternoon it can't be all that serious. On the other hand, for an American, cricket seems more like a puzzle than a game. They shake their heads at the thought of a sport so leisurely that it can last for days and so patient and open-ended that the score can run into the hundreds without either side winning.

These two sporting peas of course come out of the same athletic pod so there are a few important similarities. There is for example a sweet romance about both games. In America there is nothing quite so evocative as the dusty baseball diamond etched in the field behind a neighbourhood school. And in England, the green cricket pitch laid out on the village common is a rural idyll. Both sports also have a natural lackadaisical charm, they both prize an easy grace, unlike the hectic pace of most other games cricket and baseball are not played against the clock, they are played despite the clock.

The pieces of the two games are alike but the rhythm of play is different. Professional baseball is an altogether coarser game than cricket. The stands bustle and the crowd hoots and hollers, the fans nibble peanuts and shout insults, there is a party atmosphere about a baseball stadium. Cricket on the other hand is, well, a little posh. It still is a game where manners count. I have also noticed that cricket fans do not *go to* a cricket match; they drift to it. Come late, leave early, no matter. Cricket fans glance at the Sunday newspapers or rummage around in their picnic baskets; cricket is a day out. Occasionally a subdued moan rises from the crowd in recognition of particularly good play.

These respective national sports probably do reflect something about our respective national characters, although cricket and baseball are games, not social metaphysics. Nor are they as national as we like to pretend; cricket seems to belong to the English, not the Welsh or the Scots and for many Americans baseball is too dulcet when set beside the clamorous clashes of other professional sports. Still, in these two games, it seems to me, we each remember the way we were, or the way we think we were. In America, baseball recalls an imagined innocence and in England cricket stirs an imagined past. Most Americans, I think, believe that the world would be a better place if there were a little more baseball in it. When Americans compare baseball and life, baseball comes off better. The English are not so earthbound. I suspect most Englishmen believe that if there is a sport played in heaven, it is almost certainly cricket. The English may be right; after all, cricket comes as close as anything in sports to eternity.

TEST 4 PART THREE

You will hear part of a radio programme about Marconi and the history of radio. For questions 16–25, complete the sentences.

PRESENTER: Nowadays the air is alive with man-made signals – radio, TV, radar and the rest. But the ether was silent till Guglielmo Marconi sent his brother to the next field to signal with a gunshot if anything came through. As a teenager in a prosperous middle-class family, Marconi experimented in his attic in Italy. His experiments proved that signals could be transmitted through empty space. Marconi understood the huge potential of this. He saw that it could replace the telegraph, the wires and cables that carried signals around the world. His dream was telegraph without wires, or wireless telegraphy. He tried to sell his idea to the Italian government. He predicted the value his invention would have at sea but they were confident that if they needed more capacity they just had to lay more cables. They couldn't see the point in fragile wireless equipment that only sent signals over a few hundred metres. The 21-year-old inventor was politely refused. So Marconi went to England, although the process of getting there had its problems. He was stopped by the customs, who, suspicious of the equipment he was bringing in, dismantled it.

In 1896 Marconi, at the tender age of 22, gave his first public demonstration. To the astonished audience, it must have seemed like a magic trick. It wasn't. It was what must be the most far-reaching demonstration of the age. He showed that day how an electric spark at one end of the room could make a bell ring at the other.

In December 1901, Marconi launched his most ambitious experiment – a radio transmission across the Atlantic. With the curvature of the earth, the ocean was like a mountain 150 miles high. He didn't then understand that the ionosphere in the earth's surface could bounce signals round the globe, he just knew that somehow they went over the horizon. Just before the experiment, his huge aerial in England was destroyed in a storm so he had to improvize. The only way to get the aerial wire up into the air was by hoisting it in a kite. Marconi had set up a receiving station in Cape Cod around 2000 miles from the transmitter in England. The wind howled around the building as Marconi took his turn at listening for the signals which were being transmitted from England. Shortly after midday on December 12 1901, they started to come through. He now felt certain that the day would come when mankind would be able to send messages without wires not only across the Atlantic but between the furthermost ends of the earth.

The great Australian soprano Dame Nellie Melba was responsible for a great landmark. She was the first performer in a public broadcast, which was highly advertised by the Marconi company back in 1920. There's a very famous photograph of her standing in profile very gently holding the handle of the microphone in her right hand. And there she is in a grand hat singing *Home Sweet Home* and afterwards, to mark the occasion, she signed the microphone, which has a sort of rather crude-looking taped-together cone which focuses the sound.

The Marconi Company was granted a licence for a weekly half-hour programme. Broadcasting had truly begun. But if you wanted to listen to the radio, you had to make your own. Even the least skilful could knock up a servicable set with one of the plans published in specialist magazines. Marconi now had a lead in the manufacture of transmitters, microphones and other professional equipment but listeners were making their own receivers. Marconi couldn't allow this to continue for long. He developed the Marconiphone, the first factory made radio, which brought entertainment straight into the home. But other companies were not happy with his monopoly of radio. The government decided the only fair way forward was to form a single company made up of a number of manufacturers. This was to become the British Broadcasting Company in November 1922. There was great concern even then that the interests of the listening public should be scrupulously cared for. The company said that 'to exploit so great a scientific invention for the purpose and pursuit of entertainment alone would be an insult to the character and intelligence of the people'. What was broadcast was almost entirely wholesome; anything else was described in the schedules as 'variety to fill'.

Was this the culmination of Marconi's efforts? Far from it. The entrepreneur inventor was by now off onto new ideas, many years ahead of their time, like microwaves. When he died in 1937 all the broadcasters and radio stations around the world as a mark of respect let their transmitters fall silent for two minutes.

UNIVERSITY OF CAMBRIDGE
LOCAL EXAMINATIONS SYNDICATE
INTERNATIONAL EXAMINATIONS

ENGLISH AS A FOREIGN LANGUAGE

FOR SUPERVISOR'S USE ONLY
Shade here if the candidate is ABSENT or has WITHDRAWN

SAMPLE

Examination/Paper No. 9999/01 99/D99

Examination Title ANY CAMBRIDGE EXAM

Centre/Candidate No. AA999/9999

Candidate Name A.N. EXAMPLE

- Sign here if the information above is correct.
- Tell the Invigilator immediately if the information above is not correct

MULTIPLE-CHOICE ANSWER SHEET

HOW TO ANSWER	HOW TO CHANGE YOUR ANSWER
Like this: A B C D E	Like this: A B
NOT like this: A B C D E / A B C D E / A B C D E	NOT like this: A B C D E

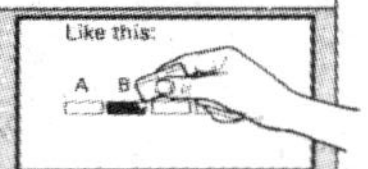

DO
- use an HB pencil
- rub out any answer you wish to change

DON'T
- use any other kind of pen or pencil
- use correcting fluid
- make any marks outside the boxes

1	A B C D	11	A B C D	21	A B C D	31	A B C D
2	A B C D	12	A B C D	22	A B C D	32	A B C D
3	A B C D	13	A B C D	23	A B C D	33	A B C D
4	A B C D	14	A B C D	24	A B C D	34	A B C D
5	A B C D	15	A B C D	25	A B C D	35	A B C D
6	A B C D	16	A B C D	26	A B C D	36	A B C D
7	A B C D	17	A B C D	27	A B C D	37	A B C D
8	A B C D	18	A B C D	28	A B C D	38	A B C D
9	A B C D	19	A B C D	29	A B C D	39	A B C D
10	A B C D	20	A B C D	30	A B C D	40	A B C D

FCE/CPE-1 KENRICK & JEFFERSON Printers to the Computer Industry DP134/11

CAMBRIDGE
EXAMINATIONS, CERTIFICATES & DIPLOMAS
ENGLISH AS A FOREIGN LANGUAGE

University of Cambridge
Local Examinations Syndicate
International Examinations

FOR SUPERVISOR'S USE ONLY
Shade here if the candidate is ABSENT or has WITHDRAWN

SAMPLE

Examination/Paper No. 9999/04 99/D99

Examination Title ANY CAMBRIDGE EXAM

Centre/Candidate No. AA999/9999

Candidate Name A.N. EXAMPLE

- Sign here if the information above is correct.
- Tell the Invigilator immediately if the information above is not correct.

LISTENING COMPREHENSION ANSWER SHEET

ENTER TEST NUMBER HERE →

FOR OFFICE USE ONLY → FCE CAE CPE 1 5 3 | 0 1 2 3 4 5 6 7 8 9

1		1	21		21
2		2	22		22
3		3	23		23
4		4	24		24
5		5	25		25
6		6	26		26
7		7	27		27
8		8	28		28
9		9	29		29
10		10	30		30
11		11	31		31
12		12	32		32
13		13	33		33
14		14	34		34
15		15	35		35
16		16	36		36
17		17	37		37
18		18	38		38
19		19	39		39
20		20	40		40

EFL-4 KENRICK & JEFFERSON Printers to the Computer Industry DP150/31

ASSESSMENT CRITERIA

PAPER 2 COMPOSITION

Marks are given out of 20 for each composition, according to:

- the relevance of the composition to the question set
- the organization of the composition, including paragraph structure and linking
- the range, level and appropriacy of vocabulary, including spelling
- the range, level and appropriacy of grammatical structure, including punctuation
- the appropriacy of style

Individual mistakes do not lose marks. There are no 'right or wrong' opinions and lack of knowledge of a subject is not penalised. However, marks are lost for compositions that are too short or perhaps too long. The following provides a general guide to the marking of compositions.

16–20
- approaching or achieving a high level of native-speaker fluency
- no irrelevance, padding or waffle; task fully addressed
- substantial proportion of sophisticated structure and vocabulary, including varied and appropriate linking and accurate spelling and punctuation
- well-controlled organization and appropriate style
- few if any errors of the kind unlikely to be made by a native speaker; no basic errors and little if any totally inapproptiate vocabulary

11–15
- natural and flowing well with some errors resulting from attempts to use sophisticated structure and vocabulary but not quite getting it right
- little or no irrelevance, with task fully addressed
- some accurate sophisticated structure and vocabulary: good linking and generally accurate spelling and punctuation
- coherent organization and appropriate style
- not many errors and few, if any, basic ones

8–10
- competent and clear but limited and unadventurous
- task reasonably addressed with some irrelevance and/or repetition
- accurate structure, vocabulary and linking, although much of it basic; few basic errors that impede understanding
- clear organization; style not wholly inappropriate

5–7
- errors substantially impede communication
- task not addressed to any significant extent, with much irrelevance and/or repetition
- structure, vocabulary and linking too basic and with many errors
- poorly organized

0–4
- composition rendered incoherent by number and nature of errors
- mostly irrelevant and/or too short for any real assessment to be made
- basic structures inaccurate; no attempt at linking; vocabulary only very basic; many basic errors
- no coherent organization

PAPER 5 INTERVIEW

The interview,which lasts 12–15 minutes, uses a combination of visual and verbal stimuli, and ranges from simple identification of material to discussion of related topics and theme-related communicative activities. It is marked according to the candidate's performance regarding the following:

a) fluency
b) grammatical accuracy
c) pronunciation of sentences
d) pronunciation of individual sounds
e) ability to communicate effectively with others
f) range and appropriacy of vocabulary

Marks are awarded out of 5 for each of these categories, giving a maximum of 30 marks, which is then converted into a mark out of 40. The following provides a general guide to the marking of the interview.

5 approaching or achieving native-speaker level in all categories

4 a) little hesitation; b) few errors even in sophisticated structrues and no basic errors; c/d) clear and easy to listen to and understand; e) communicating mostly with ease and effectively with only the occasional minor difficulty; f) few occasions when appropriate vocabulary cannot readily be produced and these only in specialized areas

3 a) little hesitation when talking about everyday matters, some when talking about abstract matters; b) competent and accurate use of more than basic structure with few if any basic errors; c/d) competent with understanding not impeded; e) communicating effectively or adequately in all contexts; f) adequate if limited vocabulary in all but specialized areas

2 a) some hesitation when talking about everyday matters and too much when discussing abstract ideas; b) adequate structures for everyday contexts but significant number of basic errors; c/d) pronunciation making understanding difficult; e) communicating adequately in everyday contexts but significant difficulty when discussing abstract ideas; f) adequate vocabulary but too much of it basic

1 a) constant hesitation; b) many basic errors; c/d) pronunciation making understanding almost impossible; e) poor communication even in everyday contexts; f) inadequate vocabulary even for everyday contexts

0 a) no connected speech; b) not even basic structures correct; c/d) impossible to understand; e) failing to communicate at all; f) only the most basic vocabulary produced